EN-GENDERING INDIA

En-Gendering India

*Woman and Nation in
Colonial and Postcolonial
Narratives*

Sangeeta Ray

Duke University Press

Durham and London

2000

© 2000 Duke University Press
All rights reserved
Printed in the United States of America on acid-free paper ∞
Typeset in Sabon by Wilsted & Taylor Publishing Services
Library of Congress Cataloging-in-Publication Data appear
on the last printed page of this book.

CONTENTS

Acknowledgments

The writing of a book, an intensely solitary activity for the most part, cannot come to pass without the support and help of many generous friends, colleagues, and relatives. This book, the seeds of which were sowed during a dissertation written in 1990, is deeply indebted to the work of leading and emerging scholars in the field of postcolonial studies. I am even more grateful to those who either read all or parts of the manuscript and to those who responded to my work presented at conferences and talks: Jenny Sharpe, Carla Peterson, Peter Hulme, Jose Rabasa, Mustapha Pasha, Martha Smith, Marilee Lindemann, Robert Levine, R. Radhakrishnan, Merle Collins, Marshall Grossman, Beth Loizeaux, Susan Leonardi, Linda Kauffman, Malini Schueller, Caryl Flinn, Deirdre David, Kathleen Blake, and Susan Jeffords. The chapter on Bankim and Tagore could not have been written without the intellectual support of Henry Schwarz. His unceasing generosity, whether it was providing yet another bibliographic reference, actually procuring hard-to-obtain material, or gently reminding me of that which needed to be said, remains unmatched. I thank Liz Deloughrey, Crystal Parikh, Virginia Bell, Mona Shah, Eleanor Shevlin, John Fisher, Sharon Groves, Kevin Meehan, Kimberley Brown, Rodrigo Lazo, Rob Doggett, and Nels Pearson for many stimulating discussions on issues of gender and nation around a desk or over a glass of wine.

I am indebted to Purnima Bose and an anonymous reader for Duke University Press for their especially generous and detailed critical assessment of the manuscript. No writer of a first book could have hoped for a better editor than Ken Wissoker, whose enthusiasm and belief in the project was highly infectious. This book owes a great deal to his finely honed editorial skills.

Brian Richardson taught me the fine art of being succinct. My greatest debt is to him for being my most meticulous reader and arguing against every turn of infelicitous prose. Sharing my life and work with him these last eleven years has been exhilarating.

While this book was being revised, my mother, Shukla Ray (née Tagore), died suddenly in an unfortunate accident. Everything I ever learned to question about gender and its relationship to things at large I learned from this one remarkable woman. Widowed at the age of forty, she lived and celebrated a life absolutely different from the one she was supposed to have lived. To her, I dedicate this book.

Portions of Chapter 4 appeared in *Genders* 20 (1999) as "Gender and the Discourse of Nationalism in Anita Desai's *Clear Light of Day.* I thank the editors and New York University Press for permission to reprint the material in this volume.

INTRODUCTION

I'd like to begin with an anecdote. At a semiofficial gathering at the residence of the Indian ambassador to the United States in 1996 celebrating the tentative ties recently developed between India and the United States, the ambassador showed his appreciation for the large Indian expatriate population by constantly referring to their obvious (to him) allegiance to the "homeland."[1] He assumed that most of the Indian audience had been born in India, had close, personal ties to the country, and frequently returned there for a visit. He encouraged them to invest in the future of India by participating in the various U.S.-Indian corporate collaborations in the making. India's entry into the twenty-first century as a major player in global capitalism was assured with this crucial transnational alliance evolving around corporate culture. And then there was a significant pause. Any nervousness we (Indians) might feel at the dilution of "our" culture as a result of these mergers and incursions was false, he said.

To prove his point he asked the Indian women in the audience to stand up. Look, he said—and the men and white women in the room turned and duly observed—at what they are wearing. These "daughters of India" are all dressed in saris or *salwar kameezes*. Not one is wearing a Western dress. Indian men, however, with a few exceptions in Nehru jackets, had, I presumed, been co-opted because they wore Western suits.[2] Two lessons can be gleaned from the ambassador's use of this visual aid. Generally, tradition is a hard thing to let go of, and more significant, even if men had to adapt because they were part of the ephemeral public life, women could always be counted on to affirm the continuity of tradition. Thus, if Indian women continue to wear Indian clothes while living in the United States, then the fear of "tradition" and "culture" being contaminated in India was minimal.

The ambassador had maneuvered carefully around a potentially explosive ideological minefield. He had begun by assuming that every Indian person in the room that night was a voluntary expatriate and had then gone on to appeal to their national sentiment by evoking nostalgia for the homeland. Having achieved that, he then asked them to imagine themselves as pivotal players in a transnational global economy by addressing their larger, more cosmopolitan fiscal interest. Instead of leaving us (men and women) delighting in or debating our positions as economically motivated citizens of the world, however, the ambassador, preempting a possible backlash against his privileging of monetary concerns, closed with a decisive return to a substantial symbol of national proportions. In doing this, the ambassador did not just reproduce a gendered separation of spheres. He allowed men to function as citizens of the world while always cognizant of their primary role as an Indian subject; Indian women were part of the ambassador's global vision *only* as uncontaminated purveyors of an inherent national culture.

I recount this incident out of many to suggest the continuing presence of the nation in discourses that seek to supersede and subvert its constrictive confines such as internationalism, transnationalism, global capitalism, academic multiculturalism, and even corporate-style multiculturalism.[3] And no matter which strategic discourse we deploy in our turn away from the nation, the mobilization of the category of "woman," despite all the debates in feminist studies ranging from woman as essence to woman as difference to woman as concept-metaphor, appears to return us once again to its threshold.[4]

Perhaps one could argue that the ambassador was deploying a strategic nationalism to produce an identity around which a diverse group of displaced Indians could cohere. As Spivak has said, "a strategy suits a situation," yet the repetition of the reproduction of nation under the sign of "woman" prevents a "critique of the 'fetish-character' (so to speak) of the masterword."[5] This absence of persistent critique of the strategic use of an essence results in the overdetermination of the essence and produces an unproductive essentialist position long after the event demanding the strategy is resolved. The anecdote establishes at least one substantive trajectory in a supposedly postcolonial diasporic moment of the legacy of national identifications. It helps illuminate the vexed historical continuity between colonial and nationalism and other global movements such as diaspora and transnationalism.

In this book I participate and intervene in key discourses that have surrounded nationalism over the last decade, engaging particularly with the paradigm of identity and its investment in nationalism. More important, this book challenges the androcentric bias of most modern national imaginings. In the variously inflected critical pronouncements on the invention, imagination, and narration of nations, the inclusion of woman under the sign of the nation repeatedly lays bare the deep ambivalence of the relationship of woman to nation.[6]

Most theorists of nationalism have been male, but conveniently to disregard the play of sexuality and gender as an integral element in the separation of the libidinal/private from the public/collective seems to come perilously close to the discourse of nationalists who continue to yoke gender to the articulation of the nation even as they seek forcefully to separate the micropolitical from the macropolitical.[7] The desire to keep the two spheres distinct is mandated by the use of the ubiquitous trope of nation-as-woman in all nationalist discourses. As the editors of *Nationalisms and Sexualities* point out, the efficient functioning of this particular trope depends "for its representational efficacy on a particular image of woman as chaste, dutiful, daughterly or maternal" (Parker et al. 6). Kumari Jayawardena has argued convincingly that the emergence of feminist movements in various parts of the so-called third world is intricately tied to anti-imperialist and nationalist struggles waged by a modernized and "enlightened" middle class. But this alliance has exacted its toll on women whose claims for recognition as equal citizens in the new, independent nation-state have been repeatedly set aside by an indigenous government that has to attend to more "pressing" concerns. The form and content of these nationalist movements and independent nation-states, both secular and religious, are multifarious, but it is crucial that discourses and practices concerning the role and specificity of gender and its relation to the positions of women be analyzed when we seek to examine the proliferation of nationalisms and nationalist discourses.[8] Here I attempt to do more than pay mere lip service to "the woman question." I underscore the necessity of a more comprehensive understanding of gender as a category, one that goes beyond an initial commitment to the representation of a specific constituency to an inquiry that challenges the assumptions behind the masculinist, heterosexual economy hitherto governing the cultural matrix through which an Indian national identity has become intelligible.

Despite McClintock's subversive formulation that "all nationalisms are gendered, all are invented and all are dangerous—dangerous not in Eric Hobsbawm's sense of having to be opposed, but in the sense that they represent relations to political power and the technologies of violence" (352), Ernest Renan's 1882 lecture "What Is a Nation?" continues to provide the framework for many theoretical peregrinations. Renan's foundational text, operating within an unmarked masculine frame, cannot position woman as anything other than a reproductive vessel necessary for the proliferation of populations in the various countries he uses to advance his theory of the nation as "a large-scale solidarity, constituted by the feeling of the sacrifices that one has made in the past and of those that one is prepared to make in the future."[9] In more contemporary inventions, imaginations, and narrations of nations, one can clearly trace an itinerary of forgetting, when in the interest of producing and maintaining a paternal/fraternal extended community, most male theorists fail to critique nationalism's repressive and homogenizing relationship to gender. It might appear outdated, but it seems prescient to reiterate what seems to be obvious:[10] every aspect of our sociopolitical reality is gendered, and the presumption of a gender-neutral methodology perpetuates the fiction of a transgendered universality that is nothing but a euphemism for a universal masculinity.[11]

The issue for theorists committed to examining what Spivak has called the "homely tactics of everyday pouvoir/savoir, the stuff of women's lives" is simultaneously epistemic and political (*Outside in the Teaching Machine* 35). My recounting of the anecdote about the ambassador reveals the quotidian production of woman as *the sign* of sex and gender. In these times, the emphasis on the transnational dimension of cultural formation has made us aware not only of the multivalent ways in which cultures are constructed and traditions are invented but also the retroactive nature of most social and psychic affiliations. The inherent danger in the dispersal of local identifications thus wrought is mediated through the figure of "woman" and thereby helps contain the threat of ambivalence enabled by spatial displacements by resituating the myth of culture's particularity in the national.

If we concur with Foucault that, in the struggle for nationhood, territory itself becomes the foundation for authority ("Governmentality" 93), the assertion of that authority seems inextricably linked to discourses about the nature and function of women. Consider the views of two very differently positioned theorists to illustrate this point. First, from George Santayana, "Our nationalism is like our relationship to women: too implicated in our moral nature to be changed honourably and too accidental to be worth changing" (quoted in McClintock 353). These words offer us an obvious idealization of masculinity that rehearses the hierarchy of gender difference. Second, from George Mosse, "Woman as a national symbol was the guardian of the continuity and immutability of the nation, the embodiment of its respectability" (18). This sentiment exemplifies the place assigned to woman when such idealizations of masculinity become the foundation of the nation. The fundamental assumptions undergirding the two positions are challenged by the following assertion made by the members of the Women's Conference to the Lothian Committee on Indian Political Reforms set up in 1932 in response to the committee's decision to rule out adult franchise: "We women wish to be citizens in our own rights, independent of any of our male relations. . . . We do not think that women's rights as a citizen should depend upon her marriage, which in the majority of cases in India at present is not entirely under her control" (Chattopadhyay 99). In contrast to Santayana's and Mosse's use of woman as sign, we hear women demand recognition of their agency in the public sphere outside a conventional patriarchal framework with its rigid structures of gender identity.

En-Gendering India explores the manipulation of gender politics in the exercise of national rule. In examining certain aspects of the nationalist movement in India, I show how Benedict Anderson's observation that "in the modern world everyone can, should, will 'have' a national identity, as he or she 'has' a gender" (16), accurate on one level, fails to take into account the systemic differential relationship between identities constructed at the intersection of gender and nationality. Over the last decade, a number of scholars have shown in myriad ways how the adoption of a feminist standpoint can transform our understanding of nationalism. In the Indian context alone, feminist scholars from various disciplines have revolutionized our understanding of British colonial discourse, Indian nationalism, and the role of women in colonial and modern India.[12] Earlier evaluations of the Indian feminist movement, such as those offered by Joanna Liddle and Rama Joshi and by Kumari Jayawardena, revealed its close connections to nationalist and anti-imperialist maneuvers. Liddle and Joshi paid meticulous attention to the ways in which factors such as class, caste, and urban and rural locations tended to complicate any easy connections presumed to exist between modernization and emancipation. Religious diversity and communalism, on the other hand, were not seen as significant categories of analysis. Only in retrospect, given the contemporary politico-religious situation not only in India but elsewhere in the subcontinent as well, does one feel the need for a reevaluation.

The anthology *Recasting Women: Essays in Indian Colonial History*, edited by Kukum Sangari and Sudesh Vaid, is particularly significant in this context because it marks a turning point in feminist research in India. Writing toward the end of the eighties, the editors argue for a crucial understanding and rearticulation of the present in terms of the "regulation and reproduction of patriarchy in the different class and caste formations within civil society" in colonial India (1). Even though their desire is to depict women from every stratum of society, they mourn their inability to do so because the essays focus mainly on the dominant Hindu middle class in North India under direct British rule. I read this emphasis as a telling moment in the genealogical excavation undertaken by the essayists in this collection. It is precisely the self-reflexive nature of much of the essays, the return to the present as a middle-class space (occupied by most of the researchers), that marks the impossibility of producing other genealogies.

The innovativeness of this anthology lies in its careful uncovering of the manner in which a particular kind of "new woman" emerged in the liminal space between colonial subjection and an incipient nationalism. Yet the unearthing of the lineage of this new woman fails to provide the kind of "dialectical relation of 'feminisms' and patriarchies, both in the inventions of the colonial state and in the politics of anti-colonial movements" (5) that its editors seek to explicate. The absence of any discussion about the Muslim community and other castes makes such dialectical relationships, however implicit, extremely friable, especially because communalism would appear to be quite central for the operation of any such dialectic. As we move from the eighties to the nineties and witness the premeditated demolition of the Babri Masjid at Ayodhya in 1992 and the increasing visibility of militant women activists in the Hindu Right, we gradually see a more concentrated effort among the intelligentsia in India and abroad to come to grips with the issue not only of communalism but also of its manipulations of gender ideology.[13]

A number of feminists are deeply committed to undertaking such a reassessment. Much like the contributions in *Recasting Women*, the work of these researchers too is marked by a self-reflexive turn, this time in relation to the manner in which their earlier leftist feminist presuppositions were marked by errors and omissions as a result of their particular, often hegemonic, location in a hierarchical society. Tanika Sarkar's uneasiness, for example, in the face of women's empowerment enabled by and within the Hindu Right organizations is quintessential ("Woman as Communal Subject" 2057–62). Today, feminists can no longer ignore the appeal of a communal sensibility for women who are increasingly reshaping the emergent public sphere of the new Hindu nation. This specific historical reemergence of right-wing Hindu ideology demands a long and careful backward look at the nationalist movement's own ambivalent relationship to the woman question and its imbrication in the production of a putative, secular, socialist India that merely glossed over rather than addressed the diverse claims made on one's identity as Indian. The unexamined nature of our investment in a modern secular India exploded from within in the early 1990s, and many feminists in India and Indian feminists elsewhere realize the need to evaluate their hitherto unmarked subjectivities as upper-caste, middle-class, and Hindu women.

In *En-Gendering India* I endeavor to chart the multiple and shifting articulations of such an ambiguous relationship in three historically linked discourses—British colonialism, Indian nationalism, and postcolonialism—by concentrating on the representation of the "native" woman. I establish how the figure of the "native" woman as upper-class Hindu woman becomes the crucial site through which Indian nationalism consolidates its identification with Hinduism. I thus underline not only the links between colonial and nationalist discourses but also the presence of sectarian religious mobilization in the very inception of the nation that, in the early 1990s, would lead to the implosion of India's secular self-image.

The historical parameters of this study are the Sepoy Rebellion of 1857 and the independence and partition of India in 1947.[14] These two events are so crucial for the representation and self-representation of India that they are constantly being retold, with each recounting rooted in the historical specificities of the moment of narration as well as the ideological predilections of the teller. The rebellion proper may be said to have begun with the revolt at Meerut on May 10, 1857, and the seizure of Delhi the next day. It technically ceased with the fall of Gwalior on June 20, 1858. The uprising changed the face of British imperialism from feigned benevolence to an unambivalent, enforced foreign rule beginning with the savage reprisals by a hysterical British population occupying the cities and garrisons at Calcutta, Kanpur, Lucknow, and Delhi. The event has produced a discursive site that continues to be mined by historians and writers seeking to rationalize and fictionalize through their representations the reasons, the horror, and the aftermath of the Sepoy Rebellion.[15]

The second date records another momentous event which occurred almost one hundred years later and which has also transfixed the imagination of writers. The partition and holocaust of 1947, the division of British India into Pakistan and India—a carving up of geographic space along religious lines that in one stroke granted independence to a supposedly Hindu India and created a new nation, Pakistan, to be predominantly populated by Muslims—continues to determine relationships between Hindus and Muslims in India, Pakistan, and Bangladesh, as testified to by the recent rise of Hindu fundamentalism in India.

In *En-Gendering India*, I argue that after 1857 the figure of the Hindu woman begins to function as a crucial semiotic site in and around which the discourses of imperialism, nationalism, an Indian postcolonialism, and feminism are complexly inscribed. As I mentioned above, the crisis marked by the Sepoy Rebellion changed the modus operandi of imperial government in India from that of a purported benevolent ruler to an unequivocal taskmaster. The English imagination was terrified by the exaggerated depictions of inhuman atrocities perpetrated by Indian men on innocent English women and children. The idea of protecting the image of the English nation threatened by rebellious indigenous mutineers could be upheld, I contend, by extending the boundaries of the imagined English nation to include the oppressed Indian woman. This incorporation is nonrealizable at its inception, however, because the female "native" body is the nonliminal site of otherness that makes possible the realization of the imagined community. Thus the rhetoric of benevolence extended toward the subjugated "native" woman by the English nation highlights the paradoxical position of the Indian woman in an imperial economy.

This putative inclusion of the doubly other (Indian and woman) threatened the myth of the homogeneity and purity of the British nation even as its various proponents struggled to consolidate the power of the empire through their writings. The Indian woman became a further contested site of appropriation when Indian nationalists sought to advance their agenda by fusing their desire for an independent nation with the independence of the Indian woman, who, they argued, could never achieve her "pure" status as an equal participant in the domestic or public spheres within the boundaries of a spurious imagined community. Thus the discourses of imperialism and nationalism became increasingly intertwined as each sought to gain control over the representations of the Indian woman.

The complex trajectory charted by these interdependent and often contradictory discourses did allow for the production of an indigenous movement centered around the "woman question" that can be loosely termed "feminism." This emergent movement further complicated the representations of Indian women by the two dominant discourses, and it is the various articulations of the problematics of gender construction in nation formation that I seek to explore in *En-Gendering India*.

What further exacerbates this embattled constitutive site of the construction of the Indian nation is the rise of communal sensibility that identified an emergent Indian cultural nationalism as pristinely Hindu. In *The Construction of Communalism in Colonial North India*, Gyanendra Pandey asserts that Indian nationalism had two clear phases. In its early stage it conceived of the nation as an aggregate of different communities coalescing along religious and class lines. In its later phase, influenced by the "modern" discourses of secularism and rationality, it attempted to interpellate a diverse body of people as citizens of a nascent nation irrespective of individual alliances along the lines of caste, class, or religion. In this latter period then, communalism was, at least on the surface, challenged as the very antithesis of a unified nation. But examining the development of the discourse of the nation along the axis of gender leads one to realize the persistent structure of the relation of women to the idea of the active, political citizen of the nation-to-come. The woman who became synonymous with the country in the second half of the nineteenth century was specifically an upper-caste Hindu woman, and the adaptation of this dynamic in the later phase of the nationalist movement continues to manifest itself in the internecine conflicts that increasingly divide the population of postindependent India along communal and caste lines.

Thus, one way to describe the subject matter of this book is to say that I examine the rival and shifting representations of the Indian woman in British imperial and Indian colonial and postcolonial writings after 1857. In addition, in each chapter I seek to theorize the enunciation of an "authentic woman" of India in texts that are equally committed to the production of a national space called "India." I use the phrase "woman of India" because it is precisely the spatial congruence between the two terms that becomes the obsessive focus of national conjuncture in the colonial and postcolonial texts I discuss. The discursive productions of the Indian woman in the various discourses of imperialism, nationalism, communalism, feminism, and postcolonialism allow me to deconstruct essentialist binary oppositions—to bring into play diverse marginalities in order to undermine the insular, homogeneous nature of "great maneuvers." By inflecting my analyses of these often contradictory discourses with a theory of ideology, I attempt materially to ground Foucault's position that power manifests itself as a multiplicity of force relations, as the interplay of various discursive fields with their immanent necessities and developments. My book both participates in and extends the area of discourse charted by earlier scholars such as Brantlinger, Vishwanathan, and Sharpe. It also attends, in the spirit of more recent works such as Suleri's *Rhetoric of English India* and Grewal's *Home and Harem*, to both sides of the colonial and postcolonial divide.[16]

I focus on the formation of a particular political community that construes political identity as the assertion of a national idenity in response to imperial government. Inclusion within the "we" of this national citizenry, however, does not depend only on a single "constitutive outside" exterior to the community. The conceptualization of the Indian nation, even as it rests primarily on the issue of self-governance, is equally predicated on a commonality that is disrupted by the particularity of identifications of those who also wish to be a link in the chain of equivalence set up by the construction of the national "we."[17] In choosing to analyze the ways in which gender and religion complicate the representation of the desired national subject, I engage with the manner in which the polarized dynamic—us and them—inherent in the discourses of both nationalism and imperialism is continually being undermined by the "shifting representations of the space of alterity occupied by women within the formation of nationalist [and imperialist] subjectivities."[18]

I have chosen to concentrate almost exclusively on literary texts, predominantly the novel, written by South Asian and British authors of the later nineteenth and twentieth centuries. Yet my focus on the novel should not suggest to the reader that this book is about the emergence of the novel in the subcontinent and the ways in which the novel was shaped and transformed by the expectations and class biases of a particular audience. Neither is it about the confluence of different literary traditions.

What I attempt in this book is a particular analysis of the intersections of the discourses of gender and nation formation and their representations in certain novels and other narratives. The novel in India emerged at a specific historical juncture, and like all cultural productions, the "Indian novel" (this designation is merely instrumental) reflects and refracts the political, social, and economic needs and desires of certain social groups that have the power to shape and interpret "reality." One could claim that in the early part of the nineteenth century, many Indian languages had produced prose writings that claimed to be novels, though it took about two decades for the form to consolidate itself. In retrospect one could see the emergence of a new literary form in both *Yamuna Paryatan*, published in Malayalam in 1857, and *Alaler Gharer Dulal*, published in Bengali in 1858.

The rise of the novel and its popularity among the reading public was no doubt aided by the enormous growth in the second half of the nineteenth century of the publishing industry, which, as Tapti Roy points out, was "perhaps the largest indigenous enterprise in Calcutta" (30). The growth of print culture benefited both literate and nonliterate audiences as books transformed existing urban performances. For example, "Kathakatha, a conventional form of recital of Pauranic tales accompanied by singing and theatrical performance, . . . found a new textual medium in the printed book" (46). Wenger's catalog of Bengali books available for sale in 1865 shows a total of 901 books as opposed to only 332 in 1857 (in Roy 50). More pertinent to my purposes here is the striking increase in works of prose fiction and drama.[19] Other catalogs of the time also confirm the growing popularity of varieties of prose fiction and drama. This unprecedented proliferation of printed texts created a problem not only for the colonial state, which sought to discipline the content and form of texts in circulation, but also for the indigenous elite, who sought cultural hegemony. As Roy puts it, "the new intellectual elite sought to demarcate a cultural zone that would be regulated by normative practices laid down and enforced by institutions set up and run by the dominant practitioners of that culture" (54). In the 1870s Bankim Chandra Chatterjee, the first Bengali novelist and perhaps the leading literary figure of his time, became a relentless advocate of literary taste, using the journal he edited, *Bangadarshan*, to define and enforce literary and aesthetic standards. The criteria for this new "high culture" was derived from two sources—classical (read "Sanskrit language and literature") and modern (read "English"). To quote Roy, "The two sources were united into a conception of a high culture by their supposed relation to the building of a 'nation'" (56).[20]

Thus it would be accurate to state that the novel emerged in the mid–nineteenth century in colonial India as a result of the spread of English among educated Indians. As Meenakshi Mukherjee notes, "It is not an accident that the first crop of novels in India, in Bengali and Marathi, appeared exactly a generation after Macaulay's Educational Minutes making English a necessary part of an educated Indian's mental make-up were passed" (3). This is not to say that the novel as it developed in India was purely derivative. When we talk about the Indian novel we must pay close attention to the recasting of this genre in a unique milieu with its own complex historical and literary evolution. Thus, for example, despite the efforts by nineteenth-century Indian writers consciously to produce a novel, we see distinct traces of prenovelistic forms of storytelling. To put it succinctly, the novel in India was a curiously productive amalgam of indigenous narrative traditions and certain formal and thematic elements of contemporary British Victorian novels. The influence of the colonizer's culture was, of course, mediated by what was actually being read by educated Indians, in translation or in English, such as Wilkie Collins, Marie Corelli, Benjamin Disraeli, G. W. M. Reynolds, and Walter Scott. Though the novel did not develop uniformly in India, one can suggest, based on the various texts produced in Bengali, Marathi, Assamese, Tamil, Malayalam, Telugu, Kannada, Hindi, and Urdu between 1858 and 1899, that the emergence of the Indian novel was a pan-Indian phenomenon.[21]

Mukherjee divides the novels being written in India in the nineteenth century into three categories: the novels of purpose that utilized the new form "for social reform and missionary enterprise" (16); historical fiction/romance that combined historical detail with supernatural ingredients to re-create a past ethos; and realist social novels. Thus as the nationalist spirit began to take root among the Indian intelligentsia, one could see it being reflected in all its contradictions in the writings of the time, particularly in the new genre flourishing among the educated elite. If nationalism is a discourse that constructs its own narrative, one can imagine the imbrication of the novel, as an emerging genre, in the construction of that narrative. If, again, the significant accomplishment of English education was the transformation wrought in modes of knowing, the novel and the narration of a nationalist discourse essentially represented a Western rationalist worldview. Thus as Shivarama Padikkal demonstrates:

> Whether the novels are reformist or revivalist in content, their fundamental shaping force is rationalism. For rationalism, the nation is basically a cultural concept. . . . If one kind of nationalist response is to bemoan our lack of cultural unity and the specific cultural qualities which had laid the foundation of European progress and the stable modern nation-state, another response was to revive the traditional culture in order to prove that India too had a great civilization, and to cull out from old histories, records and stories those elements which would aid the conception of nationhood. (223–24)

Between 1870 and about 1930, both historical and social novels were published; they were most immediately concerned with the idea of progress and its achievement within the parameters of the yet-to-be-realized nation. The idea of an independent nation and the creation of a novel identity for the unfettered national citizen was marked by the conflict (which continues today) between "modernity" and "Indian-ness," a conflict particularly fraught with difficulties for the new educated class that sought to create a "homogenous, unified, pan-Indian 'common sense' of ethical, epistemological and social beliefs. It was as part of the larger enterprise of imagining a modern nation that the English educated class tried to construct an identity for itself" (Padikkal 224). In a significant departure from the Western novel that reiterated as its dominant theme the rupture between the individual and society, the novel in India during the heyday of nationalism took as its moral and ethical obligation a recasting of social identity in an ongoing confrontation with the colonizing power. Thus the novel often became the site for the expression of the political and social ambitions of the upper caste and middle class as they sought to imagine a culturally powerful Indian nation grounded in a common tradition. The three Indian novels on which I focus embody the internal contradictions of the Indian discourse of nationalism in my vernacular, Bengali. My choice was also guided by the emphasis in the three novels on the figure of the Indian woman to capture these contradictions. The female Indian protagonists in the three novels—*Anandamath, Devi Chaudhurani*, and *The Home and the World (Ghare Baire)*—variously epitomize, often simultaneously and differentially, the revival of an ideal, an ideal which is yet to be realized and which is being destroyed in the imaginative renditions of the Indian nation.

I believe it is imperative to move beyond the colonial scene to include contemporary postcolonial Indian and Pakistani writers who are recharting the political and epistemological field of colonial India, because it reminds the postcolonial subject how crucial it is constantly to deconstruct a given or accepted historiography by introducing other genealogies that have hitherto been precluded from investigation. To this end, in this book I have included two novels by women writers from the Indian subcontinent who re-create through the voices and depiction of the fraught lives of their female protagonists the conflicting and violent years leading up to the partition of 1947.

Informing the issues discussed throughout the book—most insistently in its last chapter—are current debates about the nature and status of third world literature, a debate that attained prominence with the publication of Fredric Jameson's essay "Third World Literature in an Age of Multi-National Capitalism." Aijaz Ahmad's response to Jameson's essay captured the fierce resistance of a number of postcolonial scholars to Jameson's sweeping formulations about third world literature and nationalism. In "Jameson's Rhetoric of Otherness and the 'National Allegory,'" Ahmad primarily focuses on the impossibility of postulating a global theory of "third world" literature. He attempts to invalidate Jameson's major premise that all "Third World cultural productions" can be read as national allegories because they have something in common, namely, that "the story of the private individual destiny is always an allegory of the embattled situation of the public third world culture and society."[22] The most recent entry in the ongoing debate is Madhava Prasad's "On the Question of a Theory of (Third World) Literature." Prasad offers us an innovative way to theorize about literature by reintroducing the allegorical dimension at the level of class, thereby denying the inviolate bifurcation of the globe into the first and third worlds. Prasad argues for a perception of certain social formations as "a time-space of subject formations, necessarily determined by imperialism, colonialism, developmentalism, and experimentation with bourgeois democracy and other forms of nation-statehood" rather than as a "geography with its millenia [sic] of cultural history" (58); one could then retain the signifier "third world" as used by Jameson in its strategic relational aspect in order to highlight the inequalities that remain the hallmark of global capitalist economy. Prasad's emphasis on subject formations as primarily constituted by their entry into some form of nation-statehood allows him to draw a trajectory that defines all social formations "as structures of administration by representation on the model of the bourgeois democracies of Europe. The nation-state, with a representative rule approximating in varying degrees to the primary models, is the politically, economically and ideologically privileged unit of participation in the global order" (71).

In this formulation, Jameson is faulted not for reading third world texts as national allegories but for restating the opposition between first world and third world texts as that between Freud and Marx. According to Prasad's hypothesis all literatures at this point in socioliterary history should be inscribed in their national context to underline the hypervisibility of the national framework in third world configurations and its apparent invisibility in the Western context (73). This would entail a collapse of the distinction between the aesthetic and the political in Western literary theories which, in claiming the invisibility of the national framework in Western literatures, seeks to read the individualist emphasis solely in terms of a private, libidinal thrust. The repression of the allegorical is neccessary to advance the theory of a depoliticized realm of the aesthetic that foregrounds the "individualist" and autonomous status of the Western text.

To move beyond a binary representation of world literature as an opposition between the first world and the third world, Prasad insists on a theory of literature that would begin by "redefining the libidinal/private in its allegorical status (its relation to particular nations but especially to particular classes—a class allegory) and collapsing the distinction which originates in capitalist ideology" (78). In this reconfigured allegorical reading, the distinction between first and third world texts can still be considered within a theory of modes of production. This time, however, the theory is wrenched from its developmental framework, which posits a center of free space, ensuring the formation and participation of a free citizen who enjoys full representation in a putative, liberal pluralist democracy that foregrounds a cultural rather than a national identity based on the notion of "free will." To this center is opposed a magnetically charged involuntary field that necessitates the formation of collective communities that in their stage of secondary or tertiary development advocate a nationalist will at the expense of individual subjecthood. Prasad's notion of class allegory would reintroduce the idea of privilege into the center of free space, which in turn would highlight the obscured formation of class-based communities. This would enable us to distinguish between the bourgeoisie who thrive under a nation posited as "a community of private individuals" (75) from other classes who continue to conceive nation-states in terms of territorially biased imagined communities.

Prasad's emphasis on class as an overdetermined signifier that cannot and should not be overlooked in any discursive undertaking takes away with one hand what it bestows with the other. Even as he forces us to recognize the importance of class boundaries in the literary productions of the first world, he fails to address how gender intersects with class to confound and contradict class affiliations. One wonders whether Prasad foresees a kind of socialist-feminist coalition with class-based labor forces along the lines of that suggested by Christine Delphy.[23] It is difficult to assess because his discussion is so centered on the interjection of space-time-class subject formations in what has been the divide between the first world and the third world. Prasad does not merely emphasize class in writing from a loosely marxist "positionality." My point, which is not just a matter of splitting hairs, is that the widespread influence and practice of feminist studies in every field today should suggest to all theorists and critics that feminism is not merely a choice "among competing perspectives" but rather "a choice which cannot but undergird any attempt at a [critical/theoretical] reconstruction which undertakes to demonstrate our sociality in the full sense, and is ready to engage with its own presuppositions of an objective gender-neutral method of inquiry" (Sangari and Vaid 2–3). The emphasis in the three essays discussed above is the positing of the discursive formation of nation as a significantly masculinist, public discourse independent of the machinations of the domestic/familial. The essays yet again ignore my point here: that the study of nationalism and "third world literature" as such *must* be made to acknowledge the reality of the feminist intervention as both micropolitical and macropolitical.

Dipesh Chakravorty echoes the above sentiment when in an evaluation of the work done by the Subaltern Studies historians he admits that, though the enterprise of the collective was motivated by an "explicit spirit of opposition to the elitist and teleological narratives that both marxist and nationalist traditions . . . had promoted in Indian historiography" (10), their engagement with feminism as a significant oppositional theoretical grid came only after Gayatri Spivak's critique of the male orientation of their reconstructive projects. In her brilliant essay "Can the Subaltern Speak?" Spivak reveals that any theory of representation dealing critically with the domains of ideology, subjectivity, politics, the nation, the state, and the law must attend to the specific discursive uses of the category of gender in order not to generate yet another moment of theoretical epistemic violence. She argues that the peasant "consciousness" evoked in the various subaltern countermovements uncovered and charted by the Subaltern Studies collective is always already male because "the 'subject' implied by the texts of insurgency can only serve as a counterpossibility for the narrative sanctions granted to the colonial subject in the dominant groups" (287). Even though the methodology of the collective cannot be accused of reifying the notion of the feminine as indeterminate, it, in its originary moments, has failed to trace the "doubly effaced" trace of sexual difference in the "itinerary of the subaltern subject" (287). The archival, interventionist historiography of the collective needs to confront the aporia in its methodology that progresses on the assumption that all forms of silences can be equally measured, retrieved, and represented via the lost figure of the indigenous, insurgent classed/cast(ed) subaltern.

Spivak addresses a particular gendered issue—sati (widow burning)—not only to complicate the notion of free will but also to suggest that in every act of retrieval and reconstruction by the collective, "the ideological construction of gender keeps the male dominant" (287). Carefully scrutinizing both Brahmanic codes and texts as well as imperialist discourses surrounding the abolishing of sati, Spivak comes to the conclusion that "between patriarchy and imperialism, subject constitution and object-formation, the figure of the woman disappears, not into a pristine nothingness, but into the violent shuttling which is the displaced figuration of the 'third-world woman' caught between tradition and modernization" (306). Jenny Sharpe provides an impassioned reading of Spivak's critique of the methodology of the collective. According to Sharpe, Spivak does not fault the collective for ignoring women's participation in rebellions—the collective is scrupulous in documenting such instances. What remains problematic is the failure on the part of the members of the collective to examine critically those instances where "the symbolic exchange of women appears at crucial moments . . . for explaining the mobilization of peasants across villages. . . . Spivak notes that the project of writing a history from below repeats the subaltern male's indifference to sexual difference."[24]

In the various narratives considered in this book, I repeatedly raise the question of the haunting absence of the myriad ways in which gender inflects discourses of nationalism. In the particular examination of *Clear Light of Day* and *Cracking India* I show how two representative novels by South Asian women writers approach the complex interweavings of diurnal domestic life and the political upheavals of a colonized country on the verge of independence from the point of view of its female protagonist. Even as they can be read as national allegories, they also reveal how the production of a unified, homogeneous entity such as the two nations created by the partition hinges, to a large degree, on the determinate subject position of "woman" for its articulation. In choosing novels by two women writers, I am not only concerned with reading women's lives and highlighting women authors. Throughout my book I have taken very seriously Joan Scott's cautionary remark that to "study women in isolation perpetuates the fiction that one sphere, the experience of one sex, has little or nothing to do with the other" (32).

In Chapter 1 I discuss Bankimchandra Chatterjee's political and philosophical writings and the role of the female revolutionary in his novels *Anandamath* (1882) and *Devi Chaudhurani* (1884).[25] Bankim Chatterjee is an important intellectual figure of the Bengal renaissance who sought to renew a supposedly debased Bengali vernacular with feminine undertones with a vigorous infusion of masculine rationality. In doing this, he created a body of nationalist literature that was militaristic and combined "the moral firmness of the neo-Hinduism emerging after the Sepoy Mutiny period with secular English science and efficiency, a combination to be realized in the 'world' by rhetoric, persuasion, intellectual and verbal force" (Schwarz, "Sexing the Pundits" 240). I open the book with consideration of these two novels because they are engaged in the production of a particular Indian Hindu identity during the initial moments of the empire's consolidation of its presence in the colony. Bankim's novels project into the present a constructed glorious Hindu past that is then eulogized by militant nationalists in their demand for an independent "Mother India" during the height of the independence movement.

I closely analyze the discourse of an incipient Hindu nationalism advocated in both texts and critically examine the function and representation of the Indian woman as militant leader and activist in a chiefly male and ascetic guerrilla organization. *Anandamath*, in particular, echoes some of the tenets of the contemporary Hindu Right. Bankim's emphasis on the need to eulogize a virile Hindu community in his elaboration of a timeless and pure Hindu India is echoed in the current polemical discourse of communalism that seeks to erect a Hindu nation via a systemic erasure of the body politic represented by the Muslim minority. In my consideration of Shanti, the female revolutionary who infiltrates the all-male rebel group in *Anandamath*, I underscore how the anomalous presence of a woman in drag shores up the a priori construct of the Hindu subject as male. I explore the manner in which, in both novels, woman's power is celebrated and curtailed in its evocation of a glorious Hindu past—embodied, as I will contend, in the very essence of a Hindu woman—as a fertile ideological ground for the unveiling of a viable modern Indian/Hindu nation by the Hindu subject who is masculine, aggressive, and not vitiated by a rampant sexuality.

Chapter 2 returns us to the scene of the Indian Sepoy Mutiny of 1857, a rebellion at least partly fueled by English ignorance of the significance of certain Hindu and Muslim religious tenets. I examine Harriet Martineau's popular history *British Rule in India* (1857), Meadow Taylor's novel *Seeta* (1872), and Flora Annie Steel's *On the Face of the Waters* (1896), concentrating on an imperial determination of the social and spatial imaginary of India as necessarily Hindu. Ronald Inden argues that "historians of religion and Indologists have not only taken their Hinduism to be the essential religion of India; they have viewed it as the exemplification of the mind of India. . . . The essence of that mind was its 'feminine' imagination, source of the dream-like world-view of Indians. She was an inferior substitute for the West's masculine, world-ordering rationality" (4).

The mutiny marked a crucial shift in the colonial imagining of India as unantagonistically feminine. The three texts, separated by fifteen- and twenty-year intervals, articulate a certain recasting of this fundamental characterization of India as Hindu and feminine by embodying its typicality in the Indian woman. Martineau's history is especially intriguing because of the structural modality of the gaps in her representations of Indian women. In Taylor's and Steel's fictional accounts of the mutiny, the depiction of the Indian woman not only helps contain the rising threat of the desire of the "natives" to free themselves but also contributes to an absolute othering of India as immutably Hindu. Taylor's reworking of the Hindu epic *Ramayana* in his portrayal of the character of Seeta and Steel's evocation of the image of the Indian woman as always already "sati" participates in the narration of an essential unity called India.

In extended investigations of Martineau's history and Steel's novel, I use the abolition of sati as a point of entry into two very different texts: in her book, Martineau refuses to evoke the *gendered discourse of the white man's burden*; Steel ultimately validates this discourse in the image of the Hindu widow Tara setting fire to herself even as the British soldiers quell the mutineers and take back Delhi. I will argue that both Martineau's reticence and Steel's loquacity on the subject of sati mark sites of uncharacteristic disempowerment in an otherwise empowered discourse of colonialism. My reading of the structural aporia in Martineau's text and the "structure of feeling" that undergirds Steel's novel undercuts both the fiction of absolute colonial domination and the fallacy of the totality of otherness by insisting that the narratives which secure the position of the colonizer necessitated the repression of certain internal cultural facts that resurface as unspeakable sites in the territory of the other.

Chapters 3 and 4 focus on two partitions, the temporary partition of Bengal in 1905 and the division of the subcontinent in 1947. Chapter 3 plunges us into an India quite different from that imagined in the pages of Chatterjee or the British writers. In this chapter I read Rabindranath Tagore's novel *The Home and the World* in conjunction with his writings on nationalism and the woman question. Tagore's novel is quite well known in the West, and not only because Satyajit Ray made a movie based on it. Recently, in the pages of the *Boston Review*, the novel was resurrected as an admirable exemplification of the principles of cosmopolitanism in a debate about "education and political identity" in the United States. I discuss the ramifications of this debate at greater length in the chapter.

The novel, published in 1915, revolves around the nationalist furor generated by the partition of Bengal by Lord Curzon in 1905. In response to the typical British tactic of divide and conquer, the nationalists advocated the *swadeshi* movement—the boycott of British goods. The palimpsest-like structure of the novel and its complex points of view articulated in the narrative voices of the three primary characters—Nikhilesh, Sandip, and Bimala—make the text especially suitable for a complex dialogic reading. The novel addresses issues of communalism, nationalism, and the "woman question" via the changing relationships between the three individuals. I focus primarily on the evolution of the character of Bimala as she moves, literally and figuratively, from the home to the world. Of particular interest is Tagore's complicated position on the status of women and the manner in which the sign of the "new woman," as depicted in the character of Bimala, an upper-caste Indian wife of a Hindu zamindar (landowner), becomes the flash point, in the rhetoric of the Indian nationalists, for igniting the cultural destiny of the Indian nation.

I conclude the chapter with an analysis of "Sultana's Dream," a feminist utopia written in 1905 in English by Rokeya Sakhawat Hossain, a Bangladeshi Muslim literary scholar and activist. This utopia, with its outline of the positive gains achieved by women no longer restricted by purdah, provides another destiny for the sign of the "new woman" that challenges those eulogized by nationalists envisaging a new nation.

While the chapter on Tagore addresses the repercussions in a colonial space of the partition of Bengal along religious lines, Chapter 4 concerns the legacy of the partition of 1947 for two emergent postcolonial nation-states as detailed in Anita Desai's *Clear Light of Day* and Bapsi Sidhwa's *Cracking India*. Set in Delhi and Lahore, respectively, both novels offer a critique of the nationalist agenda that led to the partition and allow the postcolonial reader to engage with the deconstruction of identities that are posited as necessary for the formulation of coherent political communities. I attempt to bring to the surface the contingency and ambiguity of every identity, especially that of "woman," as illustrated in these two novels.

Even though the primary texts in this book are "literary" ones, my analysis of the discourses of nationalism, imperialism, and gender construction in Indian and British texts is greatly indebted to what Grewal characterizes as "an emerging field of transnational feminist cultural studies" (18). It is through the deployment of a carefully scrutinized, differentially positioned, and geopolitically refracted feminist theoretical lens that I bring into play novels and tracts written in nineteenth-century Bengal, Victorian novels and histories, and contemporary, postcolonial South Asian novels written in English. I resist a purely literary comparative framework for the examination of contradictory narratives in the construction of a Hindu India and a Hindu female identity. By consistently questioning the liminal form of the nation through the ideological emphasis on gender, I suggest how these narratives are themselves implicated in the production of history and knowledge not only in the more obvious diachronic sense (as in the chronological passage from colonialism to postcolonialism) but also in its paradoxical differential synchronicity. The construction of a Hindu India by both the nationalists and the imperialists not only occurs in a colonial moment but equally anticipates the possibility of a realm beyond imperialism and independence. In the Epilogue I suggest how such constructions persist in the discourses of the Hindu Right both in India and the United States. As India follows the celebration of its fiftieth anniversary of independence by exploding nuclear devices, we need to pause and take stock of the various narratives of decolonization and postindependent national histories that continue to deploy "woman" as both sign and subject.

CHAPTER ONE

Gender and Nation: Woman Warriors in Chatterjee's *Devi Chaudhurani* and *Anandamath*

I have never been defeated. Today I acknowledge defeat by you. My daughter, I am like your son. Have compassion on your child. Save Jibananda. Save your own life. Accomplish my work.

—Bankimchandra Chatterjee, *Anandamath*, 1992.

Behold I am not new but am the old. I am that eternal Word. Often did I come here, but you have forgotten me. So I am here again. To succour the good and destroy the evil doers, and to confirm the right am I in every age born.

—Bankimchandra Chatterjee, *Devi Chaudhurani*

The characterization of the Bengali male as effeminate and weak is by now part of the lore of colonial discourse.[1] Bankimchandra Chatterjee, probably the most well-known literary figure of Bengal in the nineteenth century as well as one of the more singular proponents of a Bengali cultural and Hindu nationalism, generally supported this portrayal of the Bengali male in his own evaluation of contemporary Bengali temperament and culture. As Tapan Raychaudhuri points out: "Despite references to occasional periods of glory and cultural achievements of great value and his doubts concerning the ascription of weakness to Bengalis even in the historical past . . . [Bankim believed that] the climate and Turkish rule had induced a degeneration in the Bengali personality and over time it had *lost all dignity and manly feelings*, though not a certain acuteness of intellect" (196; emphasis added). Bengal's lengthy subjection to alien rule had destroyed its moral fiber and left the male population "crushed and spiritless" (197). The epigraphs from Bankimchandra's two historical romances with which this chapter opens encapsulate the possibility of a cure for the prevailing contagion of effeminacy plaguing Bengali men by the very injection of the "feminine" in the public sphere. The first demonstrates the intellectual defeat of the ascetic leader of the rebel group "Children of the Gods" (Santans) at the hands of the heroine Shanti; the second epigraph functions as the epilogue to the novel *Devi Chaudhurani*, in which Prafulla, its main protagonist, is heralded by the omniscient narrator as the incarnation of an eternal force that returns every time India (read "Bengal") faces regression and ruin.[2] In what follows I provide a close analysis of two novels—*Anandamath* (1882) and *Devi Chaudhurani* (1884; henceforth referred to in references as DC), that suggests how "the feminine," embodied in a certain variant of the upper-class, Hindu Bengali woman, manifests itself within the representational framework of a historical romance. Bankim's novels seem simultaneously to valorize man's essential martial nature as that which distinguishes him from woman, even as they intimate that "woman" is the eternal warrior.[3]

The historical parameters of *Anandamath* and *Devi Chaudhurani* are the years between 1765 and 1787, which document the passage of the administration of Bengal from its Muslim emperor to the East India Company. In 1765 the emperor appointed the company to the fiscal administration of Bengal; between 1765 and 1772 the company collected the revenues using native agents; in 1772 Warren Hastings took over as the governor-general of Bengal, and between 1772 and 1786 the company experimented at rural administration by means of English officers; and on the March 29, 1787, the British government formally undertook the "direct administration of the two great frontier principalities of Lower Bengal" (Hunter 1: 13). The brief sketch of these years, however, fails to address the famine of 1769, "whose ravages two generations failed to repair" (18).[4] The famine wreaked havoc on the land, and according to a letter written by Warren Hastings in 1789, Bengal suffered "the loss of at least one-third of the Inhabitants of the Province, and the consequent decrease of the Cultivation" (381). It is the famine and the rapacity of the revenue collectors that provides the rationale for the organization of the rebels in *Anandamath*.[5] If, as the writer of the *Annals of Rural Bengal* documents, English historians' "treating of Indian history as a series of struggles about the Company's charter enlivened with startling military exploits" (19) disregarded the importance of the famine, Bankim amply compensates for the lack in his treatment of the disaster in his novel. In

Anandamath, he collapses the years between the famine that ravaged Western India and the ascendancy of Hastings to governor-general. In fact, the famine becomes both the point of departure and a trope for an exploration of the rapaciousness and callousness of the East India Company. The company, the seed of British power in India, is depicted as a relentless plunderer whose only intention is to deplete Bengal of its riches, and as the representative of its authority, Hastings comes under indirect attack by the author in both novels.[6]

More significant, the "banditti" referred to only in passing in the *Annals of Rural Bengal* as either "bands of cashiered soldiers, the dregs of the Mussulman armies . . . frequently dressed . . . in the Company's uniform, with a view to wholesale extortion from the villagers—a fraud rendered so plausible by the disorderly conduct of [British] troops on the line of march" or as "bands of so-called houseless devotees [who] roved about the country in armies fifty thousand strong" (70) are glorified as national revolutionaries in Bankim's *Anandamath*. In *Devi Chaudhurani*, the primary aim of the *barkandjas* (bandits) is to rob the collectors as they travel from one village to another and then to distribute the wealth among the poor peasants. In both novels certain "real" events and historical names, such as Captain Thomas, Bhawani Pathak, Mr. Goodland, and Lieutenant Brenan, as well as the historical figure of Devi Chaudhurani and her soldiers, are used to provide, as the author himself puts it, "a slender historical foundation" (DC xii) to an imaginative rendition of eighteenth-century Bengal.[7] This reconstruction of a particular historical period in *Anandamath* and *Devi Chaudhurani* partakes of the genre of romance which, as Henry Schwarz points out in "Sexing the Pundits" was appropriated and turned to alternate uses by Indian writers when they began to imagine the conditions for the formation of an independent nation.

In his *The Unhappy Consciousness* Sudipta Kaviraj provides a nuanced analysis of questions of historicity and fictionality and the countermnemonic possibilities in some of Bankim's key works. Kaviraj asserts that "every colonial intellectual understands the ironical, dual gifts history offers him. The word history . . . meant two entirely different things: it meant the course of happenings in time, the seamless web of experiences of a people; but its great promise lay in its second meaning, the stories in which what had happened are recovered and explained. . . . This duality of meaning, without any mystification, is constantly exploited by Bengali middle-class intellectuals in various innovative ways."[8] In 1882, Bankim outlined in detail in *Bangadarshan* his agenda for an Indian historiography. Ranajit Guha has argued that Bankim refused to grant all previous historicizations of the Bengali past the status of history, because they were representations authored by foreigners—Muslims and the British. Thus "true" history was capable of being written only by a "true" Bengali, whose first claim to authenticity lay in his fundamental denial of the truth claims of non-Indian historiographical endeavors. Guha has pointed out the motivating desire inherent in Bankim's words: "There has to be a history of Bengal. . . . Who is to write it? . . . Anyone, who is a Bengali, has to write it" (Bankim quoted in Guha 57). This was a revolutionary demand, for it took for granted the right to self-representation even or especially on the part of subjected peoples. Guha noted that to "insist on self-representation, even in terms of its past was, therefore, for such a people [the colonized], already a signal of its impatience with the state of subjection. Considered thus, the urge for an autonomous historiography could be understood as the symptom that it really was of an urgent, insistent though incipient nationalism" (57). But this autonomous historiography also made clear that there was only one truth and that only the Bengali who chose to write it could be the true Bengali. Thus writing, history, and identity become intricately connected in Bankim's definition of the Bengali. And all three were linked to the question of power by the concept of *bahubol* (physical strength) that was systematically denied in the foreigner's representation of a Hindu past. Thus the task of the Bengali historian was to re-present those occasions in the past that displayed bahubol on the part of the Hindus in the face of Muslim prowess.[9]

The emphasis on the Muslims was crucial because, as Guha points out, Bankim failed to engage directly with the British colonial force. His recovery of a glorious Hindu past consolidated as an exercise of bahubol against Muslim shows of strength imparted a "purely Hindu identity" to the Indian national character. If the Muslim is defined as the other for the construction of the pure Hindu inhabiting precolonial India, the very same Hindu is posited as the negative cultural other of the British when Bankim critiques the failure of the true Hindu to translate that unadulterated religious character into an Indian national identity. Once the presence of bahubol is established as constitutive of the essential masculinity of the Hindu, Bankim, as Partha Chatterjee has demonstrated, shifts his argument from a discourse of essentialism to that of culture to explain the lack that prevented the true Hindu from considering himself part of a nation. Benedict Anderson's explication of the formation of a nation along the lines of an imagined community occurred among the Hindus only after their entry as a colonial subject in an imperial cultural economy. It is through our contacts with "the English that we have discovered for the first time the true basis of liberty and nationality. . . . If only Hindus become desirous of liberty, if they can convince themselves of the value of liberty, they can achieve it" (quoted in P. Chatterjee, *Nationalist Thought* 55). This belated discovery of ideals that bind an imagined nation is concentrated by the necessary and vigorous animosity against the foreign rulers. In his essay *Jatibari* (Conflict between nations),[10] Bankim writes: "So long as the conflict between the native and the foreigners, the conqueror and the vanquished continues to exist, we shall remember our past glory, and there shall be no possibility of a resolution of the conflict between nations."[11] We have come full circle. The account of the rise of nationalism in the face of British conquest is seen as a necessary condition for the reinterpretation of a glorious past, which reintroduces the Muslims as the original foreigner against which Hindu prowess first needs to be established, before the nation can engage in open confrontation with the British. As Partha Chatterjee puts it, in "talking about the subjection of India, Bankim encapsulates into his conception of the cultural failure of the Indian people to face up to the realities of power a whole series of conquests dating from the first Muslim invasions of India and culminating in the establishment of British rule. To Bankim, India has been a subject nation for seven centuries" (*Nationalist Thought* 55–56).

The formation of a civil society in India revolving around the concept of a juridical "person" familiar with the ideas of individual freedom, equality, fraternity, and equal justice for all was, according to Bankim, and perhaps accurately, a direct result of British occupation, even though these very ideals were contrary to the act of territorial possession. What complicates this picture is that Bankim posits British colonialism as a positive force against Muslim tyranny. In his enunciation of the politicization of an Indian civil society through a rejuvenated Hinduism, the Muslims function as the supplemental remainder in an otherwise complete equation. Thus not only did the Hindus possess bahubol, they also were intellectually superior to the Muslims because they were able to recognize and adapt to changing sociopolitical patterns, a prerequisite for the building up of political autonomy. Thus the Hindu complaint against British colonialism was always tempered with a recognition of the positive social effects it had wrought. On the other hand, the Muslims, as on the part of the gentry, lived in comparative isolation from the changes overtaking Indian society: "Everywhere in Bengal . . . Muhammedans complain of the 'Ingilabi-zamanah' or 'the bad turn of circumstances' and the 'ashraf-gardi' or 'the upsetting of respectable classes.' The two terms I have heard thousands of times. They sum up the present dissatisfaction of the Muhammedans" (Bankim, quoted in Haldar 140–41). Other Muslims seemed stuck in a time warp and failed to realize the inadequacy of "old education" for the present time.[12] Despite Bankim's rhetorical emphasis on the need to evaluate the present in terms of the past, he failed to explore the necessary function of bahubol in British India given the presence of a number of armed conflicts.[13] This deficiency in Bankim's evaluation of the past has been variously explained by critics. Guha's criticism is perhaps the harshest but also the most cogent: "By putting *bahubol* in the wrong place in Indian history, that is, by displacing it to the precolonial period, it robbed the concept of its true historical vocation as an indispensable element of the critique without which the formation of nationhood, hence the writing of history, would not be possible in the era of imperialism" (67).[14]

At this point, I would like to return to the two historical romances, *Anandamath* and *Devi Chaudhurani*, that read as testimonials to Bankim's insistence on the presence of bahubol in India's past confrontations with the enemy. The actuation of bahubol in these two novels is intimately tied to the idea of the intellectual leader who would impart to the masses the concept of *anusilan*, a complete cultural system—dharma—that took as its foundation the practice of bhakti, with its unification of duty and knowledge. This cultural system is, for Bankim, based on his version of a regenerated Hinduism, given his belief that there was "no serious hope of progress in India except in Hinduism" (B. Chatterjee, *Letters on Hinduism* 13). His emphasis was always on what he perceived to be the correct application of the immutable principles of Hinduism. He concentrated on "the modes of application" of these "fundamental principles which underlie various religious faiths of the modern Hindus" (15) to the present time. Bankim systematically derives the fundamental principles of Hinduism by the principle of negation—by defining Hinduism as against "what the foreigners who use the word mean by the term" (7). Thus Hinduism is not, as Sir Alfred Lyall describes it, "[a] jungle of disorderly superstitious ghosts and demons, demigods and deified saints, household gods, tribal gods, local gods, universal gods with their countless shrines and temples, and the din of their discordant rites" (quoted in

Letters on Hinduism 4). It is, above all, to be restricted to "the articles of religious belief accepted by Hindus generally at the present day in exclusion of the Vedic and Brahmanic faiths out of which Hinduism evolved itself" (11). The search for a pure, untainted Hinduism was an ongoing one for Bankim. His definition of the true Hindu was synonymous with his representation of the perfect leader who would engender, through the spread of the doctrine of true Hinduism, the spirit of national solidarity: "To the Hindu his whole life is religion. To the European, his relations to God and to the spiritual world are a thing sharply distinguished from his relations to man and to the temporal world. To the Hindu, his relations to God and his relations to man, his spiritual life and temporal life are incapable of being so distinguished. They form one harmonious and compact whole" (7). It is this religious integrity that translates itself into bhakti as duty without the expectation of reward and forms the core of dharma. And when that is achieved the "Hindus will gain new life and become powerful like the English at the time of Cromwell or the Arabs under Muhammad."[15] The theory of political nationalism advanced by Bankim hinged on its harmonious unity with a renewed Hinduism. And he saw this harmonious principle incarnated in the figure of Krishna, whom he characterized as "a householder, diplomat, warrior, law giver, saint and preacher."[16] Krishna was both powerful and compassionate and articulated the essential virtues or duties necessary for a spiritual and political regeneration of India—rightful self-defense, just war, the concept of *ahimsa* (Bankim does not valorize nonviolence under any given condition; his notion of nonviolence is refraining from violence unless morally justified), and the practice of controlling one's senses.[17] Present India needed an avatar of Krishna to lead her out of subjection, but the first step to achieving that liberation was a necessary unlearning of a false past and a reinstatement of the ideal of a Hindu masculinity. Thus instead of producing an enabling critique of British colonialism, Bankim turns to past historical moments wherein he finds fitting illustrations of the ideal Hindu man. Both *Anandamath* and *Devi Chaudhurani* contain elaborate explications of Bankim's religio-political principles, as well as emblematic figures representing the idealized Hindu male warrior and guide.[18]

I do not seek to engage with the corpus of Bankim's writings that, as Tanika Sarkar has pointed out, "was notoriously elusive and that continued not only to raise very different questions and offer contradictory resolutions in many places, but also to satirize and laugh at whatever seemed closest to an agenda" ("Bankimchandra" 177). Despite the very real inconsistencies, however, I think it is accurate to assert that after 1882 he sought to provide an epistemology based on Hindu doctrines that could supply the foundation for the development of a nationalist ideology. And crucial to this epistemology was training in the rigorous religion of self-discipline (*anusilandharma*) garnered from the best in Hindu traditions. Both *Anandamath* and *Devi Chaudhurani* celebrate the potency of anusilandharma in the repeated triumphs of the Hindu rebels against the Muslims and the British representatives of the East India Company.

Both novels also illustrate Bankim's belief in the application of the practice of anusilandharma to Hindu men and women. The heroines of the two historical romances lay claim to that position precisely because they can sustain and survive the rigorous regime of self-discipline. Yet lest we think that these characterizations made Bankim an uncompromising champion of equality between the sexes, we need to examine the two texts closely to recognize how that which appears to be universally accessible is actually circumscribed by one's gendered location in terms of body and space.[19] As we read, we must remind ourselves that despite the representation in these novels of two very powerful women, their presence functions much more forcefully as a sign of that which is marked as "feminine." Derrida has critiqued the consolidation of the Western humanist subject, which occurs as though "the sign 'man' had no origin, no historical, cultural, or linguistic limit," because it cannibalizes the other by digesting information about it (116). In contrast, one could argue that the separation of the gendered other for the consolidation of the renewed male religio-political subject of Hindu nationalism is repeatedly emphasized in the two novels. The organization of the armed rebels, especially in *Anandamath*, is predicated on the removal of every association that the men may have with individual women. This is not only decisive in determining the success of one's self-discipline but also allows for the transference of the "feminine" to the land, which becomes gendered as the "motherland." Thus female rebels armed with the same self-discipline could find themselves in complex relationships with the "motherland" that lead them and us (women) to imagine the possibility whereby the sign "woman," to return to Derrida, could begin to operate a priori. That the sign "woman" could so function is not within the realm of Bankim's imaginative recuperation of history, and women's participation in men's work and their access to human resources (such as anusilandharma) is attained only by also maintaining strategically the binary opposition of "inside" and "outside." But the novels should not be read merely as inscriptions of a failure on the part of yet another Indian male exponent of nationalism to address women's issues. More significant, we should examine how the novels provide us with the occasion for raising the issue of what Spivak has called "the politics of interpretation" when dealing with "woman as the ideologically excluded other."[20] Both novels attempt to chart a movement from the "narrow and gender specific to the universal" only to confront the structural problems inherent in imagining "the ideologically constituted-constituting sexed subject in the production of and as the situational object of historical discourse."[21]

The elaboration of the principles germane to the development of a Hindu nationalism is arguably the primary intention of both novels. The dissemination of an epistemology that would harness the forces of a dispersed people in the name of the motherland forms the crux of both novels, and the intense suffering of the people in the early days of the company's rule provides the occasion for a religious-nationalist propaganda. Both novels, however, especially *Devi Chaudhurani*, also contain descriptions of gender-specific travails that are a direct result of the exercise of certain Hindu social codes. And it is on the significances of these moments and their differential relation to the overarching ideology of sanctioned Hindu cultural authority that my analysis concentrates. I begin with a summary of both novels.

The plot of *Anandamath* revolves around the lives of two married couples, Mahendra and Kalyani and Jibananda and Shanti, and their involvement with a band of rebels who call themselves Children of God. The famine, as I have said, provides the immediate occasion not only for the formation of the rebels but also as a device to involve Mahendra in the service of Bengal. Mahendra's initiation into the rebel organization provides the narrative space necessary for the articulation of the regime of self-discipline enforced on the disciples by the leader of the guerrilla organization, Satyananda.[22]

The narrative resorts to melodramatic events to accommodate the alleged death of Kalyani, and the novel turns to the representation of the life and travails of the heroine, Shanti. We are provided with a lengthy and vivid description of Shanti's early childhood, her marriage to Jibananda, her training in the art of warfare among the Sanyasins (wandering religious mendicants), and her initiation into the Children of God. The novel's penultimate ending celebrates the triumphant victory of the armed rebels over the army sent to India by Warren Hastings. True love and dedication to the country pays off for our protagonists, and in the end, Mahendra is united with his family, while Shanti and Jibananda decide to spend the rest of their life together as wandering pilgrims.

The novel, however, does not close with the victory. The last chapter includes a conversation between Satyananda and a sage (who appears a few times in the novel and has supernatural powers) in which the latter provides a rationale against further need for rebellion against the British.[23] In response to Satyananda's plaintive cry, "Alas Mother! I have failed to rescue you, you will again fall into the clutches of the Mlechhas (Non-Aryans)" (191), the sage justifies the necessary presence of the British "for the renaissance of the eternal religion [Hinduism]" (191). In a curious reversal, the sage suggests that the Santan (Children of God) rebellion would help transform the English from mere merchants to overseers of a responsible colonial government: "The Santan rebellion has come only to put the British on the throne. . . . The British are our ally and friendly power. Besides none has the requisite power to be victorious in the long run in a war against the British" (193).

The plot of *Devi Chaudhurani* is less complicated, because it basically revolves around the plight of its heroine, Prafulla, who is repeatedly victimized by various social forces. But it too has its share of incredible and melodramatic moments. The opening section of the novel is overburdened by the tragic events that befall Prafulla. Disbarred from her husband's house, her mother dead from grief, Prafulla is sold by a friend to a pimp. She manages to escape when the palanquin bearers carrying her to her buyer are attacked by robbers. She flees into the heart of the jungle, hoping to meet up with a wandering band of *sanyasis* (holy men), but instead chances upon an old *vaishnav* (a holy man dedicated to the worship of Lord Krishna) who, on his deathbed, gifts her his hoard of gold. Subsequently, she meets Bhawani Thakur, a rebel bandit, who robs the wealthy landowners in league with the East India Company's officers in order to help the poor villagers.

Bhawani Thakur is a self-appointed king of north Bengal who has taken it upon himself to rule the land until order is restored. Prafulla agrees to become his disciple and undergo strict training for five to six years.[24] After completing the training she is set up by Bhawani as Devi Chaudhurani, glorious in her splendor, and every subsequent raid is committed in her name.[25] Prafulla publicly lives the life of Devi Chaudhurani with her retinue of soldiers and ladies-in-waiting, acts as a decoy during raids, masterminds attacks on the British and the rich landowners, and distributes captured wealth among the poor, but she never participates with the rebels in any of the actual raids.

The familial plot is picked up again when Prafulla discovers that her husband's estate is about to be forfeited because of her father-in-law's inability to pay his debts and his weakness for an epicurean life. The melodramatic and sentimental reunion between husband and wife is prolonged and garrulous, and Prafulla is able to explain to her husband, Brajeswar, her symbolic role as Devi Chaudhurani. Despite her desire to excoriate her father-in-law, Prafulla restrains herself and calmly narrates the events that had led her to this position, telling her husband the reality behind her charade; the only concession she makes is that she reveals her father-in-law's inexcusable behavior toward her. Brajeswar is deeply ashamed at having condemned her without knowing the truth and is apologetic for his father's inhumane treatment. His respect for her is further heightened when he realizes that she had deliberately walked into a trap set by the British in order to see him one last time. He venerates her as "a real devi (goddess) indeed! How unworthy I am of her!" (212). Prafulla is captured by the British but through a series of clever maneuvers manages to defeat the sepoys and capture the very lieutenant sent to vanquish her.[26] The novel ends on a happy domestic note, with Prafulla reconciled with her husband and praised and loved by the very people who had once rejected her.[27]

In *Devi Chaudhurani*, as in *Anandamath*, direct criticism of the English is avoided; for example, Bhawani Thakur's role is justified because of the present lawless state of Bengal. Muslim rule, we are told, is in total collapse; the English have yet to assume control. If in *Anandamath* the Santan rebellion is legitimized as a necessary precondition for British succession, Bhawani Thakur's interim reign is vindicated as time earned wherein the British learn how to rule. Once the British have realized their genuine role in India and "the wicked found their proper punishment in the hands of the British officers" (277), Bhawani Thakur can surrender to them and serve his sentence. Critics have explained the discrepant conclusions of both novels, with their unqualified praise of British rule, as Bankim's lip service to the pressures of censorship. As Tapan Raychaudhuri suggests: "Official sensitivity to seditious intent in literary works was well known at the time when Bankim wrote these novels. The later editions of *Anandamath* had to be censored by the author to excise passages which were considered anti-British. Apprehension of official displeasure might have influenced even the first version of the novel, and *Devichaudhurani* was published after the author had been in trouble over the earlier novel" (183). It is also true, however, that Bankim's evaluation of British rule is quite complex, and elsewhere he concludes that the English have taught Indians a number of new things, among them love of independence and nation building.[28]

Most critics, writing in English, have evaluated Bankim's use of various strands of Comtean positivism, utilitarianism, and French socialism and their often quixotic juxtaposition to the Nyaya, Sankhya, Vedantic, and Bhakti schools of Hindu philosophy and religion.[29] Tanika Sarkar suggests that there is a tendency in these critics to read in Bankim's writings "a thwarted desire to escape from the prison house of derived meanings imposed by a European Enlightenment epistemology. This prison house either made a non-colonized epistemology impossible, even within a nationalist framework, or suppressed the very desire to transgress the chains of reason and rationalism and made it only possible to express this desire in the broken utterances of assumed madness" ("Bankimchandra" 177). Whatever the pitfalls of Bankim's elaboration of a patriotic Hindu cultural consciousness within the rationalist framework of a colonial epistemology, in the two novels it did provide an occasion for a vivid delineation of Hindu valor fueled by an enthusiastic religious semiotic. The novels had a tremendous influence on the new nationalist intelligentsia who used Bankim's hymn "Bande Mataram," with its unequivocal celebration of a militant nationalism, as their slogan.[30] As Partha Chatterjee puts it, "It is not surprising that in the history of political movements in India, Bankim's direct disciples were the 'revolutionary terrorists,' the small groups of armed activists drawn from the Hindu middle classes, wedded to the secret underground organization and planned assassination" (*Nationalist Thought* 79).

In both novels, the revolutionary terrorists are chiefly male. Yet Bankim does not deny the absolute exclusion of women from participation in the active work of freeing a nation from subjection. Instead he develops a paradoxical structural logic to encompass women in the authorized space of a revolutionary politics of nationalism. The novels seem to insist on the exceptional circumstances of such women who seek legitimate inclusion within the otherwise gender-specific domain of an insurrectionary organization. Shanti in *Anandamath* and Prafulla in *Devi Chaudhur-*

ani are already outside the general domestic space before their initiation in an exorbitant formation. In some ways, then, both women move from the margins of the domestic to the margins of the public sphere, and it is this marginality that allows the possibility of a return to a sanctioned private space. Though *Devi Chaudhurani* was written after *Anandamath*, I will consider the character of Prafulla in *Devi Chaudhurani* first and then examine the role and function of Shanti as a female in drag in an all-male rebel organization.

While the title of Bankim's novel—*Devi Chaudhurani*—derives from the name acquired by the protagonist, Prafulla, this eponymity can obscure as much as it reveals. Prafulla's incarnation as Devi Chaudhurani is something that is thrust on her, first by her social circumstances and then by her chance encounter with Bhawani Thakur. While it is true that the novel affirms Bankim's belief that the upper-class Hindu woman was capable of completing a rigorous course in the art of self-discipline and the study of the *sastras* and Indian philosophy, the novel equally underscores Prafulla's interpellation as a domestic subject.[31] Despite the many hardships encountered as a daughter, wife, and daughter-in-law, she never relinquishes her desire to function in these capacities and constantly seeks to legitimize assigned gender positions. Even in the chapters that are devoted to the careful delineation of Prafulla's training, the reader is reminded of Prafulla's adherence to domestic rituals. Though she never questions the strictures placed on her and masters the art of self-abnegation, she systematically defies Bhawani Thakur, her teacher, on one account: on the eleventh day of the moon she insists that she be served fish. The narrator tells us why: "That day is a Hindu widow's day in Bengal. On that day no Hindu widow . . . touch [*sic*] fish at all by way of penance in memory of her departed husband. So long as one's husband is alive the idea of putting on a widow's mode of living is shocking to every Hindu woman. Prafulla too could not get rid of that sentiment" (94).

She does not disclose her identity to Bhawani, but her one desire is to be reunited with her husband, Brajeswar, and be accepted by his family.[32] Therefore, Prafulla adopts the mask of Devi Chaudhurani but is never completely comfortable underneath it. She constantly awaits the moment when she can rip the mask off and resume her domestic position. She is an example of traditional female acculturation; she never imagines that women might desire an existence other than the prescribed one. When she hears and witnesses the ignominies that the poor tenant farmers were condemned to suffer under feudal tyranny, she willingly resolves to help them by acceding to Bhawani Thakur's plan to enshrine her as the rich warrior, Devi Chaudhurani, and use her money for the "cause of the poor" (105). But one realizes that had Prafulla not been abandoned by her husband, she would never have willingly left home to follow what she sees as a very unnatural path. She always strives to instill womanly virtues in her companion Nishi, who tends to be defiant and often a little tired of Prafulla's sanctimonious attitude toward her husband. Nishi likes to play tricks, takes great delight in masquerades, and is determined to make Prafulla's father pay for his treachery.[33] She fights against the bonds that constrict her, but Prafulla admonishes her for her frivolity and lack of respect toward the old patriarch. In fact, the novel balances the enunciation of the principles of anusilandharma and women's abilities in grasping its subtle nuances with an unhesitating valorization of woman's traditional place in a polygamous Hindu institution. One could go further and argue that perhaps Bankim asserts that it is precisely woman's resolute devotion to her husband that makes her the ideal candidate for the realization of anusilandharma. In a conversation with Nishi, Prafulla claims that "a woman's devotion is endless!" and love for one's husband is but a step to "the higher devotion for God" (one could substitute "country" for "God," because in this novel, as in *Anandamath*, the motherland is god/goddess; 84).

The novel, in keeping with the conventions of the romance genre to which it partially belongs, closes with Prafulla as Devi Chaudhurani being allowed to fulfill the role of a loving and dutiful wife, which then enables her to return as a wife to the domestic fold. The triumph of the family is also the triumph of the motherland. Prafulla's last incarnation as the Devi is one that she inaugurates, as she tells Nishi, to save her husband and father-in-law, even though the latter was responsible for betraying the Devi to the British (214). There is no space in this novel for a transgression of domestic hierarchy from within. It is only Nishi, a young woman who has never inhabited the various domestic roles assigned to the female sex—daughter, wife, mother—who is made the vehicle for the subversion of patriarchal authority.[34] Nishi reveals to the patriarch that it was Devi Chaudhurani who had helped save his honor and life by paying off his debts. Nishi tricks him into believing that the Devi had given orders to have him impaled; reduces him to an abject, weeping coward;

and extracts from him an oath to have his son marry her fictitious sister (240–45).

The last pages of the novel present a picture of domestic and political harmony. Prafulla is celebrated as an exemplary wife and daughter-in-law, and the British, as responsible administrators and governors. Prafulla's father-in-law is duly repentant, and Bhawani Thakur surrenders because "the wicked now found their proper punishment in the hands of the British officers" (277). Prafulla has no regrets, suffering no qualms at having to give up a life of independence, wealth, and rank. Prafulla is happy as the most beloved of Brajeswar's wives. When Sagar (the third wife) asks Prafulla, "Well would domestic work please you any more? Once a queen sitting on a silver throne and wearing a crown of diadem and now these petty house-hold duties, would they please you at all?" Prafulla replies:

> Yes, they will please me very well, and that is exactly why I have come back again. They constitute a woman's true duty and not sovereignty. Quite a hard task too is to lead an ideal household life. No yoga is more difficult than this. Take for instance one fact, how daily we have to manage a number of unlettered selfish and inexperienced people. No other walk of life exacts a greater sacrifice than this and no other mode of life leads to greater virtues than this. I shall practice this sort of sacrifice and renunciation. (271–72)

Thus the sacrifice demanded of women, borne out by the events in the story and at times even critiqued by Bankim, is in the end affirmed as the raison d'être of woman's existence. This is not something Prafulla had to learn through anusilandharma; it is constitutive of her very nature and what separates her from the other women in the novel. Her own tribulations as a woman, as well as her knowledge of Nishi's betrayal by the very domestic forces Prafulla consistently champions, never disturb her unswerving belief in the efficacy of the Hindu private sphere. Her life is a testimony to the triumph of the Hindu woman's essential and incorruptible nature, one that is indispensable in ensuring the sanctity of an indigenous domestic space that can compensate for the inevitable transformations in the public domain. In *Devi Chaudhurani*, woman and womanhood are inserted into social change but are not intrinsically transmuted by it. As Kumkum Sangari and Sudesh Vaid suggest in their introduction to *Recasting Women*: "The ideologies of women as carriers of tradition, often disguise, compensate, contest actual changes taking place. Womanhood is often part of an asserted or desired, not an actual cultural continuity" (17).

The conclusion of the novel, with its evocation of Prafulla in the image of the avenging goddess, affirms the prevailing necessity of a continuous, consecrated, domestic tradition, even as it represents woman as the timeless warrior.

> Come Prafulla, come now and stand once more before the public, let us have a full view of you. Stand once more, before modern society and proclaim to the world at large:
>
>> "Behold I am not new but I am the old. I am that eternal Word. Often did I come here, but you have forgotten me. So I am here again.
>> To succour the good and destroy the evil-doers, and to confirm the right am I in every age born." (278)

The ending, on the one hand, is Bankim's acknowledgment of the presence of the British and a cautionary reminder to his readers that the Devi will rise again should the need arise. On the other hand, we have just been witness to Prafulla's unqualified acceptance of and relocation into the extended patriarchal family. She is ecstatic, functioning as the best and truest of the three wives of Brajeswar. No meal is complete without a dish being cooked by her, no decision is made about anything without first consulting her, and the children of the other two wives love and respect her more than their own mothers.[35] As a humble wife, "no display of learning is at all necessary for the discharge of [Prafulla's] domestic duties. True the learned can accomplish household work much better than other, but a home is no place to make a parade of one's learning" (274–75). We are informed, nonetheless, that it was Prafulla's "knowledge of the world, her intellectual acumen, and her sound discretion [that] soon secured Prafulla a place in the administration of Haravallabh's affair. True, *the office was located outside the dwelling house, yet when knotty questions arose requiring intelligent solutions Haravallabh solicited Prafulla's opinion through his wife*" (275; emphasis added). Thus knowledge can now be transmitted from the inside to the outside without any disruption of the home, keeping home and world connected yet separate. Prafulla is never contaminated by the forces of the outside world, and it is the security of such conviction that allows the narrator to evoke Prafulla as the manifestation of the "Eternal Word." This evocation, like the channeling of Prafulla's knowledge, can very easily bypass the materiality of woman's body preserving the cultural norm of a disembodied "feminine self" as the undisrupted reality.

In *Anandamath*, the domestic is enshrined in the character of Kalyani, and the ideological power of the private sphere is reinforced in the reunion of Mahendra and Kalyani.[36] However, this resolution is not possible for its main female protagonist, Shanti. A return to the domestic space is rendered impossible by Shanti's emphasis on the lack of any "householder" (189) space for herself and her husband. The penultimate ending of the novel captures the defeat of the British troops: "Just as a small fly is crushed between the big stones, so the huge government army was crushed between the two bodies of Santans. There was no one left to carry the news to Warren Hastings" (184). Jibananda, who had died in the battle, is miraculously restored by the sage with supernatural powers and wants to return to the Santans: "What we have taken by force must be protected by the prowess of our arms" (188). Shanti, however, convinces her husband that his return would be read as an act of cowardice by one who had "hid himself for fear of expiation, [and] now finding the Santans victorious has come forward to take his share of the newly won kingdom" (188). When Jibananda insists on his duty to "serve the Mother" (189), Shanti asserts that having died in battle, the resurrected body no longer belongs to the motherland, and now "the chief part of [his] expiation is to be deprived of the pleasure of serving her" (189). The emphasis on the male body here is crucial and quite complex. Jibananda's initial death was rendered sacred in the name of a religious victory for the motherland. His new body is sacrilegious in that it is now not quite male: his manhood/maleness has been negated through death in the service of the nation. It is this absence of masculinity that is underscored in Shanti's decision to live a celibate life as they travel as Sanyasins "all over the country on pilgrimage" (189). The Santans, such as Mahendra, who had not died could go back to becoming "householders" with all the implied sexual underpinnings, yet be always ready to renounce particular sexual desire for the surrogate ecstasy experienced through intercourse with the motherland. Masculinity in this case is not denied; it is augmented. For Jibananda and Shanti, the motherland can be approached only indirectly through God, "seeking from him the boon of the Mother's complete wellbeing" (189). The body so enshrined and disciplined by the Santans is reduced to a "trifle" in the case of Jibananda's resurrected and thereby not quite male body.

How, then, are we to read Shanti, who functions in the group as a woman in drag? Before answering this question, I would like to sketch Shanti's life to suggest that her decision to join the rebel group is in many ways a culmination of a unique adolescence. Interestingly, Shanti is the only character whose life is substantially explored and explained in the pages of Bankim's text. We are first introduced to Shanti when Jibananda returns to his village to place Kalyani's baby in his sister's care. There he is tricked into meeting his wife, Shanti, and is deeply affected by this unexpected reunion. He is moved to tears at what he considers to be an abandonment of his marital vows. Shanti, in her role as dutiful wife, tries to convince Jibananda that she is happy in whatever "existence [he has] placed [on her]" (95). Jibananda, however, refuses to be placated and asserts, "I knew that I could not return to my national duty if I looked at your divine face. . . . I do not know whether the country will be ours again or not. But this I do know, that you are mine and I am yours. You are greater than this country. You are my heaven itself. Come, let us go home. I shall not return to the Ashram again" (95–96). Shanti condemns his weakness and vacillation and urges him to return to his real duty: "Shame on you! . . . [Y]ou want to renounce the path of heroism just for the sake of your wife? Do not love me so. I am willing to deprive myself even of that happiness, but never forsake your path of duty" (96). Unlike Kalyani, who is relegated to the forgotten margins of the narrative so that Mahendra can devote himself to the greater cause, Shanti becomes its principal focus. Instead of obeying her husband's wishes to take shelter in his ancestral home until such time as they can live together as husband and wife, Shanti decides to join the band of male rebels.

Book 2 opens with a description of Shanti's life that fills in the gaps which lead up to the moment of her momentous decison. Shanti, we are told, had lost her mother in infancy. The absence of a typical female role model sets the stage for her development into a woman who consistently refuses to be confined by barriers that encircle her because of the sheer accident of birth. Shanti's father, a professor of Sanskrit, allows his daughter to attend his classes along with the other, male students. Shanti's association with members of the opposite sex at such close quarters affects her behavior in some very crucial areas. First, she refuses to dress in a sari, wrapping the garment around her as one would a dhoti (the male dress). She refuses to comb her hair out in long curls and falls into the habit of streaking her forehead with holy paste, as did male Brahmins.[37] Shanti's penchant for drag is underlined from the very beginning. Despite her protests, she is forbidden from donning the Brahminic sacred thread, which is a special privilege accorded to male Brahmins alone, but no one can prevent her, given her naturally sharp intellect, from imbibing the lessons imparted to the students. Her father, realizing his daughter's intellectual potential, teaches her the rules of Sanskrit grammar as well as a few books of Sanskrit literature.

After her father's death, Shanti is left an orphan. One of the students, Jibananda, decides to take her home to his parents. It being impossible for a man and woman to live in the same house without any socially sanctioned bond, Jibananda's parents insist that the two get married. Shanti, however, refuses to let her change in status transform her behavior. She still "stubbornly refused to dress as a girl. . . . She was scarcely ever at home, but would mingle with the boys of the neighborhood and play with them like a tomboy. She used to enter the neighboring jungles alone and search for peacocks, deer, and rare fruits and flowers" (109). Her in-laws finally decide to confine her to the house, but Shanti, unable to bear this constant surveillance, runs away. She escapes into the forest, disguises herself as a sanyasi, and joins an ascetic group. The sanyasis of that period (as opposed to the time when Bankim actually wrote the novel), as the narrator tells us, were very different from those described in the texts of Sankhya philosophers. These sanyasis, though religious and ascetics, were not disposed to the "excessive otherworldliness" criticized by Bankim in his philosophic tracts and essays.[38] The band that Shanti joins "were united, well educated, strong; and knew the science of warfare. . . . Generally they were rebels against the British occupation of India. They lost no opportunity in capturing the properties of the alien government. They never failed to gather strong children every chance they got. These they educated and trained in the use of arms, and thus added to the strength of their own community" (110). Her physical appearance (disguise fails to hide Shanti's slenderness and delicacy) causes some doubts, but her powerful intellect and her diligence finally convince the sanyasis to accept her without qualms. She quickly learns "gymnastics and the use of arms, and soon became strong and hardy" (110). She travels widely with the group and takes part in a number of skirmishes.

Shanti's cross-dressing and cross-coding temporarily liberate her from what Bakhtin calls the tyranny of "hierarchical rank, privileges, norms and prohibitions."[39] After her true gender is revealed, Shanti is still al-

lowed to continue as an initiated male member of the band. But like Jibananda, who at the mere sight of his wife was ready to relinquish his devotion to the nation, Shanti's sexuality undermines the ascetic consciousness of one of the sanyasis who resorts to an uninhibited explication of
sensuous, romantic poems as a means to assault Shanti with his amorous
desires. Shanti has to leave the band, but only after she incapacitates the
sanyasi. This encounter with a sexual predator, however, transforms
Shanti in a fundamental way. Shanti, we are informed, experiences feminine feelings for the first time. These feminine emotions of "bashfulness,"
"modesty," and "radiance of feminine grace," euphemisms for a burgeoning sexual desire, convince Shanti to return home. Despite opposition from his parents, Jibananda takes her back. The two fall in love and
decide to go to Bharuipur, where Jibananda's sister, Nimi, lives with her
husband. His brother-in-law gives him a plot of land, and Jiban builds a
little cottage where he lives with his wife and tills the land to make an idyl-
lic life for themselves. But eventually Jibananda has to forsake heart and
hearth to join the Children for the sake of the motherland.

After Jibananda's unexpected visit, Shanti determines to carry out
what she had been thinking for some time. Once again she disguises herself as a sanyasi, and this time we are privy to how she dons her costume.
First she dyes a sari yellow after tearing off the borders of the cloth. She
scissors off her long hair and braids the rest of it close to her head—this
then resembles the *jatas* (a style of headdress) of the sanyasis. To hide the
curve of her breasts she ties a piece of yellow cloth tightly around them,
draping herself with the remainder of the material. With the hair she has
cut off she fashions a mustache and a beard. She covers herself entirely
with a deerskin, thus completing her masquerade.[40]

The narrative's focus on the material female body as it is made to perform in drag situates the body as the site on which sex is inscripted. We
already know that Shanti can successfully elude the social significations
of gender, for she has mastered certain elements of the performance of
masculinity in her earlier training with the male sanyasis. Yet she still
needs to be inscribed as male, which she tries to achieve by erasing specific
physical attributes that constitute female signification. In this case, the
cultural character of gender demands a connection to a material body
that needs to be marked as male to be recognized as such. The performative construction of Shanti as a man reveals the modalities of erasures and
exclusions by which the subject of gender is produced. It suggests, as Butler has argued in her critical evaluation of constructivism and essen-

tialism, "that there is an outside to what is constructed by discourse, but this is not an absolute 'outside,' an ontological thereness that exceeds or counters the boundaries of discourse; as a constitutive 'outside,' it is that which can only be thought—when it can—in relation to that discourse, at and as its most tenuous borders."[41] Bankim allows his character to stretch the parameters of this constitutive outside far beyond what could be expected in the particular historical moment of the writing of his novel. As I will show, however, the pronouncement of an "ontological thereness" was overwhelmingly necessary for the success of Bankim's ideological mission.

Even though Shanti differs significantly from Prafulla, both times we see Shanti engaged with the British soldiers, we see her removing her disguise in order to outmaneuver them. Just at the moment when Captain Thomas, the leader of the British troops sent by Warren Hastings to overpower the rebels, feels reassured that the young and handsome sanyasi he encounters sitting passively in meditation under a tree in the forest is just a harmless ascetic, "the sanyasi fell like lightning upon the Englishman and snatched his rifle from him. Then he dropped the skin from around his body, and the matted locks of hair from his head. And the Englishman found himself confronted by a ravishingly beautiful Hindu woman" (147–48). Shanti takes advantage of the captain's discomposure to ridicule him by reducing him to the level of a caged pet monkey (148). Captain Thomas's troops are defeated, but Hastings, refusing to accept defeat, sends another batallion under the captainship of Major Edwards. Shanti and Jibananda discover the encampment of the British army, and Shanti decides to get information from them in order to help the Children. Her last and most successful foray into the domain of men is in the guise of a mendicant woman. She not only gathers information about the British camp but also volunteers false information about the Children to the major, who typically underestimates the abilities of a woman, especially an Indian woman. Having received the information she desired, Shanti realizes the urgency of conveying it to the Indian rebels. Knowing that it would take her too long to get to them on foot, she tricks Major Edwards into providing her a horse. The major, presuming that Shanti is a gullible beggar woman, offers her five hundred rupees and the services of a young officer, Lindsay, to return with information regarding the true strength of the Indian soldiers. Shanti pretends to be a shy Indian woman too embarrassed to mount a horse while surrounded by men watching her. Edwards, complacent in his "positional superiority," falls into the trap carefully laid by Shanti. Shanti demurely follows Lindsay out of sight of the camp until they enter a solitary meadow. She at once drops the charade, throws Lindsay off the horse, and, leaving him helpless on the ground, rides away.

It could be argued that Bankim reveals how women are essential for the success of the indigenous forces. It is precisely Shanti's ability to perform as male and female that allows her to outwit Major Edwards and Lindsay. Jasodhara Bagchi points out that "in creating Shanti, . . . Bankim delinks wifehood from the 'enclosed space' of domesticity."[42] Bagchi contrasts Shanti to Draupadi, the heroine of the epic *Mahabharatha*, concluding that "while Draupadi was a mere camp follower of her five husbands, the first to fall on the way, the neo-Positivist heroine of Bankim marches abreast with her fellow traveller husband in their joint quest for the welfare of the Motherland. . . . The restoration of Order in the tortuous situation of a colonial society transforms the man-woman relationship into an allegory of heroism that crosses the boundaries of naturalism" (61–62). Shanti's easy return to her ascribed sexed/gendered body, however, reveals the ideological force of that which is considered "natural" and reasserts the proscriptive power of normative forces.

A crucial distinction between the men involved in the rebel group and Shanti revolves around the individual's relationship to the domestic—the men had to renounce or suppress their familial ties, especially the role of husband. Shanti's ability, on the other hand, to perform as a "male" participant (being a female in male disguise) is closely tied to her marital status, which is indelibly underlined by her sexed as well as gendered body. After Shanti is initiated as a disciple, she has to undergo a confrontation with Satyananda, the rebel leader. He immediately uncovers Shanti's identity as female and rips the false beard off her face. According to him, no disguise could alter her "voice, the glances of [her] eyes" (104)—essential and behavioral characteristics that distinguish women from men. The conversation between the two after this disclosure is enlightening. Shanti raises the question: "My Lord, what fault have I committed? Is there never strength to be found in the arms of a woman?" (104). The first question is slightly postponed while the issue of strength is settled. Satyananda wants her to string a steel bow with wire. Only four men, including her husband, were able to string the bow without unbending it and being thrown backward as a result. Shanti passes the test without difficulty, and the leader is "surprised, *afraid* and astounded" (105; emphasis added).[43] His resolution of this fearful and extraordinary event is phrased as a question: "Are you a goddess or a *mere* woman"? (105; emphasis added). Although Shanti answers that she is "only a woman," Satyananda concludes that she, with her obvious strength, cannot be a child widow who lives on one meal a day.[44]

Once it is revealed that she is married, Satyananda realizes that she must be Jibananda's wife and attacks her integrity: "Why have you come to commit this sin?" (105). Woman's presence would necessarily distract men from their purpose, because the "mind [*sic*] of ordinary men are attracted by women. . . . Because of this the vow of the Santans is this, that, they will not be seated on the same seat as a woman" (106). Shanti insists that she had been fulfilling her role as dutiful wife by following the path chosen by her husband; she had come exclusively to practice her religion; she was not "overwhelmed with sorrow" at the separation from her husband, but had come instead to strengthen her husband's purpose. Satyananda cannot entirely accept Shanti's determination of her subject position in her logical exposition of the religio-political discourse. Though he grants that she is a "chaste wife" (an oxymoron in and of itself), "a wife is only a partner in the duties of a householder. What place can she have in his heroic deeds?" (106). The chapter ends with Shanti being allowed to spend the night in Anandamath, even as Satyananda expresses his trepidation that her "brow [that] flames like fire," like the goddess Bhawani, "might burn the Santans" (107). The sexual connotations could not be more explicit. In this conversation, despite the elevation of woman to goddess, the power of the metaphor made explicit in the syntactic emphasis on the adverb "as" cannot quite displace "woman" from her anchoring in a naturalized, biologically sexed category. Thus every position that she determines or is determined by is circumscribed by a sex that is perceived as inherent and inevitably defines her as an object of heterosexual desire.

Jibananda's immediate recovery of Shanti as his wife underneath the male disguise confirms again that the female sex cannot escape recognition by the discerning male eye. The conversation between the two does not merely illustrate a playful encounter between husband and wife. Though the dialogue illuminates Shanti's sophistry in language games, it simultaneously elucidates what Diane Elam, adapting Kant, calls the "synthetic judgment" model for gender and sex determination. She writes: "the synthetic judgement would insist that the experience of sex and gender is the correct basis on which to draw the distinction. Within this model, the *a priori* would privilege 'sex' because sex is proposed as a category before thought: sex determines thought."[45] To explore the ramifications of the proposed model, I provide the following discussion between Jibananda and Shanti:

Although Shanti was dressed as a man he immediately recognised her and said, "What is this, Shanti?" . . .

"Who is Shanti, Sir?"

Jibananda was amazed. . . . "Who is Shanti, Sir? Why, are you not Shanti?"

Shanti replied with contempt, "I am Navinanda Goswami. . . ."

He said, "This is a new farce indeed. Well Navinanda, why are you here?" . . .

Shanti: I have come this day to embrace the religion of the Santans and I have been initiated.

Jibananada: What terrible misfortune! Is it true.

Shanti: Why misfortune? You too are initiated?

Jibananda: You are a woman.

Shanti: How is that? How did you come to that conclusion?

Jibananda: I thought my wife was a woman.

Shanti: Have you a wife?

Jibananda: At least that is what I knew.

Shanti: It is your belief that I am your wife? . . .

Shanti: If such a ludicrous thought has assaulted your consciousness, then, pray tell me what should be your duty?

Jibananda: I should forcibly take off your upper garment and kiss you.

Shanti: . . . When you were initiated you swore, you would not sit on the same seat with a woman. If you believe me to be a woman—this kind of mistaking a rope for a snake often occurs—then you should sit on a different seat. It is against your duty too to talk to me. . . .

Being defeated Jibananda made a separate bed for himself and retired for the night. (110–11)

By refusing to respond to the naming of her self as Shanti and by insisting that she is Navinanda, Shanti underscores her new identity as male (the irony of the name is not lost; *navin* means "new"). Starting from this new identity, Jibananda can use nothing from her past, such as their shared home in Bharuipur, to reclaim Shanti. When she discloses that she has been initiated, the discussion shifts to the issue of grounds—when is a woman a woman? If women are initiated into the group it is a misfortune, in this case not because women should not participate in the group but because women are wives and a wife is a woman. And a woman-wife who refuses identification as woman and as wife and claims to be a "new" man undermines the grounds on which the ascetic male organization is founded. Further, the tautological argument suggests the impossibility of thought outside of predetermined sex categories. Jibananda believes her to be his wife, and despite his relinquishing of his role as a desiring male, heterosexual, domestic subject, the woman-wife's mere presence is enough to shift his allegiance from the motherland to woman-wife. In response to Shanti's question as to what his duty should be if he believes her to be his wife, Jibananda's answer at once affirms man's ever ready sexual desire—he wants to disrobe and make love to her. This is exactly what the leader had confirmed in his conversation with Shanti. But Shanti proves him wrong by affirming man's governing desire under which all other desires are to be subsumed—desire for the gendered nation. The name of the motherland spatiotemporally displaces the name of the father (the organizing principle for heterosexual desire), and the determination of thought by sex to which men seem to be individually bound is now metonymically contained by the generalized figure of nation as woman-mother. The transposition of "woman" from wife to mother helps direct Jibananda's desire to its proper object, even as woman-wife's relationship to the mother-nation is restricted to performance in male garb.

The question that the text begs is whether an unmarried woman could have maintained her position as a female in drag in an ascetic, male, guerrilla organization. The narrative closure of Shanti's life suggests otherwise. When she discovers her husband's body, it is as a bereaved wife—the question of drag is completely erased. And her decision not to return to the fold could be a recognition of the fact that once her identity has been revealed to all in the group, she can no longer participate in their rebellious activities in drag. Thus in this sense gender identity becomes intricately connected to sexual identity, and male identity is underlined as "compulsory" because women can at times act like men but can never be men. In an incipient nationalist discourse of the kind offered in the novel, a reinforcement of a compulsory male identity is crucial if Bankim's theory of bahubol is to be upheld. A Hindu nation is dependent for its manifestation on the Hindu male, even though the disciplinary knowledge that produces him can be made accessible to extraordinary women. Here, drag does not undermine notions of proper gender but rather bolsters it. Butler argues that there is no " 'proper' gender, a gender proper to one sex rather than another, which is in some sense that sex's cultural property. Where that notion of 'proper' operates, it is always and only *improperly* installed as the effect of a compulsory system. . . . *[G]ender is a kind of imitation for which there is no original*; in fact, it is a kind of imitation that produces the very notion of the original as an effect and consequence of the imitation itself" ("Imitation" 21). In Bankim's novel, parody does not underscore the idea that gender is nothing but an imitation—it does just the contrary. In *Anandamath*, male gender is affirmed again and again as the original, even as the female sex appears to function as the a priori category before thought. This does not so much privilege thought as female as it suggests the possibility of male access to thought unmediated by a gender that for all purposes is assumed to be the originary given.

In another conversation between Shanti and Satyananda, the hierarchy between genders and its relationship to thought is further underscored. Shanti is allowed to remain in the rebel group after she convinces the leader of her superior intelligence. The leader acknowledges defeat and asserts that he is like her son, yet he does not refer to her as his mother but as his daughter, thereby keeping the hierarchy intact. He commands her to save her husband and accomplish his (the leader's) work (139). Lest we believe that woman is successfully elevated above man in this dictum to save him, Shanti separates her religious task from that of her husband's. According to her, "my husband is great, but my religion is greater, but greater still than that is the religion of my husband" (139). Thus despite woman's access to the pedagogy of anusilandharma and Shanti's more astute understanding of its spiritual concepts, woman herself avers the truth of male privilege.

Interestingly, Bankim severely criticizes upper-caste, Hindu male privilege in "Samya" (Egalitarianism), published in 1879. Tanika Sarkar has astutely evaluated this text as "a relentless exploration of the homo hierarchichus within Hindu society and the interlocked and extreme character of class, caste and gender oppression that went beyond the hierarchical divisions in other societies" ("Bankimchandra" 195). After providing a harsh critique of the system, wherein the related structures of caste and class help maintain the privilege and power of the few in relation to the lower-caste Hindu and the poor Muslim peasant, Bankim turns to gender oppression as the sine qua non of systemic inequality. In the section on equal rights for women, Bankim argues against the governing double sexual standard that supports polygamy, demands absolute chastity from women, prevents widows from remarrying, denies the right of inheritance for female children, confines women to their homes, and denies women the right to education.[46] If in *Devi Chaudhurani* Prafulla compares the worship of her husband to that of God, in "Samya" Bankim describes this worship as "the slavery of women [that] has gone so far that the ideal wife Draupadi could, with pride, tell Satyabhama how she served even the other wives of her husband just to please him" (190). Bankim's repudiation of this critical reformist stance in favor of an authoritarian reaffirmation of Hindu domestic ideology is, as I have shown, driven by a political agenda that seeks to produce a Hindu masculinity as a necessary condition for the emergence of a Hindu nation. In his radical revision of the representations of the Hindu male in existing discourse, Bankim felt it imperative to maintain an exclusive separation of genders and their correlated spheres. Moreover, he endorses precisely the image of women in the Sastras that he sought to contest in "Samya."

Both *Devi Chaudhurani* and *Anandamath* illustrate Bankim's desire to exemplify "woman" as the metonymic ideal of the disembodied feminine that helps generate a particular Hindu masculinity, while marking "woman" as the signifier of a sacrosanct traditional domesticity. This paradoxical double gesture is perhaps epitomized in Bankim's valorization of sati, not only the execution of the wife burning on the funeral pyre of her husband but also "willed sati" (another oxymoron)—woman as the good wife—in "Kamalakanter Daptar," one of his greatest satires. Mourning the current condition of his devastated country and wondering if the country would ever be rejuvenated, Kamalakanta is consoled by the image of woman burning on the sacred funeral pyre of her husband:

> I can see the funeral pyre alight, the chaste wife sitting at the heart of the blazing flames, clasping the feet of her husband lovingly to her breasts. . . . Slowly the fire spreads, destroying one part of the body and entering another. . . . [H]er face is joyful. . . . [W]hen I remember that only some time ago . . . our women could die like that then the new hope rises in me and I have faith that we, too, have the seeds of greatness within us. . . . Women of Bengal! You are the true jewels of this country.[47]

"Sati," as the most proper of female nouns, is the consummation of the domestic ideal, whereas sati as an act transforms the public sphere in its spectacular rendition of a courageous woman facing the flames that consume her body.[48] In this particular evocation of the ritual of sati, Bankim, even as he aggrandizes woman's valor, asserts that the performance of the Hindu woman's "courageous acquiescence" in her own material annihilation can best be gauged by man through his power to transfix the burning body in his gaze. The female body is then dematerialized as its strength and courage materializes in the "we" of the overwhelmingly masculine, imagined community of the Hindu nation. I choose to conclude this chapter by focusing on a nationalist writer's utilization of sati as an illustration of one aspect of an epistemological mechanism within which the Hindu woman is marked as different. In the next chapter I offer an exploration of various ways in which sati as a sedimented effect of representational reiteration becomes the Hindu woman in three Victorian texts.

CHAPTER TWO

Woman as "Suttee": The Construction of India in Three Victorian Narratives

In colonial records and in Anglo-Indian literary representations, the Indian Mutiny of 1857 was,[1] as Jenny Sharpe has pointed out, "closely imbricated with the violation of English womanhood" (2). Through her brilliant readings of a number of historical documents and mutiny fiction, Sharpe reveals how the exhibition of the mutilated and ravaged bodies of English women functioned as the "retroactive effect of a terror introducing spectacle that ushered in a new imperial authority in which a feudal hierarchy was rearticulated as a relationship of race" (81). Once the mutiny became the site for the encoding of imperial difference as racial distinction, it could be evoked whenever that distinction was seen as imperiled. Thus Sharpe reads Flora Annie Steel's mutiny novel, *On the Face of the Waters* (1896), in the context of the controversy generated by the Ibert Bill that granted Indian magistrates criminal jurisdiction over Europeans in rural districts. The assigning of absolute judicial authority to a brown man raised the specter of the erasure of racial inequality in the impossibility of a discursive representation of the rape of a white woman in a "colored" court. According to Sharpe, Steel rewrites the mutiny novel with a singular difference—she creates a place for Anglo-Indian female agency that then functions as an index for gauging the changing circumstance of white women in India in the latter part of the nineteenth century.[2] Yet this negotiation of gender power in the Anglo-Indian world could be adjudicated partly by the exclusion of the Indian woman who necessarily functions as the "ideologically excluded [racial] other."[3]

In this chapter I focus on three texts—Harriet Martineau's *British Rule in India*, Meadows Taylor's *Seeta*, and Flora Annie Steel's *On the Face of the Waters*—to suggest how the deployment of the Sepoy Mutiny in each initiates a scene of "writing that conquers" (Certeau xxv). Each recounting of the mutiny enables, to paraphrase Michel de Certeau, the production of the colonized space as a "savage" page on which British desire may be written. My juxtaposition of a popular history with two novels allows me to reveal how history, writing, and the novelization of history enable the production of a seamless narrative space that suppresses the "mutually constituting relations of Western Selves and their Others" (Inden 3). The production of a fixed English identity in the nineteenth century was at least partially enabled by a hysterical discourse of othering that even provided a space for the inclusion of English women in the name of the preservation of a necessary racial homogeneity. In her scrupulous analysis of British feminism's imperial location, Antoinette Burton discloses how the "languages of imperialism—articulating as they did the parameters of cultural superiority, political trusteeship, and sheer Englishness—[were] among the most readily available to women involved in various aspects of the British women's movement from the Victorian period onward" (2). If both Sharpe and Burton focus on the manner in which colonial/imperial historical narratives are negotiated by British and Anglo-Indian women in order to mark a kind of woman as a subject of history, my reading of the "remaking of history" in the three texts is indebted to Hélène Cixous's wonderful insight that as "subject *for* history, woman always occurs simultaneously in several places."[4] In my analysis of the scenes of mutiny violence as ones that conquer, I reveal how the other woman marks the site for the narration of an India whose proper name could only be "Hindu India." Despite numerous references to Muslim rule and individual Muslim rulers and leaders, the ethnogeography of the colonized space is rendered essentially Hindu and functions as a descriptive counterpoint to an emerging/emergent British India. This articulation of a Hindu India is intrinsically bound up with the production of the Indian woman as specifically Hindu and who then becomes the epistemological and ontological cultural principle against which the history of British India is enacted. Muslim India, in this particular representation of "colonialism's culture" (to borrow the title of Nicholas Thomas's book), functions as a backdrop for the staging of a temporal development of British ascension in India. I will read the three texts in order of when they were published, beginning with Martineau's *British Rule in India* (1857).

Volumes have been written about the history and ideology of the British Empire and its conflict with almost every other Victorian philosophy, such as utilitarianism, Chartism, and the rise of feminism. John Stuart Mill's infamous lines on the inability of the Indian people to govern themselves and the absolute necessity of English civilizing presence abroad has made connoisseurs of the Victorian age cringe with embarrassment. Yet only recently have literary scholars begun to pay attention to the work produced during the so-called Age of Empire. These scholars have concerned themselves primarily with the fiction of Flora Annie Steel, Rudyard Kipling, Rider Haggard, Joseph Conrad, E. M. Forster, and Robert Louis Stevenson. This interest in the obvious imperialist texts of the last thirty years of the nineteenth century does, however unintentionally, help sustain the accepted belief that there exists a violent epistemic rupture initiated by imperialism in Victorian England. Said, arguing precisely the opposite, suggests that we need to investigate those texts which constitute the "great tradition"—Austen, Dickens, Thackeray, Eliot, Trollope— and examine their complicity with and contribution to the unassailable progress of the British Empire.[5] His reading of Austen's *Mansfield Park* suggests that we should view the earlier works of British literature "as part of the structure of an expanding imperialist venture . . . [that] opens up a broad expanse of domestic imperialist culture without which Britain's subsequent acquisition of territory would not have been possible" (*Culture and Imperialism* 95).

Harriet Martineau's *British Rule in India* occupies a space different from that inhabited either by the overtly imperialist works or by the earlier "domestic" narratives characterized as insular and exclusively metropolitan. The unique position of the text parallels Martineau's own position in Victorian England between 1822 and 1870. Martineau's is not one of those suppressed women's voices that feminist historians, literary critics, and sociologists have unearthed from forgotten archives in the last thirty years or so. Martineau occupies the coveted position of being one of the few nineteenth-century women activists whose social and political writings were regarded as valuable contributions to the production of knowledge that ratified the powers of a rapidly growing middle class. Dierdre David, using Gramsci's notion of the organic intellectual, has argued that Martineau, along with her male contemporaries, was responsible for "giving 'awareness' and 'homogeneity' to an increasingly powerful social class and performing functions of 'legitimation' and 'elaboration' for the influential ideologies of that class" (6). As a woman journalist, historian, political writer, novelist, investigative traveler, and correspondent who wrote copiously for almost an uninterrupted fifty-four years, Martineau ratifies her position as an organic intellectual who actively participated in the dissemination of contemporary Victorian ideas and ideals that led to the consolidation of the hegemony of the middle class to which she belonged. Martineau possessed an uncanny ability to grasp new ideas, and in her political, economic, social, and historical writings she was chiefly concerned with communicating new and radical propositions to the masses as lucidly as possible. Martineau consistently documented, clarified, elaborated, supported, and advocated the thoughts and beliefs of the original thinkers of her time, including Adam Smith, Thomas Malthus, David Ricardo, James Mill, Joseph Priestley, Jeremy Bentham, and such active feminists as Mary Wollstonecraft, Florence Nightingale, and Josephine Butler.

Despite Martineau's own assertion that she was merely a passive observer dutifully recording history in the making, I agree with David's assessment of Martineau's "female work of journalistic popularisation" as equally important in the "making" of Victorian society as was the "male work of banking, business, and politics" (31). I want to turn to this idea of "making"—or, as Foucault would say, producing discursive arenas that involve "sets of regulative practices" which designate their exclusions and choices—in situating Martineau's particular history of India. To David's list of "male work" one must add empire building, a venture that necessitates the elaboration of the spirit of an autochthonous nationhood. Given Martineau's role as a popularizer of contemporary intellectual and political thought, one can conclude that not only would her history reach a wide audience and participate in a validation of British presence abroad but also that it would be unesoteric, entertaining, and jingoistic. Thus the text, as regards its juxtaposition to both the later imperialist texts and the early domestic narratives, partakes of the characteristics of both genres. Because it is a ratification of British imperialism, it really cannot place India in its margins; because it is being written for a large, middle-class audience often unfamiliar and sometimes uncomfortable with the idea of its Parliament being involved in governing a land so strange and so far away, Martineau's narrative, even as it outlines the history of India from 1593 to 1857, domesticates imperialism for the British palate. This need for domestication is further exacerbated by the immediate cause that necessitates the production of precisely such a historical version—the 1857 Indian Mutiny that caught both the leaders at home and the English abroad by complete surprise.

The mutiny and the reported atrocities committed by the native soldiers and their cohorts had left the English at home and in India questioning the governing of such a vast and diverse land, a rule that before the rebellion had seemed natural and inevitable. As she herself writes in the preface, Martineau designed *British Rule in India*, written in the wake of the mutiny, to provide a narrative that would enable the general public, who were always her primary audience, to get "a clear conception of past incidents and of the present field of action" (vi). At the moment, in October 1857, "hearts are palpitating too strongly . . . to leave our judgement free and fair. When this emotion has calmed down, no doubt the natural effect of all powerful emotion will appear in the strengthening and enlightening of the judicial, inventive and reflective faculties, and India will be governed better than it has yet" (vi). Martineau's history concludes on the eve of the mutiny and documents none of the "events" that caused Anglo-Indian and British hearts to "palpitate strongly." The mutiny is described merely as that which fractured existing British life in India "like ice in spring" (35). The metaphor makes clear that Martineau sees the mutiny as an anomalous occurrence; she is convinced that her readers will at the end of their perusal of her history "be enabled the better to understand the meaning and the bearings of the measures which will be taken for the *re-affirmation* of *our* empire" (356; emphasis added).

Martineau's history primarily aims to reinterpret for the angered, shocked, and scared English population the strength and cohesiveness of the notion of an Englishness that should consolidate the nation in the time of crisis. This synchronic symbiosis between culture and nation would enable the English simultaneously to acknowledge, on the one hand, their mistake in trying to coerce the indigenous population to adopt Western religion and customs and, on the other, to reinforce their continued presence in India as standard-bearers of a progressive enlightenment. The English must appreciate and respect Indian traditions, which in the end would prove beneficial to all. The English reading public is informed, without any hesitation on the writer's part, that when the British were forced to resort to "compulsory annexation," as with that of the Burmese provinces, they were motivated not by a "territorial rapacity" but by a desire to obtain "better security for the future" and to quell the "barbaric races that lived on either side" of the Irrawaddy River, thereby facilitating free commerce between the frontiers (260–73). The sepoys involved in the mutiny were deluded if they thought "*our raj* were [*sic*] really over" (277; emphasis added), because the "bottomless chasm which yawns between the interior nature of the Asiatic and the European races" (296) is revealed by the blatant disregard for humanity by "the vast multitude of those whom we were striving to raise to a condition of fellow-citizenship with ourselves, [and] who have been waiting for the expiration of our century to turn us not only out of the country, but out of the world" (298). This explanation enforces the by now inevitable conclusion—they require us to save them from themselves. People will complain under any rule, that is the very nature of things, but in India there is this "marked feature, that there is always most to complain of where the Europeans have not been" (335).

Because Martineau does not write a narrative of the mutiny, there is none of the sensationalism and melodrama that permeate contemporary and subsequent depictions of the horrors perpetrated by the mutineers. Her aim is not to fan the flames of wrath, such as Macaulay attempts: "The cruelties of the Sepoys, and above all the indignities which English ladies have undergone, have inflamed the nation to a degree unprecedented within my memory. All the philanthropic cant of peace Societies, and Aborigine's Protection Societies, and Societies for the Reformation of Criminals, is silenced. There is one terrible cry for revenge" (103). Rather, Martineau intends to calm down the nation and renew the vigor of its "civilizing and dispassionate rule" (333).

In her ancillary status as a woman intellectual, Martineau ratified the beliefs of the rising middle class. Her account of the British in India is presented in a narrative form similar to that of some of the tales in her *Illustrations of Political Economy*; it is told simply, as a tale with the "once upon a time" element pervading the entire account. Salient incidents that reveal the corruption and childlike nature of the Indian rulers as opposed to the adult, rational, enlightened nature of most of the governors-general; her sympathy for the ignorant native who felt that his soul was being jeopardized by commands given by the British, who failed to gauge the resentment and fear generated by what they thought were sensible orders (grease the rifles, wear a hat, and so forth); her anger and contempt for some of the English in India who were content to live a life of ease and luxury with no regard to their actual purpose for being there; and brisk sketches of the actual progress of imperialism, with highlighted dates and events—these elements produce a succinct, apparently unbiased, and very readable story.

British Rule in India, despite its claim to be a history, is remarkably similar in style and tone to her depictions of other societies—America, Egypt, and even England. *Society in America* and *Eastern Life, Present and Past* are travel narratives that depend on eyewitness accounts to clarify and explicate life, religion, cultural practices, and the people inhabiting foreign spaces. Martineau's history of India emulates the narrative structure of the travel genre in which the traveler, to ground the veracity of her travelogue, provides the reader with a cartography of the landscape. Thus we have Martineau perched atop the Himalayas making visible to the mid-Victorian, middle-class reader the vast geographic expanse that constitutes "our great dependency." Martineau's adjudicating position in this text, unlike in her other travel narratives, is never marked as female, implications of which I will discuss below. Her strategy of representation can be best described by the term "anti-conquest," elaborated by Mary Louise Pratt as that which allows "European bourgeois subjects . . . to secure their innocence in the same moment as they assert European hegemony" (7). The inflection of Martineau's exploratory history, like the travel and exploration writings Pratt studies, does not echo the "imperial rhetorics of conquest," even as it adopts the subject position of the "anti-conquest figure"—"the 'seeing-man,' an admittedly unfriendly label for the European male subject of European landscape discourse—he whose imperial eyes look out passively and possess" (7).

The spatial denouement is marked by one crucial difference: it is imagined; Martineau, like most of her readers, never actually visited India. But it is crucial for the purposes of her history that she enable her readers to construct an "imagined community" whereby they are all equally implicated and involved in the management of this geographic region—the glorious India of 4000 B.C. now riven by civil wars and petty squabbles among indigenous rulers. It is not only the familiarization of a foreign landscape through vivid description that enables such an imaginary community; the pseudo-travel narrative/history is also disrupted by frequent references to a shared knowledge about India between the author and her English reader. Punctuating the narrative are such statements as "as you have heard," "as we have been told," and "as Lord Bentick's letters reveal." The letters are not revealed in the pages of Martineau's history, nor are other documents that can verify her account. And this absence of official historiographic markers is precisely what makes Martineau's history a popular text. Having provided a sketch of the history of India from

1593 to 1857, having revealed to the general audience that the Sepoy Mutiny was the fault of a few misguided and intolerant leaders (who were duly punished and removed from their offices), and having outlined a general policy requiring increasing knowledge of the conquered land and its peoples and a kinder and gentler guiding hand as befits a superior race, Martineau comes to the foregone conclusion "ascertained speedily and certainly" that India

> is a splendid country for its natural advantages and its traditional grandeur. Its capital, on which our eyes now wait so anxiously for the coming forth of a thousand of our countrymen and countrywomen, vies with the capitals of Europe in numbers and splendour. As it is the last, so it is the richest of our acquisitions; and its recent condition is as fair a warning as we could have of what must become of India, in the most peaceful times, *if our civilizing and dispassionate rule were withdrawn.* (332–33; emphasis added)

It is this last clause that allows the reader to go back to the beginning of the historical account and realize how Muslim rule is set up to be the very antithesis of the British civilizing mission. The steady and increasingly significant presence of the "Mohammedans" in India since 1193 is repeatedly decribed in terms of violent conquest by a zealous, proselytizing people brandishing swords in the name of the Prophet. The British reader is seduced very early in the history by Martineau's brilliant juxtaposition of historical events: "when our Coeur-de-Lion was fighting against the children of the Prophet in the Holy Land of Christendom, . . . the Mohammedans took real possession of the Holy Land of the Hindoos, and set up their banner and their throne at Delhi" (21). The image offered here of two ancient, holy lands that resist a common, encroaching enemy suggests the staying power of both against the "forces of fanaticism" (20). Having set up the Mohammedans as fanatical invaders, Martineau can then eulogize exceptional figures such as Akbar, "whose long reign was a blessing to the Hindoos, in comparison with every other since the followers of the Prophet entered their country" (22), and still maintain that the changes effected in "Hindoo institutions" were "much more [due] to the indigenous faults of the antique polity than to the operations of foreign [read "Muslim"] influences" (19). All in all, Martineau's history emphasizes the essential indigenism of India as Hindu, signifying the geographic space stretching from the Himalayas to the Vindhya Mountains in one direction "and from the Burramppoter [*sic*] to the Indus in the other as 'Hindoostan Proper'" (8).

To glorify the essential Hinduness of a primeval India capable of surviving the onslaught of Muslim domination, Martineau, even though she often refers to the consolidation of Muslim hegemony as the Mogul Empire, has to present the Muslims as incapable of actually making "Hindoostan Proper" a Muslim colony. Thus the "Double Government of India which all the civilized world criticizes, and which stands as an anomaly in political history" (158) is the only viable form of government "in the case of an aggregate of states, poor and misgoverned, and in such a condition of anarchy that the Commercial company was not so much tempted as compelled to overrule by its power of civilization the terrorism and corruption of its native rivals and tyrants" (159). In case her reader misses the point, Martineau hammers it home: "India has never yet been colonized" (159). Thus British rule in India will not only counter the tyrannical feudalism of Muslim and Hindu kings but will also produce its object of supervision in the recognizable geographic entity of a political and territorial colony, which is, in Martineau's treatise, characteristically Hindu. The following description will make evident my point, because it reveals how Martineau generates a conceptual cartography that, as Graham Huggan has pointed out, encapsulates certain significant rhetorical strategies implemented in colonial discursive practices such as "the reinscription, enclosure and hierarchization of space . . . for the acquisition, management and reinforcement of colonial power" (125): the Vindhya Mountains "might seem to the people of the valleys a barrier cutting off Hindoostan Proper (or the Bengal Presidency) from the true peninsula of India," but Martineau, like the "god in his 'abode of Snow,' may overlook them" and capture for her British readers "that which is now British India" (8, 13). The textual production of British India in all its vastness is firmly anchored in the all-seeing eye of Martineau and by extension her English reader in the first thirteen pages of her history. Subsequent elaboration of the Mogul Empire in India, for all its detail, is not only temporally distanced in a narrative past but also belongs to a discursive order different from that exemplified by the "perceiving and speaking subject" (Pratt 64) of *British Rule in India*.

As I mentioned, by adopting the authorizing power of the European bourgeois subject in the narration of her history, Martineau rendered her gender opaque. This subject position is in complete contrast to the narrative voice in most of her other works, including *Eastern Life, Past and Present* and *Society in America*. In her astute critical assessment of Martineau's works and career, David notes how Martineau's "attitude towards male cultural and social authority is undeniably ambiguous," making her "arguably the Victorian feminist who more consistently than any other publicly committed herself to women's causes . . . [even as] she never ceased to cast herself in the role of intellectual daughter" (58). The very theoretical framework David uses to read Martineau's contribution to Victorian economy, politics, and letters is gendered, for she casts Martineau as a female organic intellectual, an equivocal position to say the least. As David subsequently goes on to show, it is this very ambivalence that is constitutive of "the enactment of her Gramscian organic role for the English middle class" (54), which, even as it accommodated her "uncompromising feminism" (31), "expressed and helped to constitute important Victorian prescriptions for woman's role and function . . . [and incorporated] into her feminist writings the inconsistent views of women held by that class" (54). Thus one would expect to see the marked presence of a gendered female subject and/or voice in the explication of British presence in India. Not so: not only does Martineau adopt the putative nongendered position of the universal bourgeois subject, but her history of India contains no substantial depictions of the lives of Indian women.

The presence of Muslim women in India is evoked in the allusion to the zenana, in the reference to "the glorious Nurjehan [*sic*]" (35), and in the unamed daughter of Shah Jahan, who after being severely burned was restored by the English doctor Mr. Gabriel Boughton. This incident is mentioned as an example of the many "accidents" through which "the commercial fortunes [of the East India Company] were advanced, and 'a stake in the country' . . . fairly appointed to them [the company officers]" (50). The named doctor, having saved the unnamed princess, gained "great influence with her father. He used his power in obtaining freedom of commerce for his countrymen. When he was in the service of the Governor of Bengal soon after, privileges of high importance were obtained and practically enjoyed" (50–51). We do hear of Chand Bibi, "an Indian Joan-of-Arc" and "the greatest of Indian heroines, [who] fought in the breach at Ahmednugger [*sic*], in complete armour, though veiled" (23) against Akbar's invasion of the country south of the Deccan. In fact, this is the only substantial reference to an individual woman, and being exceptional, she merits an entire paragraph. Even though Hindu women are not evoked in any greater number, the form of their representation is significantly different. References include a paradoxical description of "Hindoo women," who we are told "held a low rank theoretically, but practically were like matrons and maidens in those essential ideas and feelings which are common to all races in all times" (28). Thus the intrinsic nature of the Hindu woman makes her similar to women everywhere and therefore less alien to the British reader. The second half of the above description suggests that Muslim women too must exhibit these common essential characteristics, but their marked absence in Martineau's delineation of the everyday life of people in India suggests their exclusion from an Indian polity. The description then continues: "The same may be said of the handsome children. The juvenile gentry looked and behaved like little men and women; and the children of the poor (who went to school, however, and learned writing and arithmetic), rolled in the dust, and played in the streets like any Christians" (28–29). The diurnal existence of people in India is similar to life in the Christian world, but once again the juxtaposition of Hindu and Christian leaves the "Mohammedan subjects," male and female, on the peripheries of the India being delineated in these pages.

As the contemporary reader assesses the India being unwrapped for a nineteenth-century British audience, she knows that she is going to be confronted, sooner or later, with the specter of sati, or widow burning. Lata Mani indicates that "nineteenth-century British India was marked by a series of debates on reforming the status of women. The first, and most sensational public debate, was concerned with outlawing sati" ("Production" 107). In *Eastern Life* and *Society in America*, the marked sites of difference—the harem, the Shaker women, and the slave—are vigorously critiqued. David has argued, quite correctly, that "none of her [Martineau's] criticism of the social and political status of English women is as vividly compelling as her matchless attack on the condition of women in America" (49). *Eastern Life* presents us with Martineau's harsh indictment of polygamy. Confronted with the condition of the women in the harem and the eunuchs guarding the doors to the women's quarters, Martineau tries unsuccessfully to remind herself that "every arrangement and prevalent practice had some one fair side,—some one redeeming quality" (259), but in polygamy she finds none. According to her, the longer one studies it, the more horrified one is by the "intricacy of its iniquity, and the more does one's heart feel as if it would break" (59). The emotional distress caused by her two visits to two different harems is a "constant reminder of the most injured human beings I have ever seen"

(270), and she leaves Egypt unable either to forgive or to forget. To Martineau, the Victorian feminist, the people forced to live in the confines of the harem, completely disciplined by its insidious and incestuous rules and regulations, epitomize a more degrading and dehumanized existence than do those forced to live as outcasts in the "Deaf and Dumb Schools," "lunatic asylums," and "prisons" of the Western world.

In *British Rule in India*, Martineau constantly emphasizes the tremendous power of the British race, even as she calls for certain changes in the actual governing of the empire. By juxtaposing immediate British superiority to ancient Hindu progressiveness and to contemporary Muslim and Hindu iniquity, by consistently foregrounding the former and using the structure of colonialism as the framing device for her textualization of the history of India, Martineau precludes any knowledge or desire that may exist outside the frame that she has constructed. Therefore, though the British government has sometimes made mistakes as illustrated by the Indian Mutiny, this lapse can be easily rectified because the British are by nature more suited to governing a different race than are the Asians, and this inherent trait can be enhanced by educating British officers "of the conditions and qualities of the people to be governed." The Anglo-Indian officers should not duplicate the "ignorance of Asiatics in their occasional travels in the West. They do not know an Italian from a German— a Frenchman from an Englishman; and we may conceive what would be the chances of success of an Asiatic government of Europe which should proceed on such a view" (15). Thus the discourse that makes up *British Rule in India* is a discourse of power. It illustrates dramatically Foucault's compelling thesis that knowledge is produced within the matrix of power and that power operates through the deployment of knowledge.

The reader, then, might duly expect a blunt polemic on the subject of sati. What greater claim can be made about the benevolent civilizing mission of colonial rule than its abolition of barbaric traditions in the name of an unerring allegiance to the spirit of modernity? What the text offers is about fifteen very inconsistent statements regarding the abolition of the practice by Lord Bentinck. The subject appears to be summarily and dispassionately dismissed, even though a sentence such as "The more supervision was instituted, the more frequent the practice became: and more mischief was clearly done by Government recognition than good by suppressing attendant enormities" (285) begs further elaboration. In the very next sentence the "spiritless" nature of the Bengalis (Bengal being where the practice was most prevalent) is evoked as the reason for the success of the "vigorous measures" implemented by the governor-general to curb the practice. Lest the British reader fear that this interference in a significant local custom fueled the mutiny, Martineau, in a curiously self-contradictory manner, explains how this was not possible: the "native soldiery [were not] deeply interested in the matter;" they came from districts where the practice was "least insisted on;" their "wives were not wont to be with them in cantonments"; and (this last item contradicts the first) "it was thought sufficient to avoid using their services in the suppression" (286). The next few sentences are equally ambiguous. On the one hand, we are told that the practice was quite popular in Bengal and, on the other, that the police "had but little to do;" it was very easy to extend the prohibition to the other presidencies even though "abolition was by no means so general as it was at first concluded;" and, the last two sentences on the subject, "it is impossible to say how far the sullenness of the disappointed Brahmins may have aggravated ill feelings from other causes during the interval; but . . . several native princes have proscribed the custom because the General Government did so with success" (286). These few sentences interrupt her larger discussion of the consequences of Christianizing the heathens by the missionaries, which she resumes and which is again speculative, judgmental, and detailed.

The reference to the rite of sati also consolidates the domain of British India as primarily one populated by Hindus.[6] Yet when one compares the passage on sati with Martineau's accounts of the condition of American, especially the Shaker, women, as well as women imprisoned in Egyptian harems, one cannot but be struck by the peculiar absence of any trace of her feminism or what David describes as her "trenchant and stirring language" (59).

How do we then account for Martineau's silence on the subject of sati? One could argue that Martineau did not have access to texts describing the ritual and therefore had to resort to a nonhorrified, abbreviated summary. But the presence of numerous tracts by missionaries and other officials documenting and delineating the elaborate ritual for public consumption, as well as accounts written by travelers to India who consistently emphasize its horror and their sentimental sympathy for the "victim of superstition," repudiates this assumption. Just two texts, one written by Henry Bushby, a civil servant (*Widow-Burning: A Narrative*), and the other by J. Peggs, a missionary (*The Suttee's Cry to Britain*), can suggest the range of records available to Martineau. Peggs's text was already in its second edition by 1828, and the full title and its contents, which are listed in the preface, suggest the dramatic potency of the subject of sati.[7]

Early-nineteenth-century depictions of sati are deeply influenced by what Paul Courtwright calls the colonial iconography of self-immolation. Much British literature on the subject, as Monika Fludernik shows, "can be classified as an exoticist watered-down version of the generic features prominent in the eighteenth-century literary traditions of the sublime and of the sentimental novel" (2). In a number of fictional accounts, the British officer sent to prevent sati rescues the distressed woman in the nick of time, though historical documents more often than not reveal his halfhearted intervention that is largely futile. In most cases, as historians such as Lata Mani have shown, he does not attempt intervention at all. The aestheticization of sati thus "uncovers a fundamental ambivalence in the British emotional response to the ritual, and this ambivalence can be demonstrated to interfere with the professed Christian and humanitarian agendas of witnesses and officials alike as voiced in their administrative reports or interventionary exempla" (Fludernik 2).

Bushby's *Widow-Burning: A Narrative* (1855) is a sensationalist and sentimental rendition that seems to take a salacious enjoyment in the spectacle of the woman burning to death. But Bushby's narrative, with its depiction of "a scene of a terrible solemnity" (5), coupled with his fascination with "the *thrilling* moment antecedent to . . . death by fiery torture" (245), is not unusual. The following description, found in an 1825 report of the General Baptist Missionary Society, is emblematic of the manner in which sati both titillated and horrified the British viewer, as opposed to the "Hindus," who either demonstrate shocking indifference or levity when confronted with the sufferings of their women.

> Thus attired, she looked the picture of all that is degraded and wretched. Altogether I never saw anything so infernal. The barbarous indifference of the multitude to every feeling of humanity . . . altogether pressed upon my mind that the feeling beggars description. . . . [T]he woman could not utter a syllable distinctly, all that could be understood was . . . "juggernaut is my pleasure." A *thrill of horror* ran through my veins. (Sabin 6)

I asserted earlier that *British Rule in India* is very much part of an imperial discourse that shores up the violence and power necessary for the maintenance of the putative yet crucial binaries of colonizer/colonized and self/other. In the light of recent theories on alterity, however, one has learned to interrogate the appearance of an absolute power which is inherent in such discourses of knowledge and which seeks to control and manipulate that which threatens the discourses by confining them within an allegory of otherness. Despite the ratification of British hegemony evidenced in *British Rule in India*, I would suggest that the spectacle of the other resurfaces in Martineau's discourse as a kind of surplus or supplement that ruptures the structural economy generated by binary oppositions—it emerges in her denial to engage with the practice of sati. British policy over sati in India, as well the ambivalence that characterizes prototypical vignettes of early-nineteenth-century accounts of sati with their fluctuatiiong emotions of terror and pity, awe and secret pleasure, denies Martineau recourse to the very binary language that permeates other sections of her history and her other two travel narratives. When she goes to America, she has etched in her mind the words of the Constitution. Therefore, when she is confronted with the institution of slavery she can accuse the Americans of hypocrisy, barbarism, and much more. Her visit to an Egyptian harem leaves this energetic, independent woman, who had dedicated her life to the uplifting of bourgeois women at home, enraged by the segregation and restriction that the harem initiates and appalled by the inertia and sexual proclivity that characterized the women confined by this particularly repressive cultural practice.

If the British were truly committed to their purported mission of civilizing the despotic natives in India, if they wished to transplant the domestic ideology of the angel in the house to foreign shores, then the abolition of sati should presumably be clear-cut. As such recent historians as Mani have revealed, however, British policy vis-à-vis sati was centered primarily "around the issue of the tolerance of such a practice in 'British India'" ("Production" 32). Thus, on the one hand, we have Lord Bentinck's impassioned words, which capture the extent to which this practice occupied British imagination and politics:

> Of the rite itself, of its horror and abomination not a word need be said. Every rational and civilized being must feel anxious for the termination of a practice so abhorrent from humanity. . . . But to the Christian and to the Englishman, who by tolerating sanctions, and by sanctioning incurs before God the responsibility of this inhuman and impious sacrifice not of one, but of thousands of victims, these feelings of anxiety

must be and ought to be extreme. The whole and sole justification is state necessity—that is, the security of the British empire, and even that justification, would be, if at all, still very incomplete, if upon the continuance of the British rule did not entirely depend the future happiness and improvement of the numerous population of this Eastern world.[8]

This language precludes any discourse of cultural relativism by which the practice could be sanctioned. On the other hand, the controversial positions often adopted by British officials regarding sati—the refusal to acknowledge sati as a demeaning social practice by the officials in order not to endanger the East India Company's economic and political stakes, the refuge taken by some English officials in the scriptural validation of sati and their self-motivated desire not to interfere in indigenous religious practices, and their division of this terrible infliction into "good" (voluntary) and "bad" (coercive) satis—does precisely that. Willed sati could therefore be encoded in the discourse of cultural relativism, thereby enabling British officials to condone the act when it suited their purpose. Because this chapter is not about the discourses surrounding sati in British India, I must be very sketchy, but I want to assert that Martineau could have deciphered the very tangible rhetoric of tolerance hidden under the unanimous denial of sati put forth in the abstract. In other words, to quote Mani, Martineau could not participate in a written debate that "was primarily about the feasibility rather than the desirability of [the] abolition [of a heinous practice]."[9] The symbolic economy of a political practice based on the precarious foundation of cultural relativism would not further the ultimate aim of Martineau's history—the necessary presence of the British in India in order to continue the empire's civilizing mission in a benevolent and dispassionate manner.

Even more significant, I would suggest, British policy surrounding sati, instead of enabling the conservative ideology based on the representations of us and them, collapses the distance that such a binary structure seeks to maintain. Martineau's failure to use the practice of sati, as she does that of the harem and slavery, cannot be dismissed as a consequence that accompanies the kind of text that *British Rule* claims to be—"a convenience" by which the general British public could obtain "a general notion of what our Indian Empire is, how we came by it, and what has gone forward in it since it first became connected with England" (v). Martineau's silence marks a site of disempowerment in this otherwise empowered discourse of colonialism. S. P. Mohanty, addressing the potency of the agency of alterity, raises this question: "Just how other, we need to force ourselves to indicate, is the other?" (5). Confronted by the vexed idiom of British policy on sati, Martineau can no longer set herself up as the excluded, privileged outsider untainted by the cultural dynamic that seeks to plot the other in a differential and hierarchical economy. The prerogative of racial difference is here occluded by the threatening presence of the same—alterity can no longer be contained by the allegory of difference, nor can it be transcended in a kind of Hegelian sublation. The very idea of a superior autochthonous nationality that enables the rhetoric of binarism essential to the imperial mission is made impossible by the dawning realization that not all members of the nation have equal access to the privileged notion of the same. The contested ground of gender at home is made all the more visible because of the treatment of Indian women by the Englishman. This is not meant to generate a causal dialectic but to indicate, as Suleri notes, that "colonial facts are vertiginous" (6). A recognition of the interdependency of the terrains bounded by the terms of nationalism and colonialism should allow us to entertain, even as early as 1857, the precariousness of the imperial endeavor that can sustain itself only through the overdetermination of the trope of an absolute alterity inhabiting the peripheries of the English nation. Thus I suggest that Martineau's significant reticence on the subject of sati is an instance of supplementarity, a silent acknowledgment of the hypocrisy that often accompanied British claims to civilize and protect. This silence is all the more telling because the abolition of sati has been celebrated as a paradigmatic example of British benevolence. The reading I have attempted to formulate undercuts both the fiction of absolute colonial domination and the fallacy of the totality of otherness by insisting that the narratives securing the position of the colonizer necessitated the repression of certain internal cultural facts that resurface as unspeakable sites in the territory of the other.

Unlike Martineau, who had never been to India, Meadows Taylor exemplifies the true definition of the Anglo-Indian. He spent a large portion of his adult life in India and was perhaps Rudyard Kipling's most successful precursor in the domain of Anglo-Indian fiction. Shipped out to India in 1824 at age fifteen, Taylor ended up in the service of the Nizam of Hyderabad, one of the (ostensibly) independent "native princes." He married a Eurasian woman whose grandmother had been a princess of Delhi, and his close, often sympathetic, identification with Indians and Indian social patterns gave him a perspective often critical of British racism and misgovernment.

Meadows Taylor's *Seeta* (1872) is a novel primarily about the Indian Mutiny. It is the third book in a trilogy concerning critical periods of Indian history. *Tara* (1863) illustrates the "rise of the Marathas, and their first blow against the Mussulman power in 1657;" *Ralph Darnell* (1865) describes the "rise of the English political power in the victory of Plassey in June 1757;" and *Seeta* deals with "the attempts of all classes alike to rid themselves of the English by the Mutiny of 1857" (Taylor vii). Unlike the numerous other Anglo-Indian novels about the rebellion, Taylor sees the mutiny as affecting "all classes alike," not only sepoys and a few native princes.[10] Taylor does not dismiss the caste violations suffered by the sepoys because of the greased cartridges as mere superstition. He depicts it as a serious threat to Hindu and Muslim orthodoxy, viewing the rebellion as a religious striving for purity: "The Sepoys had completed their contract of a hundred years of faithful service, and yet their masters were now seeking . . . to defile them and pollute their social caste, which was more precious than life, for without it life and honour would be dead" (215).

Taylor's novel has two focal points—the imaginative account of the mutiny, and a detailed account of the growth and consummation of an interracial romance. In his introduction to the novel, Taylor writes that it had not been his "purpose to write history; but to give, as it were in an episode, a general impression of the time, which of all others in the history of India is the most absorbing and interesting to the English reader" (viii). Instead of concentrating on the "sickening details of pitiless massacre and suffering," Taylor, in an interesting move, devotes special attention to the events of the Sumbut year 1914, which began on March 25, 1857, and closed on March 19, 1858. In the Hindu calendar,[11] the year was significant because it embodied a prediction "in the form of an astrological deduction from a conjunction of planets [and] had been repeated in every Hindoo Almanac for a century" (ix). The planets foretold great mayhem, natural disasters, and political turmoil resulting in the expulsion of the foreigners from Indian soil. According to Taylor, much that was predicted did occur. This exercised great "power over the native mind, among all classes and in all localities of India [making it] one of the most prominent and exciting causes of general combination and action in that year" (viii–ix). Ironically, "the deposition of the East India Company from power, held to signify the expulsion of the English from India, was literally fulfilled. But, while the Company died, the Queen of England ruled in its stead!" (ix).

The emphasis that the introduction places on the various causes for the mutiny is significantly belied by the epigraph to the novel, Shakespeare's 116th Sonnet ("Let me not to the marriage of true minds / Admit impediment"). The episode that Taylor uses to write his general impression of the particular historical moment is a love affair beween an Indian Sudra widow and the local British magistrate.[12] The eponymous title of the novel indicates that it is around the Hindu female heroine that the tale of the mutiny will unfold. The name Seeta resonates with immense social and religious significance in the diurnal lives of Hindus. The great Indian epic *Ramayana* has enshrined its heroine Seeta as the embodiment of a chaste Hindu wife, a chastity that is hyperrealized in the powerful image of Seeta emerging unscathed through a column of fire.[13] This exemplification and mythologization of female purity is paradoxically contradicted by the other image of the Hindu wife burning herself on the funeral pyre of her husband as an illustration of her abiding virtue. "Sati," a specific Hindu ritual globally (under)translated as the practice of widow burning in India, is more significantly an achieved state of being. John Hawley writes that "the term *sati* has a wide semantic range, with marked differences of emphasis. . . . *Sati* can refer to an action or event whereby a woman is being immolated on her husband's pyre, to the woman who is at the center of this spectacle, or to Sati as a goddess" (11). In its second signification, it represents a particular kind of woman—a good woman (*sadhvi*); a woman devoted to her husband (*pativrata*); a truly faithful wife, a "nonwidow woman" (*avidhava nari*)—a mode of being/becoming for woman/wife not often cited in Western translations of the word. Meadows Taylor's novel, I will argue, situates his female protagonist in the overlapping spaces between these two discursive traditions—Seeta and sati—of the proper Hindu woman. In doing so he recasts one of the main themes of the *Ramayana*, the overdetermined concept of the faithful wife, and thereby consolidates through reiteration the discursive construction of the Indian body politic as Hindu.

In *Ramayana*, Seeta is captured by the evil ruler of Lanka, Ravana. During her captivity she remains faithful to her husband and on her safe return to the kingdom of Ayodhya proves her sexual constancy to her husband, Rama, by walking through fire. In Taylor's novel, Seeta is a widow whose husband is killed in a raid organized by the Brahmin dacoit Azrael Pande. Pande later reappears as one of the chief conspirators of the mutiny, using religious and patriotic rhetoric to rouse the masses into rebellion. Seeta and her family epitomize the loyal Indian subject who even at the height of the mutiny had "a strong, deep-lying attachment to English rule, to English faith and honour, and to that ample protection of property to the meanest as well as to the richest, which a powerful English governemnt had afforded, that pervaded all the most valuable portions of the population, and bore good fruit in time" (315–16). It is in this spirit of allegiance that Seeta gives testimony against Pande at the British court summoned by its local magistrate, Cyril Brandon.

Seeta is not a Brahmin widow. This aspect is crucial to the development of the events in the novel. It allows Seeta a relative mobility as compared with a Brahmin woman, and it enables Taylor to cast the Brahmin priests as corrupt instigators of the religious ferment that, in the novel, appears to be the chief cause of the mutiny. No matter which caste Seeta belongs to, she is portrayed as an exceptional Indian woman. Her refusal to inscribe herself as a good Hindu wife by performing the "duties and ceremonies of a widow in full—have her beautiful hair shorn off, and break her ornaments on the place where [her husband's] body had been burned" (49)—and her relinquishing of traditional notions of modesty to testify in court against the dacoits signal her difference from the usual Indian women that Cyril Brandon had met during his stay in India. Before meeting Seeta in his court, Brandon had concluded in his own mind that "she would be in no wise different from other women of her class; quiet, modest, and timid, yet in no degree interesting" (60). When Brandon actually lays eyes on her, he is dazzled: "For a native woman, Cyril Brandon, had never seen any one so fair or of so tender a tone of color. Such he remembered, were many of the lovely women of Titian's pictures. . . . One in particular came to his memory like a flash—the wife of Duc d'Avalos, in the Louvre picture; or Titian's Daughter, carrying fruits and flowers, at Berlin" (61).[14] Brandon's evaluation of Seeta's physical beauty enunciates the "politics of seeing," the perception of the visual overdetermined by location (hooks 2). In this case, Seeta's beauty makes it possible for Brandon to detach her from her indigenous location and imaginatively reposition her in the more familiar geosocial realm of the wives and daughters of European men captured on canvas by one of Europe's most famous painters.

If Seeta's physical characteristics make possible a certain dilution of her concrete otherness, Brandon's exceptional character and his love for India and its people further help decrease the cultural and material distance that separates the two. Unlike many British men who came to India, Brandon had chosen to enter the civil service of India deliberately. "India, and its history and people, had always fascinated him: and he studied the great characters who had gained fame there, and burned to emulate them" (67).[15] In his six years of service, he had obviously succeeded tremendously in his chosen path, because "many a dame, humble as she might be, repeated his name with that of her household gods each night as she lighted the lamp before the shrine of her faith, and taught her children to say it. Nay a rude village poet had written ballads, and the minstrels had sung them to his praise, at village festivals" (69). Brandon's accommodation within the pantheon of local gods and heroes and Seeta's visual conformity to Western aesthetic norms creates an interstitial space between the two distinct worlds and makes possible the expression of an interracial romance. Seeta's child from her previous marriage conveniently dies, further enabling the romance. Not only would Seeta's motherhood undermine her signification as the indigenous, virginal bride of an Englishman, but the incorporation of a "native" child within this interstitial space would corrupt the "white" space that Seeta is made to occupy in Brandon's aesthetically imagined community.[16] The love affair thrives despite opposition from both British and Indian quarters, and in a quite unusual move, Brandon marries Seeta in a Hindu ceremony.[17]

In an ironic reversal of the *Ramayana* myth, Seeta's foray into another world is sanctioned by the Brahmins and legitimized through marriage. If Seeta's aunt sees in this marriage an elevation of her niece to "'the very Queen of all the provinces,'" Seeta envisages herself as Cyril's "own 'Savitri' now, not of duty only, but of love too—a faithful wife till she died" (132). Thus Seeta's marriage to an Englishman allows her to realize herself as "sati"—not as a woman who immolates herself but as the incarnation of the goddess Sati. As John Hawley writes: "Strictly speaking Sati [the goddess] does not commit sati—at least not in any major version of her myth. True, she does sacrifice herself for the sake of her husband Shiva . . . [and] the Sati legend provides a general paradigm for a woman's boundless devotion to her husband" (14). Brandon's popular elevation to god and local hero, his stoic acceptance of "a red bridal dress and a turban," his willingness to follow all that "Baba sahib told him to do" (132) makes him a legitimate Hindu husband for a true daughter of

India. His "kindness and love" for Seeta transforms him to a Shiva-like husband, allowing Seeta to become a Sati-Savitri by throwing herself before the spear meant for her husband (377).

Once married, Seeta dutifully lives out the role of the traditional Hindu wife. Despite the initial sanctioning of the marriage by the Brahmin priest, however, growing religious tension and the machinations of the rejected suitor, Ram Das, force Seeta's family to treat her as a not-Hindu. If the mythological Seeta had to prove her sexual virtue as a result of being kidnapped by Ravana and forced to live in captivity in another country, Taylor's Seeta is denounced as religiouly impure because she inhabits a Christian house. Unlike the epic Seeta, our Seeta cannot prove her religious purity, for that which is now considered impure—her physical and social contamination—had earlier been authorized by the religious institution of a Hindu marriage. This leaves Seeta forever outside the domain of a Hindu domestic space, because her reentry into it can be achieved only by her renunciation of her status as a Hindu wife. Thus her very iconization as Seeta is what renders her impure.

If Seeta's paradoxical enshrinement as a true Hindu wife separates her from her originary society, her status as an English wife is equally dubious. Any potential that this marriage may contain for a subversion of colonial power is undermined in Seeta's initial ignorance of English law that will not recognize a Hindu marriage as legal. Seeta does not realize, until the very end, that she would not be Cyril's wife in England and that their son, if they had one, would not inherit his English estate. Brandon does expect gradually to convert Seeta and marry her a second time by Christian rite, and the novel participates in the English missionary zeal to introduce Christianity into the Hindu world. Thus, Brandon looks forward to the "dawning of true light" in Seeta's mind, and so, apparently, does Taylor. At different points in the text we see Seeta struggling between her Hindu upbringing and her attraction to the words in the Bible. She even admits that the words in the Bible are more egalitarian and accessible to the average intellect than is the Bhagavad Gita, which requires constant interpretation and elucidation by the Sanskrit-educated priest. On her deathbed, we are witness to a mawkish and sentimental scene as Seeta reaches a near conversion. Though her final expressions of faith are more ambivalent than those expressed in polemical, evangelical stories, she hears a blending of "strange snatches . . . Sanscrit prayers . . . with lines of simple Christian hymns" (382–83). Patrick Brantlinger suggests that *Seeta* is "a study of how religion in degenerate forms—superstition, prejudice, Mrs. Grundyism on both sides—helped spawn the violence and race hatred that flared up in 1857" (214). But the presentation of religious intolerance on both sides is, to a certain extent, negated in the deathbed scene. In the end we, along with Seeta's friends and husband, are convinced that, had she lived a little longer, Seeta would have realized that Christianity was the one true religion that could bring eternal happiness.

In "Mobilizing Chivalry: Rape in British Novels about the Indian Uprising of 1857," Nancy Paxton argues that "*Seeta* reasserts interracial marriage as an alternative to rape and revenge by recalling the marriages in Indian epics where daughters are exchanged to establish stronger and more peaceful political alliances between conquering and conquered warriors" (16). This particular reading allows Paxton to emphasize the novel's exposition of the theme of sexual rivalry between Azrael Pande and Cyril Brandon for the possession of the Indian woman, "a conflict that is nearly always obscured in other English Mutiny novels and histories" (18). Yet Paxton in her brief discussion of the novel does not raise the issue of the other woman who acts as a foil to Seeta.[18] Paxton's stress on the elaboration of the motif of rape in the novel enables her to contrast "Brandon's love for Seeta with Pande's desire to abduct, humiliate, and exploit her" (18) but precludes a comparison of Brandon's feelings for Seeta with his growing desire for Grace Mostyn. Despite Seeta's virtues, fair beauty, education, and desire to learn English ways, she falls short of something—she is, after all, not English. Another character in the novel, Grace Mostyn, the perfect Englishwoman, would be the ideal wife for the English hero Brandon. Though in love with Seeta, Brandon constantly hankers after Grace. He does not betray Seeta but fails to come home on time every evening because of Grace's English charm and beauty. Grace "*was very fair*, and the *pure English colour was as fresh as ever*; that gentle mingling of the most delicate carnations with white which no women's complexions but those of England can boast of. . . . A *fair Saxon face*, with not a shade of guile about it: as tender as it was full of grace" (170; emphasis added). Once Grace enters the scene, Seeta is doomed to die; she has no real place in Brandon's life and cannot return to England with him after his period in India is over. Taylor cannot have Brandon abandon Seeta; that would undermine Brandon's chivalric character and Taylor's/Brandon's "romantic perspective on the power of sympathy and sexual passion to overcome racial prejudice and accommodate cultural difference" (Paxton 17). But Taylor does not identify with Seeta left alone in her house as Brandon goes out to "play." If Brandon had once admired Seeta's intellectual abilities as that which separated her from the poorly educated Englishwomen one encounters in India, he now finds Seeta too innocent and childlike in her desires. Indian women, even someone like Seeta, who has experienced true love for the first time, do not have the usual expectations of mutual companionship that the Englishwoman desires in a "true" marriage. Seeta, no matter how hard she tries, cannot remove all traces of her "Indianness," and the "sweet, fresh face of Grace" haunts Cyril more and more. He "must . . . go away, leaving her [Seeta] alone. She did not know what kept him so long away, but accepted the plea of business—without a doubt or suspicion" (190).

Among the English posted at Saddley Peeroo station, even those who liked Seeta and treated her as a friend, was the pervasive feeling that had Grace come to India a little sooner, Brandon would have been saved from a relationship that could only end in failure. Philip Mostyn, who is not representative of the typical intolerant English person and who believes that "if there were not our horrible social prejudices against it, many of us would be happier with such a wife [Seeta] than with some of our own people" (87), cannot help but voice the bitter "truth" after he sees Cyril and Grace together: "But Cyril, poor fellow, will get tired of the monotony of that girl [Seeta], brilliant and wonderful as she is. He will miss the freshness of an English intellect. That pleasant talk under the trees today; could that girl have followed what they said? Impossible! . . . No! this won't do. It can't last. There must be *unity of thought*, or no thought at all, to provide married happiness" (196; emphasis added).

Therefore, the reader knows that this relationship must end. But how? Taylor has built up Seeta as a virtuous, loyal, educated, loving wife, and Brandon as the ideal, dedicated, unprejudiced English soldier who loves India more than the average Indian. His mission is to save the empire from the misguided rule of the average Englishman but also to prevent it from being ruined by the overzealous Indian as embodied in Azrael Pande and the Rani of Jhansi. Even though the novel does not concentrate on the crucial events of the mutiny, it does evoke the presence of a significant player in that event in the person of the Rani, who is invoked by the English, including Brandon, as an unnatural woman who is almost a megalomaniac and totally devoid of any "womanly feelings" (265). Taylor does not spend many pages on her, but we hear of a collusion between the Rani and the dacoit turned patriot, Azrael Pande. Seeta becomes a foil for the irrational, manipulative, power-hungry Rani, who would rather see innocent men die to save the throne than join hands with the English to protect the Indians and India from a fate worse than death—the reign of a thug such as Pande. Seeta's "blood was up. Her soul revolted at the idea of treason to the English and danger to her Lord" (271). But the Rani, consumed by hatred and revenge, sees the Englishmen in India in 1857 as "a mean, covetous race. . . . I would rather have shaved my head and wandered on foot as a poor Bairagan . . . denouncing these English as tyrants and oppressors. . . . I had them slain. They were ruling where I ruled; they were collecting my money, they were changing the old customs of my people, they were corrupting our priestly caste" (411). Whatever the truth behind the Rani's claims, she is revealed as the one responsible for the massacre of women and children in Meerut and Jhansi during the days of the rebellion.[19] She is the source of destruction, even more threatening than Pande, a queen "gloomy and vindictive, a very tigress at heart; so beware of her" (412).[20]

Jhansi is retaken, and the rest of the Rani's life is quickly dismissed: "I need not follow the fortunes of the Ranee of Jhansy, who has no other connection with this tale than as regards the Nawab" (415). Yet the Rani's connection to the tale is quite significant—she functions as Seeta's doppelgänger. The Rani is seen as an unequivocal threat to the consolidation of British power in India, and not only in terms of her military capabilities. She is neither a version of the epic Seeta, who is willing to repeatedly prove her sexual innocence, nor Taylor's Seeta, the ideal Hindu woman, educated and intelligent, who can learn to appreciate Christian tenets and who will face religious ostracism for the sake of the love of an Englishman. The Rani functions as the incarnation of alterity—the Hindu woman in her "natural" destructive capacity. Seeta, by contrast, signifies an accommodated alterity that can be strategically deployed against its own community. Thus Seeta is "essentially" different from the Englishwoman who faints at the sight of blood. "We women of India are used to rougher scenes than you" (289), says Seeta to Grace and Mrs. Mostyn after her first rout with Cyril against the rebels. She "never trembled once" as she fired the shots against her own people. In fact Cyril is convinced that Seeta "enjoyed what she did!" (289). This enjoyment of war and bloodshed, hypostatized in the figure of the rapacious Rani of Jhansi, is in the case of Seeta beneficial to the English under attack by the mutineers. However, the difference between Seeta and the Englishwoman once again introduces the structure of imperial ideology in all its contradictions—even as Seeta is valorized as an exceptional Indian woman who can be accommodated within an Anglo-Indian community, her difference needs to be marked to shore up the identification of English national character with the Englishwoman in the empire.

Brantlinger's valorization of the novel as "Victorian fiction's only approach to an adequate symbolic antithesis to the Mutiny" (216) fails to address the impossibility of a sustained domestic narrative for the exogamous (Indian) woman within a teleological discursive construction of colonial home and identity. The presence of Seeta as wife in an English domestic space is a violation of the historical narratives of both colonizer and colonized. Displaced and disbarred from entering either a Christian or a Hindu domestic space, Seeta becomes a frozen image transported in a framed picture to the ancestral home of the Brandons. The preservation of an imperial spatiotemporal economy is nowhere better clarified than in the reader's final encounter with Seeta. Unlike the epic Seeta, who when asked to defend her virtue for the umpteenth time begs her mother, the Earth, to open up and embrace her forever, Taylor's Seeta, unable to create/inhabit a viable interstitial domestic space in British India, is enshrined as domestic goddess only through imagistic representation. The novel concludes on the tenth anniversary of Seeta's death with the two worlds once again being juxtaposed in ceremonial commemorations of the pure and good Hindu woman. We are first introduced to a bounded Indian space in Cyril's study at Hylton Hall. What he calls his "den" is

> hung round with Indian trophies of the chase, and Indian arms and hog spears, the addresses in their silver cases, and many sketches, and finished drawings of Indian landscapes and figures. . . . [T]wo figures are standing before the fireplace, looking up to a picture which hangs on the wall above them. It is a large masterly drawing in water colour, of a fair Indian lady, simply dressed in white muslin drapery. Below its rich frame is another oval frame made like a large locket, and lined with crimson velvet, in which are a long tress of wavy, deep brown hair, almost black, but which where the light falls, shows a tinge of bright gold. With it, there is a small withered branch of a sweet scented Indian plant, and some dried flowers tied up in ribbon, of which we know. (441)

In Cyril's initial encounter with Seeta, her indigenity had been mitigated by his comparison of her to Titian's paintings of European women. In the end she becomes one of those portraits, but without its rightful place in the Hylton familial portrait gallery. Thus although the conclusion of the novel addresses the legacy of overlapping territories and intertwined histories as a result of the British presence in India, the culture of colonialism demands a strategic containment of the other for the narration of a distinctive English familial topography. The last lines of the novel move us back to India, to Seeta's grave, now a designated place of worship, where "Brahmins offer flowers and sing hymns" and where unmarried girls pray for the privilege of becoming "sati" like Seeta (442). Thus Seeta's temporary location in another world is erased as, through worship, she is made to occupy a place among the pantheon of Hindu female deities. To paraphrase Rajeswari Sunder Rajan, despite the differences between the two structures of representation (both, of course, produced by a British colonial writer), death defines the Hindu woman's behavior and makes possible the reconstruction of her subjectivity and the narration of her life-in-death (*Real and Imagined Women* 59).

If Martineau finds it impossible to talk about sati, and Taylor reinscribes the more common image of the woman burning alive as the goddess Sati, in her novel *On the Face of the Waters* (1896), Flora Annie Steel returns us to an inexplicable Hindu "India" reified in and as the image of the burning widow. Steel said that the Indian Mutiny "was then the Epic of the Race. It held all possible emotion, all possible triumph" (*Garden* 226). Both Jenny Sharpe and Nancy Paxton have explained that the resurgence of novels about the mutiny in the 1890s was a response to the racially charged discourses surrounding the introduction of the Ibert Bill, also known as the "white mutiny," which "granted Indian magistrates criminal jurisdiction over Europeans in the rural districts" (Sharpe 89). In my reading, I will concentrate on the representations of two Indian women in *On the Face of the Waters* who, I argue, provide a sensationalized space for the articulation of a fixed notion of Indian womanhood that illustrates Spivak's explanation that "the project of imperialism is violently to put together the episteme that will 'mean' (for others) and 'know' (for the self) the colonial subject as history's nearly selved-other" ("Rani of Sirmur" 134). In Steel's novel, the mutiny enables the three principal English characters to gain a knowledge of the self that elides this "selved-othering process" by securing a progressive narrative of imperial history in the discursive fixity of the Indian woman as sati.

Rebecca Saunders points out that Steel creates in Alice Gissing "a new type of female character, one who reveals unexpected possibilities in the unusual circumstances of life on the frontier and who becomes a model for Steel of appropriate female behavior" (308). Alice Gissing perhaps partly reflects the author's own life in colonial India. Steel lived in India for almost twenty years and, unlike the typical memsahib, participated in Indian politics, learned several Indian languages, and started a school for girls. However, Alice Gissing's sexual misalliance with the husband of Kate Erlton (the novel's heroine) can be allayed only by Alice's heroic death (see Saunders), thus making way for the narration of the more conventional love story of Kate and the hero, Jim Douglas.

It is against these two British women that the Indian women are positioned. *On the Face of the Waters* opens with a delineation of an interracial relationship between Jim Douglas and a Muslim woman, Zora. In Steel's novel, unlike in Taylor's *Seeta*, the threat of this interracial relationship developing into something significant is held in abeyance from the beginning. Early in the novel we are told that James Greyman, alias Jim Douglas, had to leave the service under a cloud—he therefore inhabits the peripheries of Anglo-Indian life marked by the boundaries of the "civil lines." This marginal existence allows him certain fringe benefits without severe ostracization—an affair with Zora. The affair, though, is literally breathing its last—the "native" Zora is dying. She is ensconced in a little room on the top of a house that "was unmistakably Indian. It was a perfect rabbit warren of dark cells, crushed in on each other, causelessly" (27). The lack of cause or reason seems to extend to this affair of eight years. We are told that James had purchased Zora from a house of "ill-fame" and had her "installed" in this house. He had bought her as he would have any "horse, or flower pot, or anything else which he thought would make life pleasanter to him." But he had also pitied her because she had been a child about to be sold into prostitution, "as many are in India." Yet "his pity would not have led him to buy her if she had been ugly, or even dark; for the creamy ivory tint of her skin satisfied his fastidiousness quite as much as did the hint of soul in her dark, dreamy eyes" (27).[21] Above all the affair seems to have continued primarily because of his "reckless determination to show himself that he had no regrets for the society which had dispensed with his presence" (28).

Steel uses this relationship to represent the gap between East and West. The following description exemplifies the denial of coevality that is indicative of the power dynamics of much of colonial discourse. In this passage, Jim Douglas's position as Zora's lover replicates that of the Western anthropologist who, "in spite of sharing time with the Other . . . writes an ethnography that denies the Other coevalness, placing the object in a time other than the Western present" (Behdad 6).

> As he stood, still looking down on the sleeper, something in the lack of comfort, of all the refinements and luxuries which seem to belong by right to the sickness of dear ones in the West, smote him suddenly with a sense of deprivation, of division; . . . the bareness of it seemed somehow to reveal the great gulf between his complexity, his endless needs and desires, and the simplicity of that human creature drifting to death, almost as the animals drift, without complaint, without fears, or hopes. (37)

The use of animal imagery to describe Zora and her desires genders the other as "primitive," and in doing so it repeats the invariable binary opposition of East/West as feminine/masculine.[22] What is crucial in this discursive repetition of colonial tropes is the absolute containment of the gendered other as primitive in a decaying and noncontaminating, diseased female body. Zora is presented as "a poor little soul," "a wounded bird" who appears to have no desires other than to be hidden away in a dark house exposed only to her English lover. We are never given a description of Zora, other than that her body has been "wasted" by an incurable disease. She lacks physical substance, which reduces the threat of seduction that is often designated as an essential attribute of an Indian woman's body by the Anglo-Indian writer. In most Anglo-Indian texts the Indian woman does not actively have to seduce the Englishman—her body signifies "seduction," as an inherent trait that is both elusive and inexplicable. The only time that Zora walks and speaks is during the few moments before her death. Hearing Jim's voice, she gets up, a shadowy figure, whose presence is noticed only because the silver anklets chime as she walks slowly toward him. Though it pains her to take a step, she fulfills her desire to reach the outstretched hands of her savior, and in keeping with the spirit of gothic melodrama whispers, "I have come, I have come to my king" (40).

Jim is left with the deep feeling that somehow her death is unfair, but as he looks down from the parapet of the house into the city below, he is filled with a sense of release and relief: "Even in death a great gulf lay between him and the woman he had loved" (39). The relief is even greater because there is no offspring to remind him of his association with her.

This relationship, depicted as it is in its last stages, does not convey any depth of romantic love or passion on Jim's part. What the reader perceives, in the initial pages of Steel's novel, is Jim's loneliness and isolation from both the Anglo-Indian and Indian communities. He indicts those men who seem to be able to combine "the two lives," because "they had been content to think half-caste thoughts, to rear up a tribe of half caste children" (38). Their union had produced a child, a son, but it had been "a still morsel of humanity." Zora had been unhappy because she was afraid that he might be angry with her for not being able to provide him with a living son, but he "had never told her of the relief it was to him, of the vague repulsion which the thought of a child had always brought with it" (38). The absence of any discussion about racially mixed children in *Seeta*, as well as Jim's instinctive repulsion for a "half-caste" child, including his own, indicate the narrow boundaries of an imagined or realized exogamous relationship within a colonial power structure. Yet even this inability to envisage a racially mixed society on the part of the Anglo-Indian is recast as symptomatic of the unnatural aspect that inheres in Indian women. Immediately after Jim's confession about his feelings, he adds: "One could not help these things; and after all she cared only because she was afraid he cared. She did not crave for motherhood either. It was the glow and glamour that had been the bond between them; nothing else" (38). Zora's unnatural repudiation of the desire for motherhood places her outside the representational aesthetic governing the depiction of "natural" women, thereby further reducing any real threat of contamination to the Anglo-Indian world.[23]

The "quaint house in the oldest quarter of the city of Lucknow" (27) in which Zora has lived for eight years is not representative of some kind of interracial domestic hearth. The Indian woman as Muslim, in this novel at least, is not seen as a domestic rival for the affections of an Anglo-Indian soldier. She is completely contained within the generic framework of a putative chivalric romance that is more about the hero's crisis of self-representation within the Anglo-Indian "civil" community than about any grand prohibited passion: "Romance had perhaps more to do with his purchase than passion; restless, reckless determination to show himself that he had no regrets for the society which had dispensed with his, had had more than either. For he had begun to rent the pleasant pavilions after a few years of adventurous roving had emphasized the gulf between him and his previous life, and forced his pride into leading his present one as happliy as he could" (28). Zora, essentially, is represented as a victim of an indigenous society in which young girls are sold into prostitution. Her slow yet inevitable "decline" (28) parallels the unavoidable disintegration of an already corrupt and decaying Muslim empire at the hands of the English.

In the early pages of the novel, Steel tries to capture the Muslim atmosphere of Lucknow. We hear of the "Moulvie from Fyzabad" who was going to preach to more than half the city in the "big Mosque," and as dusk falls the city echoes with the "long-drawn chant of the call to prayer from the Mohammedan mosques, the clashing of gongs from the Hindoo temples, the solitary clang of the Christian church bell" (11). Here, Steel clearly imagines India as Hindu and Muslim. The following rendition casts India as a somber space that is simultaneously Hindu and Muslim: "There was no light in these dark shrines, save the circling cresset; none, save the dim reflection of dusk's white marble, in the mosque where the Moulvie's sonorous voice sent the broad Arabic vowels rebounding from dome to dome." Steel juxtaposes this space with an enlightened Christian haven: "But in the church there was a blaze of lamps and the soldierly figure at the reading desk showed clear to the men and women listening leisurely in the cushioned pews. . . . [T]he words were stirring enough; there was no lack of directness in them" (12). By the end of the novel, however, Steel has reaffirmed the construction of India as Hindu India by deploying, once again, the cultural practice of sati.

In "Images of Indian Women in Rudyard Kipling: A Case of Doubling Discourse," John McBratney notes that in Kipling's "writings about India, Indian women are seen, finally as *the* sign of the 'other,' the marker of what is different from (and therefore both inferior and yet threatening to) the British. . . . Indian women are seen as the primary figures of a realm defined by its difference from that of the Anglo-Indian official and soldier" (52). Steel definitely represents Zora as inferior, though not threatening. However, the doubleness of the Indian woman as other is monstrous and menacing in Steel's delineation of the character of Tara, the Rajput woman whom Jim had rescued from being burned alive at the funeral pyre of her husband. Unlike in Kipling's stories, Jim is never tempted to fall in love with Tara. After Zora dies, Tara determines to attempt sati again, this time by drowning in the holy Ganges. Jim, fully cognizant of Tara's desperate attachment to him, tries to manipulate her into abandoning her decision by taking a strand of her shaved hair for his locket. He believes his action will work because he "had found such suggestions of ritual had an immense effect, especially with womenkind who were for ever inventing new shackles for themselves" (78).

But Tara's determination to perform a ritualized death because the end of her life has already been narrated—"Hinder me not again! before God I am *suttee*! I am *suttee*!" (79)—places her beyond the realm of Jim's typical "woman." Initially, Jim believes he has triumphed over Tara's fears of "eternal damnation," but when he "closed the locket with a snap . . . the full meaning of the threat, of the loss—or of something beyond these—seemed to overtake her; an unmistakeable terror, horror, and despair swept through her" (78–79). In her desperation she falls at Jim's feet and clasps them with both hands. Instantly, the terror and horror that Tara feels in having to continue to live as "suttee" seem to enter the very core of Jim's being. Tara is no longer the Rajput widow who in gratitude had looked after Jim's mistress for eight years but is hypostatized as "the Eastern clutch of appeal [that] is disconcerting to the average Englishman. It [the clutch] fetters the understanding in another sense, and smothers sympathy in a desire to be left alone. Even Jim Douglas stepped back from it with something like a bad word" (79). Jim's instinctual repulsion from the "East," as incarnated in the body of the Hindu woman, reveals that he is constantly on guard against the danger of being captivated by the dark, sensual eroticism to which so many of Kipling's heroes succumb. In McBratney's words, it is as though Jim realizes that "the ineluctably material Indian woman suggests the Indian house in which she lives, in turn the city of her residence, and finally a malevolent Indian world . . . that general enveloping menace, that abstract threat to British imperial prestige" (50).

Steel's hero is venerated as the incorruptible Anglo-Indian soldier, who, despite his anger at the hypocrisy of many in the Anglo-Indian community, is also aware of the need to maintain the boundaries of its civil space. In other words, Jim can penetrate Indian spaces and use the knowledge garnered there to help maintain the sanctity of the Anglo-Indian enclave,[24] because his innate and undiluted Englishness is naturally repelled by the oppressive "mystery of such womanhood as Tara Devi's and little Zora's. . . . Their eternal cult of purely physical passion, their eternal struggle for perfect purity and constancy, not of the soul, but of the body, their worship, alike of sex and He who made it, seemed incomprehensible" (80).[25]

In contrast to Tara's and Zora's sexuality stand the sanitized feelings that the Englishwoman's domesticity inspires in Jim. Long before the first stirrings of love, Jim's paternalistic desires are evoked by Kate's desperate re-creation of an English drawing room in a hovel in an obscure part of the city where he has hidden her, along with the white baby that Alice Gissing had died saving. Initially Jim is irritated by Kate's trivial preoccupations but then finds something that transcends their situation and gives meaning to it. The following passage stands in stark contrast to Jim's emotions regarding his feelings for Zora and their dead, "half-caste" child:

> Here he was looking at a woman who was not his wife, a child who was not his child, and feeling vaguely that they were as much a part of his life as if they were. . . . The mystery of fatherhood and motherhood . . . seemed to touch him here, where there was not even love. Yet it was a better thing. The passion of protection, of absolute self-forgetfulness, seeking no reward, which the sight of those two raised in him, was better than an absorption in another self. (324–25)

Kate conjures up a vision of paternalism that is precisely what the mutiny threatened, for on a larger scale the protection of the weaker in exchange for their obedience is what imperialists such as Steel believed was the true situation of India. The vision Kate inspires guides Jim to take revenge on the Indians; any thought of what the rebellion was about in the first place is successfully deflected. The initial objective outlook with which the novel begins—with its cataloging of the various oversights on the part of the British imperialists in India that in part led to the mutiny; the almost factual presentation of certain incidents, such as the greasing of the cartridges with pork/beef fat (often dismissed as absolute lies in most Anglo-Indian tales about the mutiny)—disintegrates into melodrama of the most lurid kind toward the end. We do have a few pages describing the final outcome of the mutiny in a chapter titled "Rewards and Punishments," and the reader meets with no surprises as to which group reaps rewards and which group is cowed by severe punishments. In the end the mutiny, initially seen as a real threat to British power, is reduced to the wicked manipulations of an evil queen and a few power-hungry, corrupt men who lack real commitment to a cause and the courage of the average Englishman. Rebellion, without a raison d'être, cannot sustain itself too long, and right prevails when Nicholson retakes Delhi. Here is Steel's own explanation for the title of her novel: "I have chosen it, because when you ask an uneducated native of India why the Great Rebellion came to pass, he will, in nine cases out of ten, reply, 'God knows! He sent a Breath into the World.' From this to a spirit moving on the face of the Waters is not far" (v–vi). This sentiment is echoed in Captain Morecombe's failure to provide an explanation for the revolt. In the letter with which the novel concludes, Morecombe underlines the inexplicable enigma that is India: "Truly the whole thing was a mystery from beginning to end. I asked a native yesterday if he could explain it, but he only shook his head and said the Lord had sent a 'breath into the land' " (475).

Jenny Sharpe cogently argues that the "narrative function of the Rajput widow is to stabilize the Victorian ideal of womanhood so that the Mutiny role of the English woman might be realigned" (108). Such a realignment is achieved not only through Kate's ability to recast any space in the formal lineaments of Victorian domesticity but in the assertion of female agency in her adventurous masquerade as a willing "sati." Tara is caught between her desire to fulfill her role as a true Rajput widow and her inarticulate love for Jim Douglas. Steel can express Tara's love for Jim only in terms of the latter's desire to be of service to the man. In a manner, Tara is a lesser incarnation of Taylor's Seeta, a mute Indian woman who is doomed in her unrequited passion for the benevolent Anglo-Indian. This is best expressed when Tara returns, as she herself expresses, after having spent "few hours of freedom in a perfect passion of purification, so that she might return to her saintship once more" (396), to confront Kate ensconced in the room on the roof. Tara retreats to the religious shrine, leaving Kate with the words, "I must think. . . . I am alone; but I am suttee!" (396). At the shrine, she is regarded as a saint commanding the worship of other women who "crept close to kiss the edge of her [Tara's] veil humbly!" (397), much as Seeta is commemorated after her death. At this moment she is determined to leave Kate to her devices because "she would be suttee" (397); in the end, unable to face Jim's disappointment should he realize that she had abandoned Kate, Tara returns with the knowledge that "it was hopeless trying to be a saint till she had done what she had promised the Huzoor she would do" (398).

She decides that Kate, to prevent recognition as a white woman, must adopt the garb of a sati by shaving her head and removing her jewels. Her conviction that Kate would never concede to shaving her head is constantly troubled by her sense of the religious impropriety of having a

Christian woman enact the ritual of a sati: "She had no right to do it! The mems were never suttee. They married again many times. And then this mem was married to someone else" (399). However, Tara's termination of Kate's masquerade as a sati indicates a different motive. Kate is eager to cut off her hair, "for, in truth, she was becoming interested in her own adventures, now that she had, as it were, control over them" (400). Sharpe reads these words, quite rightly, as an indication of the "racial difference between the English woman, who had agency over her actions when she enters the space of sati, and the Indian woman, who is a slave to her domestic role" (108). Yet Kate is as much an aborted sati as is Tara. When Tara sees Kate cheerfully "sawing" off her hair, she is reminded of another very different scene—"Why! when she [Tara] had had it done for the first time, she had screamed and fought. Her mother-in-law had held her hands, and—" (400). Tara stops in midthought and decides that the "foolishness" must stop; "with a sigh of relief" she plaits up Kate's remaining hair so that no one will see the difference. Kate as sati is now replaced by Kate as a "screened woman . . . a Hindoo lady under a vow of silence and solitude" (401). One could read this scene as Tara's jealous acknowledgment of the strength of Kate's true feelings for Jim or as Tara's ultimate refusal to see a Hindu ritual being defiled by its displacement on a Christian body. But Tara's anguished recollection of her first ceremonial initiation into the role of a sati could suggest the beginning of a bond between the two at the recognition of women's fate in a patriarchal society. Such an interpretation is sustained by Kate's ultimately sympathetic recognition of Tara's futile love for Jim (463–64).

But even as I offer such an explanation, I am aware of the transient nature of such a moment of identification. In Steel's depiction of colonial India, the incommensurable differences between the domestic economies in which Kate and Tara are encompassed are made clear in the impossibility of Tara ever being able to achieve Victorian domestic propriety. Even though Tara attempts to transform the room on the roof with such singular cultural signifiers as a tablecloth and a vase of flowers, along with fitting food for a sick Anglo-Indian hero such as chicken broth, milk and eggs, and brandy, her presence is enough to render them improper in their significations. It is only Kate's presence that can actually invest these signifiers with their relevant meanings.

The two aborted satis can no longer occupy the same space—the room on the roof—now recognizable as a domestic English space. Tara leaves the two lovers and retreats to her own bare room in the building behind the shrine after she has taken the lock of her hair from the sleeping hero's locket. This room is "bare set round with her one scrap of culture . . . an old basket . . . [that contained] her scarlet tinsel-set wedding dress" (465). At this point the narrative underscores Tara's mental instability, emphasizing her trembling hands and her "wild eyes [that] blazed like fires themselves" (467). If we read this final scene along with two other moments, however, we can recognize the sense of agency in Tara's actions. The first scene is when she prevents Kate from completing her disguise as a sati. In this she duplicates Jim's role in rescuing Tara herself from a literal sati. The second is where she dresses as a uniformed and mustached sepoy in order to lead Kate to a boat that would take her to Metcalfe House where the English were lodged.[26] In this disguise as sepoy, she inverts the role of Jim Douglas, who, as a spy for army intelligence, manages to move incognito between the city and the garrison. Even though Kate too eludes capture by masquerading as a Hindu woman, she is constantly under the purview of Tara. Thus in Jim's absence Tara enacts Jim's role as a savior of the virtue and lives of English women. This agency is simultaneously enabled and circumscribed by her liminal status as a not-quite-sati, and in the end, Tara's decision to be engulfed in flames on the top of a burning building needs to be examined in relation to the two moments just presented. Further problematizing the final exhibition of the woman burning as a realization of sati is the spectacle of Tara dressed in her red wedding dress with her arms laden with ornaments.[27] This rendition of sati undermines the normative body of the unadorned widow in white being consumed by flames on her husband's funeral pyre. Jim's decision to save Tara from a barbaric death reinforces the historical narrative of imperialism not only as necessary to the establishment of good society but also its particular "espousal of the woman as object of protection from her own kind" (Spivak, "Can the Subaltern Speak?" 298). The mutiny ruptures the unidirection, to paraphrase Foucault, of the materiality of colonial power operating on the body of the individual and, by extension, the social body. In this text, the retelling of the mutiny with its already narrated conclusion serves to underline the constitutive interdependence of forms of knowledge and power apparatuses. With the introduction of the anomalous character of Tara, however, the description of the mutiny as an allegorization of the past for the present moment also has to account for the inexplicability of the "object of protection"—the Indian woman. In Taylor's *Seeta* the bridge between the two worlds is narrowed because of the extraordinary nature of Seeta that makes her similar to a good Englishwoman. Seeta relishes her role as the protected; Tara constantly fluctuates between her love for the man who has saved her and her realization of the impossibility of living as sati. Even as she chants the names of her gods while dying, not once does she say "I am suttee," a sentiment she has articulated throughout her life. In adorning herself as a bride (not a widow), she further underscores her realization that she can no longer lay claim to that sacred subject position.

Spivak has demonstrated how the general scriptural rejection of suicide is not applicable to those committed by "the knowing subject [who] comprehends the insubstantiality or mere phenomenality of its identity ("Can the Subaltern Speak?" 299). The guarantee of a state of enlightenment by such philosophical knowledge is what annuls the suicide as suicide. What makes the act of female self-immolation a (non)suicide is the recognition that the corporeality of the female body is relevant only in its possible destruction at the funeral pyre of the husband. Thus the rite of sati "may be read as a simulacrum of both truth-knowledge and piety of place" (300). It is a simulacrum of truth-knowledge because the annihilation of the female body hinges not just on the recognition of its insubstantiality but in the more substantial acknowledgment of its intrinsic connection to the body of the dead husband who is the true "extinguished subject." Because this already dead subject cannot enact its own (non)suicide, the female "(non)agent 'acts it out'" (300). It is an embodiment of the "piety of place," for the funeral pyre becomes the "metonym for all sacred places . . . where the woman's subject, legally displaced from herself, is being consumed" (300).

I provide this summmary of Spivak's argument to suggest the unlikely possibility of Tara's suicide being validated by herself as sati. Neither her dress nor the place can give Tara the status of a sati, as her act cannot be "ideologically cathected as 'reward'" (301). She dies because she simply cannot live, and her death is reinscribed by those watching her as yet another fatal accident caused by the mutiny. Steel's final symbolic rendering of the mystery of the mutiny (and all acts committed by the Indians) as the unsolved mystery of the woman "choosing" to go up in flames stages the power inherent in a literary operation that seeks to provide a hermeneutics of the other by recoding the alterity that it encounters in dominant colonial tropes. Michel de Certeau could be talking about the function of this novel as colonial discourse when he writes: "The power that writing's expansionism leaves intact is colonial in its principle. It is extended without being changed. It is tautological, immunized against both any alterity that might transform it and whatever dares to resist it. It can be taken as the play of a double *reproduction* which, as history and as orthodoxy. preserves the past and which, as mission, conquers space by multiplying the same signs" (216).

I would like to conclude by suggesting the significance for the present of my analysis of the modalities of representation of the Indian woman as sati in colonial discourse. The postcolonial production of knowledge of the colonial encounter can be oppositional if we make "use of its historical consciousness to critique the cultural conditions that continue to produce unequal relations of power today" (Behdad 9). Even though my exploration of the discourse of colonial violence has been concentrated on the novel, I assert the significance of the literary text in the production and maintenance of the structures of cultural domination and thus stress that my readings can function as political critiques of Britain's imperial cultural economy. Therefore my investigation of the textual manipulations of the practice of sati should allow the contemporaneity of the resurgence of this practice in a postcolonial, communally divided India to be situated within a critically conceived genealogy.

In this age of purported tolerance for variances in cultural practices, specific rituals performed by "others" continue to haunt the imagination as that which exists beyond the pale of acceptable ethical behavior. One such ritual is that of sati, and lest we think this a practice to be resurrected only for theoretical analysis from British colonial archives of little immediate consequence for women in postindependence India, we are reminded of the much publicized case of Roop Kanwar, a modern-day sati occurring as recently as September 4, 1987. The image of a woman burning on the funeral pyre of her husband is a powerful visual image that can easily be used as a *mise en abyme* for the barbaric status of a culture, a society, and, in this specific case, a nation. If in postindependence India a woman burns/is burned alive, then the participation of a people in the production of an imagined community that constitutes a nation is held up for scrutiny outside its boundaries. The fraught internal discourse surrounding, for example, the specific instance of Roop Kanwar is never highlighted in the rest of the world, and India continues to inhabit a space of the incomprehensible "wild" other in the Western imagination. Lest I be accused of making too much of an "other" issue, one not foregrounded

in the American cultural imaginary, let us not forget that in his much celebrated *Closing of the American Mind* Allan Bloom uses sati as *the* example of a practice marked by the extreme coordinates of cultural difference
to motivate the apathetic American undergraduate trapped by the discourse of a complacent cultural relativism: "If you had been a British administrator in India, would you have let the natives under your gover-
nance burn the widow at the funeral of a man who had died?" (26). The
question posed here continues the iconization of the representation of the
"white man's burden" in a neo-imperial geopolitical arena in the inter-
changeability of British administrator and American undergraduate.
Further, the address to the undergraduate could easily be rephrased
to authorize "white" America's intervention in cultural practices within
its own national boundaries, if its East Indian immigrant population
sought to move transgressively toward a more Hindu fundamentalist
constituency.

As an Indian academic in the West deeply engaged in colonial and
postcolonial issues vis-à-vis the Indian subcontinent, I suggest that
through scrupulous readings of colonial and postcolonial narratives, one
can plot a particular trajectory which will allow us to read the function
of the continuing evocation of sati in both India and the West as a "limit
trope." It is one that displays the ambivalence underlying colonial, neo-
imperial, and even certain postindependent authoritative illustrations of
the other as radically discrete and separate. The next chapters take us in
a different direction, moving from the Indian woman as sati to the "new"
woman whose desire to participate in the nationalist movement comes at
a tremendous price. Even though Tagore's novel *The Home and the
World* does not trope woman as sati, the narrative underscores the tragic
outcome for the "new" woman who crosses the domestic threshold too
hastily.

CHAPTER THREE

Woman as Nation and a Nation of Women: Tagore's *The Home and the World* and Hossain's *Sultana's Dream*

I do not belong to the present age, the age of conflicting politics. Nevertheless I cannot repudiate the age which has given me birth. I suffer and struggle. I crave for freedom and yet am held back. I must share the life of the present world, though I do not believe in its cry. I sit at its table, and while it fills its cup with wine to slake its unnatural thirst, I try to listen, through the noisy carousal, to the murmur of the stream carrying its limpid waters to the sea.

—Rabindranath Tagore, *Letters to a Friend*, 1928

Tagore's novel *The Home and the World* (*Ghare Baire*), published in 1915, is set during a crucial juncture in the history of colonial India.[1] In the novel Tagore attempts to question the conflicting political discourses generated by the partition of Bengal and the swadeshi movement and grapples with the sociopolitical and epistemological vicissitudes of a discourse of nationalism as articulated by the three protagonists: Nikhilesh, Sandip, and Bimala.[2] In 1876 Queen Victoria was declared Empress of India by an act of Parliament, probably the greatest discursive manifestation of imperial rule. As Schweinitz puts it, the "arrogance of a superior, but exportable civilization now gave way to the arrogance of inherent superiority" (175). During the years 1899–1905 under the viceroyalty of Lord Curzon, the British manifested themselves as supremely imperialistic and had perfected the institutions of imperial rule. At the same time that the forces of British imperialism seemed invincible, however, India was taking shape in the minds of an Indian elite as an oppressed society.

The earlier pretensions, before the Sepoy Rebellion, of a benevolent rule could no longer be sustained, and the British became more severe and reckless in order to combat increasing demands for independent rule by a diverse body of educated Indian elites. In *The Home and the World* Tagore struggles to construct a particular subjectivity for each of his main characters even as they often confound the logic of unambiguous subject positions in their negotiations with the contestatory discursive space of an Indian nationalism. Tagore uses the character of Bimala and the narrative of her tenuous passage from the domestic to the public sphere to capture the pulse points of an increasingly violent Hindu nationalism that engenders itself in the image of the Mother Goddess as Shakti (strength). Such a partisan engendering precludes a significant portion of the population, such as the Muslims, from participating in the privileged space of the imagined community necessary for the constitution of a secular nation. At the same time, the crisis of individual identity precipitated by the possibility of mobility in the transition from private to public and its simultaneous containment in the iconization of the female as nation-goddess affects not only Bimala but the two men, Nikhil and Sandip, as well. The binary logic of Tagore's emblematization of the two strands of the swadeshi movement (the moderate and the extremist) in the two male characters is consistently challenged by the homosocial bond that at times prevails over their political differences as well as the metamorphic relationship between Bimala and the two men.[3] The representation of shifting political allegiances in the guise of woman's sexual culpability cannot merely be decoded as the inevitable figurative status of woman in the gendered discourse of nationalism. What the contemporary reader uncovers is the manner in which the novel, despite itself, offers a critique of the overdetermination of particular gender configurations in nationalism's relationship to the figure of woman in its ambivalent and often self-contradictory reinscriptions of the everyday structures of femininity and masculinity.

If Tagore's novel reveals that in the cultural politics of an Indian nationalism "the home was not a complementary but rather the original site on which the hegemonic project of nationalism was launched,"[4] *Sultana's Dream*, by Rokeya Sakhawat Hossain, a consciously feminist utopia published in 1905, transforms this feminized "original site" into the very nation itself. The bulk of this chapter focuses on Tagore's writings on nationalism, the woman question, and *The Home and the World*. In comparison, the section on Hossain is quite brief. One reason for this is that the utopian fantasy *Sultana's Dream* is a very short novella and my reading of it is meant to be merely suggestive of alternative tendencies during this particular historical moment. Yet I reiterate here that the inclusion of an analysis of an overt feminist utopia characterized by contemporary critics as "a reaction to the prevailing oppression and vulnerability of our women" is necessary as a counterpoint to my analysis of the representations of Indian women by male writers.[5] These two very different texts allow the postcolonial reader to trace the manner in which the juxtaposition of various narratives of nation formation disturbs the seemingly incontrovertible binary dichotomies produced in the construction of a nationalist discourse.

Because I concentrate on a particular discourse of nationalism as expressed in Bengal between the years 1885 and 1917, the partition of the Bengal Presidency mandated by Lord Curzon on July 19, 1905, is a crucial event that needs elaboration. Despite the various reasons adumbrated by Bengal's lieutenant governor Andrew Fraser and home secretary Risley, such as greater administrative convenience, relief of Bengal, and improvement of Assam, one cannot but be aware of the obvious political motives behind the desired division—the separation of the Hindu politicians of West and East Bengal, and the latent power of a united, large presidency. Risley's forceful presentation of the necessity of such a division on two occasions in 1904 makes the intentions of the British government quite clear: "Bengal united is a power; Bengal divided will pull in several different ways. That is perfectly true and is one of the merits of our scheme. . . . One of our main objects is to split up and thereby weaken a solid body of opponents to our rule."[6] The failure of the Moderate Congress's opposition to the partition plan led to a search for new forms—the boycott of British goods (suggested by Krishnakumar Mitra in his weekly publication *Sanjivani* on July 13, 1905, and eventually accepted by Surendranath Bannerjee at the Calcutta Town Hall meeting on August 7) and later to the boycott of educational institutions and organizations. The British assumption that the opposition would be mostly bureaucratic in form was violently challenged, and for a while the antipartition movement gathered great momentum, amassing a large number of supporters and giving an extremist and militant voice to the struggle for *Swaraj* (self-rule). However, the various factions within the extremist intelligentsia, their failure to ground fervent nationalist rhetoric in material and economic reality, and their tendency toward Hindu revivalism prevented the swadeshi movement from sustaining its initial impetus and enabled the established moderate leaders to call off the educational boycott on November 16, 1905.[7]

The partition of Bengal not only crystallized the fundamental ideological differences regarding the ends and means of nationalist action and political power between the Moderates and the Extremists; it also challenged the Catholic and nonsectarian image that the Moderate Congress wished to claim for itself. The responses to the partition revealed the deep communal cleavages between Hindus and Muslims. The partition enabled formation in 1906 of the Muslim League, which was dedicated to the protection of Muslim interests, and even though Surendranath Bannerjee called for Muslim support, most politically active Muslims accepted the partition and opposed swadeshi. Whereas a large percentage of the 18 million Muslims of East Bengal saw the partition as beneficial in terms of new opportunities in education, government service, and the professions, the Hindus vociferously opposed it as an attack on the growing solidarity of Bengal nationalism. Of course, beneath the pious plea for a united Bengal lay the grim fear of the erosion of Hindu dominance. Despite the lack of active participation by the Muslims in swadeshi and the initial reservation by Viceroy Hardinge to rescind the partition because he felt that it would be interpreted as "'concession to noisy clamor,' and would alienate the Muslims," the partition was revoked in June 1911 to "remove what the Bengali Hindus regarded as a 'flagrant injustice' to them" (Hasan 53).

The swadeshi movement, for all its divisions and ultimate failure, inaugurated a new age of intense challenge to the legitimacy of British rule. The list of Bengali men involved in swadeshi as moderates or extremists reads like a who's who of the current elite population and included Surendranath Bannerjee, Aswini Kumar Dutt, Aurobindo Ghose, Satish Chandra Mukherje, Bipin Chandra Pal, and Rabindranath Tagore. As Leonard Gordon succinctly puts it, "Bengal became the temporary cynosure of Indian politics" (84–85), and the tremendous impact of the movement can be encapsulated in the image of Gandhi noting in *Hind Swaraj*, as he sails back to India from South Africa, that the spirit of swadeshi that had started in Bengal would sweep over the rest of India.

Rabindranath Tagore was initially deeply committed to and involved in the movement. Between the years 1901 and 1906 in a number of Tagore's prose writings we can see a marked ascendancy of Hindu revivalist ideas.[8] For example, in "Bharatbarsher itihas" (India's history, 1902), India's traditional strength of unity in diversity is lauded as an accomplished achievement in and through Hinduism; in "Brahman" (1902) the purported functionalist virtues of the caste system are unequivocally commended; and in his "Swadesh Samaj" address of 1904, Tagore insists on channeling all constructive work through the revival of India's traditional society. As S. Sarkar states, "The bond of unity with the country is being sought explicitly now through the Hindu religion and samaj— 'Will not Hinduism be able to bring every one of us day by day into the bonds of affinity and devotion to this Bharatvarsha of ours—the abode of our gods, the hermitage of our rishis, the land of our forefathers?'" (*Swadeshi Movement* 54). It is obvious that Tagore's political views in 1904 had failed to take into account the "problem of integrating the Muslims and the low-caste Hindus—always outside the pale of the traditional samaj—into the national movement" (55). Tagore's mandate of *atmasakti* or self-help did lead to a constructive swadeshi with the formation of a number of autonomous industries, schools, and rural developments.[9] By 1906, however, Tagore had already begun to be disillusioned by the extremist overtones in the political propaganda undertaken by certain of the Bengali intelligentsia who wished to mount a full-scale movement of resistance against the British. After the summer of 1906 he withdrew to his central Bengal estates to devote his energy to village reconstruction efforts and educational experiments at Shantiniketan. Between 1905 and 1907 the swadeshi movement grew increasingly zealous in its absolute program of complete boycott of the foreign administration. And we now encounter a different Tagore, one sensitive to the needs of the peasant classes who, in the eastern sections of Bengal, were also chiefly Muslims. In 1907, as S. Sarkar points out, Tagore underlined the class bias of the ideology of resistance mounted by the Extremists: "The peasants were expected to buy inferior and costly goods and face Gurkha lathis into the bargain for the sake of a cause that must have seemed distant and abstract to them, and that they were being asked to do all this by 'babus' who had treated them so long with contemptuous indifference or at best with condescension" (*Swadeshi Movement* 79).

Jasodhara Bagchi also points out that it was in the aftermath of the swadeshi movement in Bengal that "Rabindranath Tagore turned seriously to the question of identity and selfhood in matters relating to possible national identity" ("Secularism as Identity" 57). Bagchi goes on to discuss Tagore's essay "Self-Identity" published in the famous Brahmo journal *Tattwabodhini Patrika* in 1912.[10] She argues that in this essay Tagore deconstructs the notion of the production of identity in difference through a negotiation of his own problematic relationship to the constructedness of religious identities. She asserts that Tagore's primary aim in this essay is to explore "the problems of why he [Tagore] is a Hindu, even though he is a Brahmo, and why he is not a Muslim even though he is a monotheist. Though there is a clear attempt at *naturalizing Hinduism as the only acceptable indigenous identity, he very consciously opposes attempts to reify this identity, to make it monolithic and rigid* (52; emphasis added).

If in his 1912 essay Tagore attempted to "debate one aspect of Hindu identity that had haunted the nation building process in Bengal" (52), his critique of the extremists in his 1917 essay "Nationalism in India" was aimed at their importation of a Western model of nationalism that was impervious to the social needs particular to India.[11] He believed that unless "we in India . . . remove those social customs and ideals which have generated a want of self respect and a complete dependence on those above us—a state of affairs which has been brought about entirely by the domination in India of the caste system" (*Nationalism* 68–69)—the Extremists would merely obtain a formal decolonization that would leave us "victims for other nations" (68).

A number of moderates and extremists saw Tagore's withdrawal from the political sphere as a fundamental betrayal, and *The Home and the World* can be described as Tagore's response to his critics. Two other novels by Tagore, *Gora* and *Char Adhyay*, also focus almost exclusively on aspects of the nationalist movement, but I find *The Home and the World* the most didactic. I concur with Bagchi in her assessment of the novel *Gora*, which was serialized from 1907 in an avant-garde Brahmo literary journal *Prabasi*, as the least didactic and the novel that vigorously reinforced an indigenously modified secular outlook. Bagchi characterizes the novel as Tagore's fictional rendition of his belief in the need to fight religion as a basis for political identity. "While not denying the importance of the search for self identity, he [Tagore] searches for a secularism that is inclusive and indigenous at the same time. . . . As the class based nationalist agenda increasingly reified and homogenized the religious identity of Hindus and Muslims, Tagore searched for a secularism that was not a harsh rejection of religion" ("Secularism as Identity" 59).

Tagore's refusal to compose a song at the request of Bipin Pal to celebrate the motherland as a goddess, his reluctance to set the militant slogan "Bande Mataram" to music for the Congress session to be held in Calcutta, and the use of the slogan by the nationalists setting fire to Muslim homes in his novel *The Home and the World*—these actions testify to his mistrust of the deployment of a particularly inflected religious idiom for a nationalist movement. He constantly sought to write patriotic songs that would enable both Muslims and Hindus to celebrate their common relationship to the land. According to Bagchi, in "Tagore, there has been a systematic attempt to reach some kind of identity as consensus, though the compulsion was very great to conform to a Hindu ideology" (63).

Yet Tagore clearly denounces the uncompromising, militant nationalism secured by a Hindu ideology, as seen in the incarnation of the character of Sandip as the Ravana figure in *The Home and the World*. However, his position vis-à-vis nationalism in general is quite complex. Ashis Nandy delineates the sociopolitical scenario of the novel as "a bitter criticism of sectarian Hindu nationalism . . . [and an anticipation of] the *low-key unheroic, consensual nationalism* which Gandhi wanted a multi-ethnic society like India to follow."[12] Such an interpretation at once situates the novel and Tagore's paradoxical relationship to the ideology of nationalism despite his pious denunciation of the idea of the modern nation-state. "[The] idea of the Nation is one of the most powerful anaesthetics that man has invented. Under the influence of its fumes the whole people can carry out its systematic program of the most virulent self-seeking without being in the least aware of its moral perversion" (Tagore, *Nationalism* 25–26). But Tagore's poetic onslaught against nationalism fails to offer an alternative modus operandi for decolonization. His demand for "a basis of unity which is not political" (59) remains at the level of an emotional appeal to a universalism that must motivate man to exert "all his power of love and clarity of vision to make [a] great moral adjustment which will comprehend the whole world of men and not merely the fractional groups of nationality" (61).

The idea of the nation is a menacing one because it gives man the "satisfaction of moral exaltation" even as it denies him the free expression of his "complete moral personality" (67). Man can become a true moral being by celebrating the one history—"the history of man" (59). However, the commemoration of the one history of man is enabled first by the prior imperative of maintaining the separation between East and West. This division is not just an assertion of the geographic distance between the two; East and West for Tagore function much more crucially as discursive sites that affirm a number of Orientalist tropes. In Tagore's conceptualization of the global landscape, the governing structures of an Orientalist theory are clearly visible in its paradigmatic production of the reciprocal images

of the Orient and the Occident. Thus even though the British nation is in-
dicted for its false tutelage and "sedulously giving currency to the arro-
gant cynicism that the East is east and the West is west and never the
twain shall meet" (12), it is the impossibility of the reconciliation of East
and West that is challenged by Tagore and not a foundational tenet of
Orientalism that, as Said has pointed out, "is a style of thought based on
an ontological and epistemological distinction made between 'the Orient' and (most of the time) 'the Occident'" (*Orientalism* 2). Thus, for Tagore's brand of universalism to work, the West is commanded in inspira-
tional prose to forgo false pride in its accomplishments the better to
impart to the "East what is best in herself, and [to accept] in a right spirit
the wisdom that the east has stored for centuries" (Tagore, *Nationalism*
62). India (and the East) should not compete with Western civilization in
its own field but follow its own Eastern destiny. If it is providential that
the West has come to the East, "some one [Tagore?] must show the East
to the West. . . . Let us have a deep association. . . . I have great faith in
human nature, and I think the West will find its true mission." This goal
will be to temper the West's much needed materialism with the spiritual
wealth garnered from the East (66). The translation of this aspiring poetic
practice into the political sphere, however, remains ephemeral and fails
to provide an ideological program that would counter the empty decolonization that he sees offered by the swadeshis.

Nikhil, the wealthy landowner in Tagore's *The Home and the World*,
is an idealized figure modeled partly on his creator and exemplifies Tagore's beliefs on the function of an aristocratic, patriotic leader. Like his
creator, Nikhil spends his money in making swadeshi soaps, pencils, and
the like, which are quite inferior to the Western goods that his family
members are used to. But he continues to manufacture indigenous goods
against all odds, despite losing large sums of money in the process. Like
Tagore, Nikhil too cannot participate in the unwarranted destruction of
British goods through gratuitous acts of violence, especially when he realizes that it is the Muslim traders under his jurisdiction who were suffering
the most. They could not afford the idealistic and patriotic gestures of
lighting bonfires with imported goods and therefore become the target of
coercion by Sandip, the revolutionary, and his followers.

This concern for the poorer members of the society, who in the novel
happen to be of the religious minority as well, separates Nikhil from Sandip, the "professional politician" (Nandy 13). Sandip is a nationalist who

seeks to gain independence for India and personal glory at the same time by any means possible, including a complete disregard for the "true tradition" of India. Nikhil, on the other hand, embodies Tagore's philosophy that salvation for India lies in *a patriotism, not nationalism*, that should attempt *at the social, not political level*, to "make an adjustment of races, to acknowledge the real differences between them where these exist, and yet seek for some basis of unity" (Tagore, *Nationalism* 59). The true patriot would apply his knowledge of India's glorious past—"What India has been, the whole world is now" (59)—to prevent the parochial spirit of nationalism from delivering a putative political freedom at the expense of spiritual emancipation (73–74). Tagore's realization that the political freedom offered by the nationalists failed to take into account the internal oppression in a society ridden by caste and religious hierarchies was quite accurate. His concern for the spiritual well-being of humanity allows for some very perceptive critiques of the swadeshi movement and of nationalism in general. Yet Tagore fails to offer a political manifesto for a positive movement of decolonization.

Tagore's criticism of a bourgeois nationalism that addresses only the vested interests of an indigenous elite is echoed in Frantz Fanon's essay "The Pitfalls of National Consciousness" written almost fifty years later during the Algerian war of independence (in *Wretched of the Earth* 148–205). But Fanon, as Neil Lazarus points out, does not dismiss the importance of nationalism for a sustained movement of decolonization. According to Lazarus, Fanon distinguishes between a bourgeois nationalism, on the one hand, and "a liberationist, anti-imperialist, nationalist internationalism," on the other, which "as a form of national consciousness does not merely mobilise the 'people' but actively registers and articulates their aspirations."[13] Theories of nation formation asseverated by a bourgeois nationalism are, as Partha Chatterjee has shown so brilliantly, a "particular manifestation of a much more general problem, namely the problem of the bourgeois-rationalist-conception of knowledge, established in the post-Enlightenment period of European intellectual history, as the moral and epistemic foundation for a supposedly universal framework of thought" (*Nationalist Thought* 11). The status of nationalism as a "derivative discourse" then forever straddles the quicksand of a negation of the discourse of power that is colonialism and the assertion of a new discursive order of national power in the alien image of that which it seeks to replace.

Tagore clearly saw the emerging concept of the Indian nation put forward by its intelligentsia as being engulfed in quicksand at the very moment of its inception, and he retreated to the peripheral safety of a pastoral Bengal where his status as an intellectual and financial magus allowed him to continue his own small experiments in education and village work in a tradition that resembled a benevolent feudalism. An emphasis on changing the daily existence of a rural population as a first step before attending to the needs of a colonized country at large formed the basis of Tagore's plans for reconstruction. Tagore believed in the presence of "shakti" (strength)[14] in man and society, and he underscored in a number of passages the importance of harnessing and directing this shakti toward "some centre . . . where all could unite, where thinkers could contribute their ideas and workers their efforts; then there the generous would find a repository for their gifts. Our education, our literature, our arts and crafts, and all our good works would range themselves round such centre and help to create in all its richness the commonwealth which our patriotism is in search of."[15]

Yet the translation of this intellectual framework into a structure that would forge autonomous local knowledges into a social revolution was hopelessly inadequate. Tagore's trenchant critique of the inadequacy of a borrowed nationalist epistemology for the Indian condition is not without merit, as I pointed out earlier. But his wholesale dismissal of nationalism fails to take into account the ideological difference between bourgeois nationalism and nationalitarianism, the latter allowing for a possible explanation for "the huge investment of 'the masses' of the colonised in various kinds of nationalist struggle" (Lazarus 214). As an intellectual, therefore, one who was certainly against imperialism, Tagore's particular failure lay in his inability to appreciate that both bourgeois nationalism, to some extent, and the nationalitarianism of "the masses," more significantly, could "struggle with an entire body of systematic knowledge . . . [and] open up that framework of knowledge which presumes to dominate it, to displace that framework, to subvert its authority, to challenge its morality" (P. Chatterjee, *Nationalist Thought* 42).

Tagore's depiction of the power dynamics generated by the onslaught of the nationalist movement is in the last instance cannibalistic. The collection of three essays published under the title *Nationalism* concludes with a translation of a poem written in Bengali, on the last day of the last century, called "The Sunset of the Century." The excessively metaphorical and luridly romantic narrative of nationalism espoused by Tagore in this poem represents the drive to nation formation as self-devouringly narcissistic:

> The naked passion of self-love of Nations, in its drunken
> delirium of greed, is dancing to the clash of steel and the howling verses of vengeance.
>
> The hungry self of the nation shall burst in a violence
>   of fury from its own shameless feeding
> For it has made the world its food.
> And licking it, crunching it and swallowing it in big morsels,
>   It swells and swells
>
> . . . .
>
> . . . —the self-love of the nation—dead under its own excess.
>
> (80–81)

In this discourse of nationalism, the ambivalence that underlines the liminal image of the nation is completely elided. If, however, we take this statement as Tagore's last word on nationalism and move forward to his rendering of the repercussions of the swadeshi movement in *The Home and the World*, we realize the complex nature of Tagore's disavowal of nationalism. In his depiction of the transformation of the micropolitical as a result of the dominance of nationalism in the macropolitical, it is Bimala who is denounced by her sister-in-law as "cannibalistic" and therefore ultimately held responsible for the tragedy that befalls her husband, Nikhil, and the household in general. In this representation, then, nationalism is not merely gendered but sexualized, and it is in the imagining of nationalism as a devouring female that Tagore's critique is rendered shrilly censorious.

I turn now to an extended reading of the novel, beginning with a brief summary, to flesh out the implications of Tagore's syncopation of the nationalist narrative into the body and space of the upper-caste Hindu woman.[16] Bimala is married into the family of a wealthy landowner, Nikhil, who cares deeply not only for the people living and working in his constituency but also for abstract equality in the relationship between husband and wife. He provides Bimala with a modern education (complete with its requisite presence of an English governess), allows her to come out of the "zenana" (women's quarters) to meet and communicate with his friend Sandip without any supervision, and, when he realizes that she is increasingly infatuated with both Sandip and the nationalist movement, does not in any way curb her freedom or mistreat her. Bimala is attracted to Sandip, the revolutionary, who sways her with his fervent speeches about the glorious and necessary outcome of the swadeshi movement and captivates her with his charismatic persona. He ultimately betrays her, however, by revealing his avarice and need for personal validation. Bimala finally learns to appreciate her husband's subdued, virtuous qualities, also realizing the pitfalls of the nationalist agenda, but her participation in the affairs of the world does conclude the novel on a deeply tragic note.[17]

Though its chief aim is to deride the nationalist revolutionaries and their acts of violence, the novel allows the reader to explore, through the character and the actions of Bimala, the paradoxical functionary position that a certain class of woman inhabited (were made to inhabit?) in the spatial politics of a nationalist ideology. If power over space is one governing axis of the interplay between colonialism and nationalism, then the everyday spaces traversed and occupied by women become crucial sites of interpretive struggle. If one accepts a definition of "feminism" as a kind of spatial politics,[18] then the emphasis on movement that marks Bimala as different from other women—for example, the wives (now widows) of Nikhil's brothers—enables an analysis of the complex and competing discourses of "modernization" and "tradition" in relation to the issue of the "women's question" that in some form or another surfaced throughout the nineteenth century in Bengal.[19]

The representation of the role and status of Bimala is but one illustration of the manner in which female geography—as in woman's *place*, with its dual resonance—was constantly being scrutinized, problematized, and negotiated in the nineteenth century, first under the aegis of social reformers wanting to usher India into the "modern" era and then under the general political platform of liberty for all Indians. Joanna Liddle and Rama Joshi have pointed out that in "the nineteenth century the women's question was initially raised by men through a number of organizations concerned with general political reform" (19). And although in 1904 one can see the first steps being taken to formulate a special sphere exclusively designed to address questions concerning the secondary status of women in Indian society,[20] the politics of woman only became an issue because the Indian (primarily male) intelligentsia wished to consolidate their position and present a united front in the realm of nationalist politics. The force with which women had to contend in this stage of their emancipatory struggle was not the patriarchy but the common enemy of all India—the imperialist regime.

In their assessment of the rise of the women's movement in India, Liddle and Joshi very astutely point out the reason why nationalist politicians termed women's politics the women's movement rather than a feminist movement: "The movement did not adopt the term 'feminist,' because it suggested that the women's question had priority over the nationalist question, whereas in fact they (the native [male] intelligentsia) saw the two as inextricably linked. India was not in control of her own government, so she could hardly institute legal reforms on woman's position" (22). Most Bengali nationalist intellectuals who advocated reforms to change the subordinate status of women did so in the context of a social agenda that never questioned the role of woman as good daughter, wife, and mother. This emphasis on the domestic role of the Indian woman, as Partha Chatterjee has pointed out, was not just another repetition of the typical conceptualization of woman's role in traditional patriarchy. In seeking to reproduce their own version of the domestic to counter the one constructed in colonial discourse, nationalists endowed the domestic realm with the sovereignty of an untainted Indian spiritual essence that became the exclusive signifier of a sanctified tradition unsusceptible to the incursions of a Western modernity. In doing so, the separation of the home and the world was extended to a marked distinction of inner versus outer, material versus spiritual, and the bourgeois, upper-caste Indian woman was made to signify this differential essence. The nationalists then could continue to advocate the benefits of modernity in the material world, even extend certain of those benefits (such as education) to women, and yet be able to measure their ideological distance from the hegemony of colonial epistemology. Thus "the national paradigm in fact supplied an ideological principle of *selection*. It was not a dismissal of modernity but an attempt to make modernity consistent with the nationalist project" (P. Chatterjee, *Nation* 121).

In *The Home and the World* the various discourses engaged in resolving the "women's question" and its relation to nationalism are mobilized around the character of Bimala. When Tagore's novel was first published it generated considerable hostility among the intellectuals of the time because they felt that Tagore had completely denigrated the average nationalist intellectual in his portrayal of Sandip. He was equally attacked for his valorization of the opposition in the figure of the wealthy landowner Nikhil, whose altruistic benevolence and stoic demeanor they deemed more characteristic of a saint. Even if one subscribes to this last description of the novel, one still needs to engage with the important presence and role of Bimala, who not only becomes emblematic of the motherland but from the outset is also the site/body on and through whom the various discourses are inscribed and disseminated. The novel is divided into the various texts of the three different authors: Bimala, Nikhil, and Sandip. It is "Bimala's story" however, that frames the novel—hers is the first and the last story that one reads, allowing us to read the novel as a memoir. Malavika Karlekar points up how by the "second half of the nineteenth century Bengali women started writing about themselves as well as noting down their responses to the changing environment."[21] Of course, these women came from the *bhadramahila* class and represented a very tiny percentage of the elite section of society.[22] But through their *smritikathas* (memoirs), as Partha Chatterjee notes, we can deduce not so much the "life history of the narrator or the development of her 'self' but rather the social history of the times." Bimala's story as recounted by her, perhaps because it appears in the form of a novel, accomplishes both.[23]

It is a kind of female bildungsroman that weaves Bimala's own fraught maturation with the complex discourses of nationalism struggling to achieve independence for a colonized nation. Unlike a traditional bildungsroman, however, the novel provides no resolution to the various conflicts elaborated in its pages. The opening lines of the novel reach forward in time to the ending, filling the present moment with the tragic overtones of the future, and this logic of reversal initially leaves us in no doubt of Tagore's pessimistic attitude toward swadeshi. Yet this temporal displacement also makes possible the opening up of interstitial spaces where Bimala's texts begin to function as palimpsests on which are inscribed the rewritings of both her husband and her lover. Thus the tendency toward an absolute indictment of swadeshi captured in the image of a chastened and defeated Bimala mourning her seriously wounded husband is, if not negated, definitely subject to deferral. The deferral is occasioned by the interrogative reflections of Bimala on her changing position, first as the wife of a modern, secular zamindar; second as the nation-goddess worshiped by Sandip, the false revolutionary; and third as the mother of an incipient nation who commands the devotion of her (the nation's) true son, Amulya.

The novel seeks to endorse the image of a penitent Bimala and through it authorize the domestic realm as the signifier of an unimpeachable bedrock of tradition. "Woman," Radhakrishnan writes, "becomes the mute but necessarily allegorical ground for the transactions of nationalist history" (84). The reverberations of a material history echo in the palimpsest-like traces of Bimala's voice and challenge the idea of the body as a source for a knowledge transmitted through a neutral language that is either allowed or disallowed by a centralized form of prohibition. As Foucault has revealed, our subjectivity, identity, and sexuality are intimately linked and are actually brought into play by discursive strategies and representational practices. The relationship between the body and discursive power is not a negative one, because power renders the body active and productive. But this equation is never simple but a complex and often paradoxical interaction that struggles against the institutional desire for normalization. In Tagore's *The Home and the World*, Bimala's struggle to develop an independent identity tends at times to undermine the repressive ideology of the family, which masks itself in the guise of humanism and which ultimately seeks to uphold a particular identity for women "in line with the exigencies of [its] own discursive fields and legitimating truths" (Martin 14).

A system of social beliefs, values, and ideas that are shared by a social group has traditionally been termed "ideology." In recent years, however, in its most general sense, this overused though indispensable term has come to indicate the various processes by which social subjects are formed, reformed, and effected and thereby allowed to perform as conscious agents in an apparently meaningful world. Therefore, all practices, like all subject matter, are a production of ideology. Given this, all orientation to language as such is always already an orientation to language that is being produced from a position within "history, culture, society, politics, institutions, class and gender conditions" (Montrose 16–17). In *The Home and the World*, Bimala's performance as a social subject can be contained even less by a simple definition than can Nikhil's or Sandip's. One can sum up their position by defining them, respectively, as a virtuous and benevolent zamindar and as an overreaching, selfish revolutionary. They also enact the role of husband, lover, and friend, but the latter performances are definitely subsumed by their more public activities, so that their identity resides in a continuing reinscription of their sociopolitical roles that extend beyond the home. Bimala, on the other hand, inhabits a space that is crisscrossed by every significant sociohistorical and cultural formation. She occupies various subject positions: she is an upper-caste, educated woman undergoing rapid transformation under conflicting norms; she is Nikhil's wife and therefore the landlady of not just her house but the estate as well; she is a married woman attracted to her husband's friend; she is in charge of familial transactions inside the house; she is the emblematic goddess/mother that will rouse a nation to freedom; and, finally, she is the economic agent who helps fuel the crisis that creates a rupture in the dividing line that separates the home from the world. Bimala, then, more so than any other character in the novel, is subjected to the "equivocal process of subjectification: on the one hand, shaping individuals as loci of consciousness and initiators of action—endowing them with subjectivity and with the capacity for agency; and on the other hand, positioning, motivating, and constraining them within—subjecting them to—social networks and cultural codes that ultimately exceed their comprehension and control" (Montrose 21). In her introduction to the English translation of the novel, Anita Desai claims that "the novel ends in scenes of unbearable tension and horrific violence. Bimala realizes now that the path Sandip has shown her is *evil*; she draws back from it, but by then it is tragically too late" (11). A conclusion of the drama enacted in the novel as a simple struggle between the forces of good and evil, however, fails to take into account the dialogic context that an evaluation of Bimala's texts as palimpsest provide.

A more extended dialogic context is provided if we read *The Home and the World* in conjunction with Tagore's essay "Woman," published in the collection titled *Personality*.[24] In this essay Tagore sets up binary oppositions to define man and woman. He opposes woman's desire for stability to man's constant need for "unlimited augmentation of power." According to Tagore: "The masculine creations of intellectual civilization are towers of Babel, they dare to defy their foundations and therefore topple down over and over again. Thus human history is growing up over layers of ruins; it is not a continuous life growth" (*Personality* 171).

The present stage of history, the early twentieth century, was according to Tagore a stage in the history of civilization that was "almost exclusively masculine, a civilization of power, in which woman has been thrust aside in the shade." Because its "motive forces [were] the forces of destruction," its ceremonials could be effected only "through an appalling number of human sacrifices" (172). Tagore therefore felt a pressing need to engage women in this history, to bring their "instinctive" desire for fullness to counter the shooting of "wanton [male] arrows of curiosity into the heart of darkness" (171). He believed that the time "had arrived when women must step in and impart her life and rhythm into this reckless movement of power" (172). In the same essay female virtues are categorized as "passive qualities of chastity, modesty, devotion, and power of self sacrifice" that are "necessary for the healing and nourishing and storing of life" (173), but he does not intend for women to be restricted to the domestic sphere. Tagore believes that the power which women possess is the "power of love," and it is this emotion that allows them to embrace their fellow creatures not because of their usefulness and market value but because they are human beings—an attribute that needs to be introduced into the public domain. Therefore he does not want "domestic life [to be] the only life for a woman. I mean that the human world is the woman's world, be it domestic or be it full of the other activities of life which are human activities, and not merely abstract attempts to organize" (176). It is imperative that women use their power "to break through the surface and go to the center of things" (177). Tagore firmly advocates the importance and relevance of woman's role in shaping the history of a country, especially in moments of crisis.

Tagore insists on clearly demarcating the home from the world, but he feels that the home should deterritorialize the world and not be "crowded" out by the market. Man craves to appropriate the whole world for himself, and in doing so he hardly leaves any room for woman. "But woman cannot be pushed back for good into the mere region of the decorative by man's aggressiveness of power. For she is not less necessary in civilization than man but possibly more so" (180). As is clear from this delineation of Tagore's position on the "woman question," a marked tendency exists to essentialize female qualities as those of nurturing, rebuilding, and humanizing that would and could prevent society and the world from the destructive mayhem they were then heading toward.[25] But for women to save the world from the dehumanized state brought about by men, women had to cross the dividing line that man/society had drawn to circumscribe her. The dilemma at this point becomes crucial for Tagore. He believes that certain innate qualities constitute women, thus he must enforce the belief that, despite temporary contamination, women will eventually return to their purified state because they will be unable to deny the force of their instinctive nature. Their essential qualities will ultimately reinforce their natural position as healer and helper in the domestic realm and will not interfere with their participation in the macropolitics of the world. As is obvious by now, such a theory is inherently repressive because of the debilitating values it prescribes.

When we turn to *The Home and the World* with the above psychosocial framework in mind, the masculine and feminine qualities attributed to man and woman do not neatly correspond to the three characters. Only Sandip, the male superego engaging in systematic destruction to create his very own "tower of Babel," fits in with Tagore's depiction of the masculinization of contemporary civilization. Because Tagore's intention in the novel was to underscore the negative repercussions of the swadeshi movement, the significance of Sandip as a character is diminished by his delineation as a caricature embodying the worst attributes of an elitist nationalist. On the other hand, even this caricature is humanized by Nikhil's attraction to and long-standing friendship with him.[26] Nikhil represents many of the qualities defined as "feminine" by Tagore—Nikhil, unlike Sandip, has the capability of perceiving the true essence of things; as Bimala attests, "he did not assert his power just because he had it" (26); and by the end of the novel we are privy to his enormous capacity for selfless devotion and self-sacrifice. Bimala, who should embody these same qualities, is certainly not completely chaste and is more headstrong, opinionated, and reckless than Tagore's delineation of the ideal woman. Yet even this is more complicated by the fact that, to a certain extent, it is Nikhil's desire to "modernize" his wife which is responsible for the final tragedy.[27] As I noted, it is Bimala's character that is the most systematically developed in the novel. We see her gradual transformation from a woman with the deeply ingrained notions of the duty and function of an upper-caste woman to the wife that Nikhil shapes her to be to, finally, someone who realizes the truth about Sandip. One of the more obvious moral messages of the novel is the castigation of women who fail to reconcile tradition with modernity. Bimala's abandonment of her traditions makes her similar to the "woman of the western world" whose "certain restlessness . . . cannot be the normal aspect of her nature. For women who want something special and violent in their surroundings to keep their interests active only prove that they have lost touch . . . with their own true world" (208–9). It is only a monumental catastrophe that can finally bring Bimala "in touch with [her] own true world."

The irony is that she was, to begin with, very much in touch with this "true world" sustained for generations by an indigenous patriarchy. Tagore supported the education of women and did not believe that they should be confined to the domestic realm, therefore Nikhil cannot be condemned for emulating these very principles. Even though Tagore denounced the swadeshi movement and the nationalist ideology derived from it, his essay "Woman" echoes a number of the sentiments of such nationalist intellectuals as Bhudeb Mukhopadhyay, who sought to define the new domestic realm in terms of the material/spiritual dichotomy necessary in the modern world of the nation. This new patriarchy, of which Tagore was an integral member, "explicitly distinguished [itself] from the patriarchy of indigenous tradition, the same tradition that had been put on the dock by colonial interrogators. Sure enough nationalism [and *Tagore's own doctrine*] adopted several elements from tradition as marks of native cultural identity, but this was now a 'classicized' tradition—reformed, reconstructed, fortified against charges of barbarism and irrationality" (P. Chatterjee, *Nation* 127). For example, Nikhil is horrified when he discovers Bimala "taking" the dust off his feet one morning before he is fully awake. The moment before the entire household wakes up to the routine of daily life is appropriated by Bimala for the expression of her singular devotion toward her husband. Bimala is a careful observer of the traditions of Hindu domestic life, and as a child her one powerful recollection of beauty is the image of her mother arranging fruits, "peeled by her own loving hands, on the white stone plate, and gently wav[ing] her fan to drive away the flies while [her] father sat down to his meals" (18). The domestic realm in late-nineteenth- and early-twentieth-century India was almost exclusively run by women—the wife, mother, mother-in-law, and often a widowed sister/sister-in-law.

This was the power that automatically belonged to Bimala the minute she stepped over the threshold of a Rajah's house. Although her "father-in-law's house was old in dignity from the days of the Badshahs" (18), Bimala's husband was "absolutely modern." And he therefore wished to extend her power beyond the usual zenana space by providing her with an English governess, Miss Gilby. This was achieved despite "all the wagging tongues at home and outside" (19). The wife who found aesthetic pleasure in worshiping at her husband's feet is gradually educated "and introduced to the modern age in its own language" (19); when she later tries to capture the significant events of her life through the written word, those moments of self-fulfillment that she had realized in actualizing her love, desire, and respect for her husband appeared to "blush with shame in their prose setting" (19). The juxtaposition between the natural and artificial in its various manifestations is a key trope in this novel,[28] and Bimala understands at the moment of writing that just as being born a woman was beyond her power, "so was the element of devotion in woman's love" not only incapable of being understood by the male but also ineffable in the modern language of men that she must emulate.

Though she praises her husband for his magnanimity in elevating her from a position that is literally at his feet to one beside him, her hidden text articulates her inner trepidation at what this abrupt shifting of position might entail. Despite her embarrassment at the barefaced admission of her initial overwhelming devotion for her husband, as well as her admiration for the "greatness" and the overflowing love with which her husband flooded her, Bimala's very real misgivings over certain of her husband's opinions about equality and love make the reader question Nikhil's apparent blindness to his wife's reception of his often facile incorporation and hasty imposition of Western notions. On the issue of equality, Bimala's opinion is very different from that of her husband: "My husband used to say, that man and wife are equal in love because of their equal claim on each other. I never argued the point with him, but my heart said that devotion never stands in the way of true equality; it only raises the level of the ground of meeting. Therefore the joy of the higher equality remains permanent; it never slides down to the vulgar level of triviality" (20). Nikhil's desire that she abandon an inherited cultural accoutrement and don an entirely new social robe subjects her to internal contradictions within the different social significations such that she does not and cannot achieve the fixed identity position of a homogeneous subject. Ideally, Nikhil would have her imitate his subject position, be his representative in the home; thus, when he chose to enter her zenana space, she would be capable of understanding and appreciating his discourse without debating or doubting its superiority and validity. Bimala feels the constant need to "stand up for one's rights" (25), and she questions her husband's motivations for some of the changes that he wishes to implement. When her husband wants her to come out of "purdah," she demands to know his reasons:

> "What do I want with the outside world?"
>
> "The outside world may want you," he replied.
>
> "If the outside world has got on so long without me, it may go on for some time longer. It need not pine to death for want of me."
>
> "Let it perish, for all I care! That is not troubling me. I am thinking about myself."

"Oh, indeed. Tell me about yourself?"

My husband was silent with a smile.

I knew his way and protested at once: "No, no, you are not going to run away from me like that! I want to have this out with you."

"Can one ever finish a subject with words?"

"Do stop talking in riddles. Tell me." (23)

In this conversation, which is even more protracted, Bimala does not provide the actual reason for her refusal. She definitely does not like the way her husband presents his reasons—in riddles or in the form of a fable with its inevitable moral (24)—but her reluctance is rooted in her traditional upbringing and beliefs, which do not allow her to cause unnecessary unhappiness to Nikhil's grandmother. This older woman, who had uncomplainingly watched a "hundred and twenty percent" of the house of the *badshahs* (kings) being infiltrated by twentieth-century taste, would have accepted the violation of the seclusion code equally gracefully, but Bimala knew that she would have been extremely hurt by this ultimate Westernization.[29] At that particular moment in her life Bimala does not feel the urge to be a part of the world; as she herself says in her opening story, "I have read in books that we are called 'caged birds,' I cannot speak for others, but I had so much in this cage of mine that there was no room for it in the universe—at least that is what I felt then" (24). Once again we find Bimala questioning the validity of Western interpretations of the Hindu woman's existence. At this point in the novel, one could argue, it is Bimala who functions as the mouthpiece for Tagore's views regarding woman, whereas Nikhil emerges as a Bengali "babu" who introduces the new currents from the outside world into his home without fully appreciating the impact of the new demands made on his wife.

One cannot argue with Nikhil's desire to educate his wife, despite his insensitivity to her reception of it. But the novel does foreground the problems that accompany change in the home and the world even when the ultimate goal seems to be in the direction of progress and emancipation. There can be no question, for example, about the virtue inherent in the notion of emancipation through education for women. The problem lies in the identification of exclusive qualities for men and women that becomes even more crucially significant when these qualities denote activity and power to mobilize, on the one hand, and passivity and guidance through love, on the other.[30]

Thus, Nikhil's behavior toward his wife is impeccable. He buys her highly fashionable, modern clothes that are often derived from Western models. Verbally, he denies any notion of a hierarchical relationship, and never, even when she begins to drift further and further from him and his ideals, does he reproach her. He allows her to express her feelings and conduct herself as she desires. Even when his widowed sister-in-law is appalled at the way Bimala continues to meet Sandip in the privacy of her chambers, Nikhil does not coerce her into obeying standard norms of decorum. Yet Nikhil's inner turmoil reflects Bimala's initial dilemma when she is made to realize and rectify the error of certain indigenous practices. Nikhil, the stoic, had tested his strength of mind "by imagining all kinds of evil which might happen" to him, including Bimala's death (40). But he had never imagined the one possibility that does occur: that she might grow to love another man. His story reveals what he never articulates to anyone else in the novel, the pride in fashioning a woman/wife along lines he felt perfectly suited him: "Up till now Bimala was my home-made Bimala, the product of the confined space and the daily routine of small duties. . . . I longed to find Bimala blossoming fully in all her truth and power. But the thing I forgot to calculate was, that one must give up all claims based on conventional rights, if one would find a person freely revealed in truth" (41).

Bimala is his possession, and while Nikhil never treats her as such, the thought continues to haunt him as he awakens to the realization that he is no longer Bimala's revered idol. The very practices he had prompted Bimala to abandon, such as the garlanding of his portrait in her room with a fresh wreath every day, now assume a different symbolic significance for Nikhil. Later in the novel, Nikhil walks into the bedroom to fetch a book. Except to sleep, he had not been inside that room during the day for a considerable length of time. As he walks in, his eyes are attracted by the signs of Bimala's occupancy of the room—her sari hanging on the rack, her perfumes, pins, and the vermilion box—economic and cultural signifiers that manifest the ritualized transformation of woman to wife. But his neglected portrait in the niche explicitly states that although Bimala was still his wife as suggested by her "presence" in the room, she no longer elevated Nikhil (as she had earlier) through her wifely devotion. Bimala no longer felt the need either to take the dust off his feet or to make any gesture of homage. The "withered black" flowers scattered around the portrait were still there "because it was not felt worth while even to remove them" (87). Nikhil waxes nostalgic about the good old days when

Bimala was engrossed in pleasing him and realizes that despite his intellectual commitment to freedom for women he cannot be "unmoved" by Bimala's expression of a subject position that is not predicated solely on him.

Tagore never presents Bimala as a completely subservient wife. Not only does Bimala question Nikhil's desires to modernize her, she is also critical of his excessive probity: "I used to feel that goodness has a limit, which, if passed, somehow seems to make men cowardly. Shall I tell the whole truth? I have often wished that my husband had the manliness to be a little less good" (22). Of course she pays a heavy price for not appreciating the very quality that separates him from most men, but Bimala's silent criticism underscores the diurnal strain of living with someone excessively virtuous. She further reproaches him for allowing himself to be fleeced by Sandip: "Whenever he [Sandip] wanted to start a newspaper, or travel about preaching the Cause [swadeshi], or take a change of air by the advice of his doctor, my husband would unquestioningly supply him with money. This was over and above the regular living allowance which Sandip Babu also received from him" (27). The reader is also privy to Bimala's annoyance at seeing her husband duped by someone she did not quite trust: "There was something in his [Sandip's] features which I did not quite like . . . he had a splendidly handsome face. Yet, I know not why, it seemed to me, in spite of all its brilliance, that too much base alloy had gone into its making. The light in his eyes did not shine true" (30). Bimala also has opinions about swadeshi that differ from her husband's. The novel makes it clear that Bimala believed in swadeshi long before her infatuation with Sandip. "As soon as the Swadeshi storm reached [her] blood" (27), Bimala wanted to burn her foreign clothes and get rid of the English governess, Miss Gilby. Even when Miss Gilby is attacked by young Noren in the name of swadeshi, she refuses to indict the young man who, in his enthusiasm for swadeshi, had insulted a defenseless woman.

Thus Bimala already sees herself partaking in the spirit of nationalism before the arrival of Sandip. What is crucial is that her initial assessment of Sandip is completely overshadowed by her passionate response to his verbal magnetism. It is his words and their message that she "was no longer the lady of the Rajah's house, but the sole representative of Bengal's womanhood" (31) that for the first time allow her to elevate herself in her own eyes to not only the deity of "the household fire, but the flame of the soul itself" (31). So far her self-aggrandizing is no less than that which Tagore extends to women in his essay. The point of departure for Bimala is that she allows the elevation of her self to goddess-nation to displace the self that is goddess-home. Thus rather than having the spirituality of the home negotiate and temper the materiality of the world/nation, Bimala collapses the dichotomy necessary for the survival of a hegemonic national culture based on the privileging of an "essential" tradition. As Bimala functions less and less as the signifier of cultural essence, Nikhil begins to represent the "ideal of stability," "the life rhythm" that will combat the "reckless movement of power" now embodied in both Sandip and Bimala, "the passive element, broad and deep and stable" essential not for "mere growth but harmony of growth" (Tagore, *Personality* 172–73).

An easy valorization of the nation as articulated by Sandip is harshly condemned in this novel. What is less obvious is Tagore's dilemma over the role of women in this temporal space. The anxiety lies not in the overdetermination of woman as nation or Bimala as goddess-nation but in the indeterminacy of the individual woman (when am I a woman?); her relationship to the political indeterminacy (what can "women" do?); and the historical indeterminacy (what do women mean, and when?) of the represented chronotope.[31] Tagore's apparent resolution of these indeterminacies is to distribute the various determinations of the signifier "woman" between Bimala and Nikhil. This allows him to critique a singular woman's partial determination of what woman can do at the expense of a dilution of what women are made to mean, and yet maintain the closeness between identity and identification necessary for the performative materialization of the fixity of a gendered position guaranteed in the term "woman." As Bimala structures her new identity, Tagore in a brilliant move depicts Bimala in the very likeness of a Sandip whom she had earlier denounced. I have documented how Bimala despised Sandip for extracting money from Nikhil through manipulation. In chapter 6, in the name of swadeshi, Bimala plays the arch seducer who tempts Nikhil to act against his convictions. Bimala becomes the female reflection of Sandip, or one could even suggest that Sandip, despite his overt masculinization, always employs characteristically "feminine" ploys of seductive manipulation. In this moment of identification between Sandip and Nikhil, the negative implications of the signification of "woman" as temptress are doubled. It is this recognition of what "woman" can mean that restores Nikhil and allows him to confront the battle outside his home unencumbered by personal feelings.

In chapter 5 we see Nikhil deeply upset at the sight of his overlooked picture in the bedroom and his embarrassed withdrawal at the appearance of his wife. At the end of this chapter Nikhil blames himself for failing to recognize his wife's true character. He indicts himself for not realizing that Bimala had "only come into [his] home, not into [his] life." He castigates himself for thrusting everything else aside in the excessive object-worship of Bimala, his insatiable passion for "decorating her and dressing her and educating her and moving round her day and night" (89). The chapter concludes on an implicit condemnation of Bimala, whose very presence led him astray from the higher truths of life: "so painfully important did Bimala make the mere actualities, that the truth remained concealed from me" (90). Despite this critical appraisal of his marital relationship, the reader is still left with the image of a desolate Nikhil mourning his wife's increasing distance from him, and his sorrowful refrain, "Alas, my house is empty," haunting him.

In chapter 6, which begins with Nikhil's story, we see a transformed man who is jubilant at his freedom from and recognition of the true character of not just one woman but women in general—she who "weaves our net of enchantment at home. . . . We must beware of clothing her in the witchery of our own longings and imaginings, and thus allow her to distract us from our quest" (110). The translation highlights the intent of this passage as a warning to all men who must unite against temptation that is "woman" itself. The dialogic and palimpsestic nature of the novel, however, accentuates the irony in Nikhil's evaluation of Bimala's conduct. Before Nikhil comments on the situation, Bimala provides us with a glimpse of her changing personality: "I sent for my husband. In the old days I could contrive a hundred and one excuses, good or bad, to get him to come to me. Now that all this has stopped for days I had lost the art of contriving" (98). It is interesting to examine Bimala's thoughts as she dresses up and awaits her husband. Caught up in the tremendous surge of the glory of the nationalist movement and mobilized from her static position as wife of a zamindar by Sandip's repeated discursive aggrandizing of her powers as the "mother" of the nation, Bimala begins to believe in a self that is both beautiful and intellectually powerful enough to convince unbelievers of the relevance of nationalist practices such as the boycott of English goods from indigenous markets. No doubt she is blinded "with the brilliance of [her] own glory," but Bimala truly believes in the rationale behind the nationalist movement. Though one might wish to condemn her for succumbing too easily to Sandip's charismatic personality and for not being able to gauge the reasons for Sandip's valorization of her as the "Shakti of Delight that dwells in the heart of creation" (97), one must also realize the opportunities for the expression of power that such allegorization allowed a woman.

It seems that at times the novel, almost despite itself, strains against the reins that try to steer it toward a complete renunciation of nationalist ideology. Nikhil comes out of "that broken cage of a bedroom . . . a knight whose quest is that freedom to which our ideals call us" (119–20), in sharp contrast to the conniving, acquisitive Sandip, who in the last third of the novel is reduced to a mere villain with little regard for the movement or the motherland. The reader is asked to see Sandip as clearly as Nikhil believes he perceives Bimala—he "could see everything relating to Bimala as if vividly pictured on a camera screen" (109). One cannot help but feel inclined to remind Nikhil that cameras can distort reality as well.

Bimala has a much more realistic reaction to the same situation. Initially she is convinced of her powers of persuasion, and we leave her at the end of her story, awaiting her husband. In chapter 8, we return to her story and encounter a Bimala who questions her previous complacent self-idealization. It is moot at this point in my analysis to emphasize that Bimala is the only character in the novel who is tormented with doubts about the efficacy of her position on social and political controversies. Nikhil might reconsider his evaluation of Bimala's character and the role he has played in shaping her, but he never doubts that his decisions and judgments are correct. So does Sandip, for less noble reasons, of course. Bimala, however, expresses the construction of her subjectivity as a process that is constantly assaulted by the various social significations such that her subject position is never consistent but erratic, a result of the insistent heterogeneity and contradictions within the subject itself.

Before her meeting with Nikhil, Bimala identifies herself for the reader as a goddess who has magic powers, as the current of life that flows through the veins of such men as Sandip and Amulya. She is, therefore, ready to meet her husband "like a lightning-charged cloud" (136). After her failure to reason with him, she feels "as unreal as a dream—a dream which would leave only the blackness of night when it was over," unlike the earlier awakening color of the river at dawn. Bimala has always had to struggle to find an identity with which she is comfortable in society. She was not a beauty by Bengali standards; she resented being dark because fairness of skin was a necessary attribute for being beautiful. She reveals her vulnerability when she says, "I used to be jealous of my sister-in-law for her beauty. Then I used to feel that Providence had given me no power of my own, that my whole strength lay in the love which my husband had bestowed on me. Now that I had drained to the dregs the cup of power and could not do without its intoxication, I suddenly found it dashed to pieces at my feet, leaving me nothing to live for" (137). First Nikhil, then Sandip: she has had to derive her subjectivity from the love they showered on her, each committed to shaping her according to their image of perfection and necessary symbol, respectively. She might assume the garb of freedom, she might even be glorified as the emblem of liberty, but she is not free, for her identity depends on what the men choose to adorn her with at any given moment.

The irony is exemplified in her bitter reaction to Nikhil's supposed magnanimity in the garden when he walks up to her unannounced and, in an apparent gesture of self-abnegation, grants her independence from him. This is what Bimala has to say about such a resoundingly hollow posture: "And then the other day in the garden, how easy my husband found it to tell me that he set me free! But can freedom—empty freedom be given and taken so easily as that? It is like setting a fish free in the sky" (137). Bimala's anguished words capture the conflicting emotions generated by the changing status of women in this precarious stage of colonial Bengal. Nikhil's belief that he could modernize Bimala without indelibly transforming her proves Kumari Jayawardena's assertion that an elite native bourgeoisie often assumed "that social reform and female education would revitalize and preserve the patriarchal family system, produce more companionable wives and better mothers, and therefore have a stabilizing effect on society" (79).

I want to emphasize here that Bimala is entranced not just by Sandip but by the important role that he promises she would be playing in the independence movement. What Bimala eventually realizes is that swadeshi provides Sandip a stage where he can selfishly indulge in the theatricals of performance without worrying about the life-threatening consequences his theatrical exercises can have. Despite Sandip's powerful sway over the rest of the population to the very end, Bimala does realize the duplicitous nature of Sandip's proclamations. But she never condemns him as harshly as the author does. She recognizes her culpability and succeeds in finally repudiating Sandip's manipulations. Yet although she recognizes the greed and selfishness in Sandip, she also realizes that she is still attracted by his magnetism: "There must be two different persons inside men. One of these in me can understand that Sandip is trying to delude me; the other is content to be deluded. Sandip has power but no strength of righteousness" (149).

Nikhil, by contrast, has an overwhelming sense of righteousness but little power to prevent the consequences of Sandip's ideological maneuvers. Bimala ultimately appropriates both. She wants to "wean" Amulya away from Sandip and "save" him from death. Sandip recognizes the power that she has over his disciple. It is ironic that Bimala should use her elevated status achieved via Sandip's discursive moves and her image as the goddess-mother conceived by Sandip to sway Amulya. Sandip cannot hide his annoyance at having his position as a guru be replaced by that of Bimala, a mere woman. The contradiction in Sandip's discourse about the necessity of women in the mobilization of nationalist forces is reminiscent of the anomalous nature of Nikhil's notions concerning the emancipation of women. Though Sandip delights in Bimala's company, though he is tremendously motivated by the desire to place her on a pedestal to be worshiped as the ideal/idol representation of a glorified India, he does not wish Bimala to incorporate those very notions of freedom in order to subvert his own status as the savior of the nation. Bimala's realization of her own power liberates her from Sandip: "At last Sandip has realized that he is weak before me. That is why there is this sudden outburst of anger. He has understood that he cannot meet the power that I wield with mere strength. . . . At last have I come to a level above him" (157). Because Tagore has systematically portrayed Sandip as an irredeemable rogue, one cannot applaud Bimala's refusal to be objectified by him as a moment of singular triumph. Furthermore, the ideological encoding of the "woman question" within the boundaries set forth by the new indigenous patriarchy cannot allow Bimala to exist in a space outside the reaches of colonialism and a nationalist patriarchy.

Communalist tension is unleashed by Sandip's emphasis on the necessity of burning all foreign goods and his decision to send a message to the Muslim traders who had refused to participate in the boycott by ordering the boat of the Muslim trader Mirjan to be sunk. Nikhil's manager was Sandip's ally in this venture, but when the police identify the perpetrator, he resorts to petty blackmail. The only way out for Sandip is to buy the silence of those involved, including the police. Most people, even if guilty themselves, would have been incensed at the manager's actions. Sandip, however, articulates a certain unpalatable truth:

We all have a hidden fund of moral judgement stored away within us, and so I was about to wax indignant with the manager, and enter in my diary a tirade against the unreliability of our countrymen. But if there be a god, I must acknowledge with gratitude to him that he has given me a clear-seeing mind, which allows nothing inside or outside it to remain vague. I may delude others, but never myself. So I was unable to continue angry. Whatever is true is neither good nor bad, but simply true, and that is Science. A lake is only the remnant of water which has not been sucked into the ground. Underneath the cult of "Bande Mataram," as indeed at the bottom of all mundane affairs, there is a region of slime, whose absorbing power must be reckoned with. The manager will take what he wants; I also have my own wants. The lesser wants form a part of the great cause—the horse must be fed and the wheels oiled if the best progress is to be made. (118–19)

This is perhaps the only time that Sandip is allowed any retrospection on his role as a nationalist leader. He quickly returns to his role as archvillain as Tagore presents Amulya's account of Sandip gloating over the hoard of gold sovereigns that Bimala had taken from her husband's safe to finance the swadeshi movement. Sandip ultimately returns Bimala's ornaments, but he does so by invading Amulya's privacy (he breaks open Amulya's trunk and steals the little sack containing the jewels), presenting it to Bimala in front of Amulya in an uncouth display of jealousy and power.

Sandip ultimately leaves Nikhil's zamindari when he hears rumors of a communal riot. Fearing for his life, he takes the first train back to Calcutta. Once again one notices the author's dilemma in not being able completely to negate the nationalist movement. Nikhil, who had initially helped his friend with generous donations, who had defended him against earlier denunciations by Bimala, is now totally repulsed by Sandip's selfish motives. But in her inner speech Bimala still evokes the potential that Sandip does possess: "Yet—yet it is best to confess that there is a great deal in the depths of him which we do not, cannot understand—much in ourselves too" (178). She does not deny "his terrible aspect of Chaos,"[32] just as she is honest enough to admit that "that very vision is alluring" (178). Therefore, even though Tagore wants to insist on the destructive aspects of the movement by concluding the novel with the death of the young, honest, ultimately betrayed Amulya and leaving the reader in doubt as to the status of Nikhil (he is wounded, not dead at the end of the novel), the dialogic nature of the interactions between the characters and their voices prevent any absolute notion of one hierarchical voice subsuming all others.[33]

If I have been able to highlight Tagore's ambivalence toward swadeshi through my reading of the novel, can I do the same with regard to his feelings about Bimala? We see her in the penultimate pages of the novel, awaiting news of her husband and Amulya, who have rushed out to quell the riots, "feeling that, if only I could die, all this turmoil would come to an end. So long as I was alive my sins would remain rampant, scattering destruction on every side" (202–3). She sits by the window transfixed, unable to move or speak, concerned only with the fate of the two men. The last words of the novel announce the death of Amulya and the precarious condition of Nikhil, who has a serious head injury. The silence that often follows an announcement of death is filled with the memory of another silent, anguished moment when earlier in the novel Bimala undergoes the cleansing of ritualized confession. She blames herself for the incriminating situation that Amulya finds himself in and has a premonition of the tragedy to come. Suddenly, she is overwhelmed by her guilt and anxiety, and throwing herself on the ground, she prays for mercy. Nikhil comes upon her prostrate body and, being the generous man that he is, forgives her. This scene is enacted without any words from either person in a reversal of the usual confession in which one needs to be absolved of one's action by verbal expression.

As Foucault has demonstrated in *The History of Sexuality*, confession acts as a ritual that apparently leads us to the "truth lodged in our most secret nature." However, the confession actually functions as an institutional device that subverts our freedom by disguising the "power that constrains us." In Western societies this act of confession is "a ritual of discourse in which the speaking subject is also the subject of the statement; it is also a ritual that unfolds within a power relationship, for one does not confess without the presence (or virtual presence) of a partner who is not simply the interlocutor but the authority who requires the confession, prescribes and appreciates it, and intervenes in order to judge, punish, forgive, console, and reconcile" (61–62). If the speaking subject is also the subject of the statement, what does the lack of any statement entail for the actors in this particular master-slave dialectic? Bimala's silence here reflects her complete subjugation. Bimala imitates her early act of obeisance by touching her husband's feet. Nikhil moves to withdraw his feet, but Bimala's insistence convinces Nikhil of the necessity of such a gesture. Returning to the opening lines of the novel that initiate Bimala's recollected smritikatha does not return us to the revised temporal space advocated by nationalists for the upper-caste and bourgeois woman as they ushered in the modern Indian nation-state. The analogy that the novel sets up between Sandip and Bimala in their incarnation as temptress and destroyer prevents Bimala from being iconized in the last instance as the "new woman" who could successfully negotiate the task of female emancipation with the goal of sovereign nationhood. It is interesting to see how similar Tagore's ideas about woman are to those espoused by the new patriarchy advocating nationalism. The opening lines reach us from the very zenana whose threshold Bimala had crossed wondering if the "vermilion mark at the parting of [her] hair, the sari . . . with its wide red border" (17) would soon have to be replaced by an unmarked part and a body draped in white.[34]

The palimpsest-like structure of Bimala's "stories"; the echo of her transgressive notions about Sandip's character and the role he had played in her life; and her astute assessment of her own indeterminate subject position just before she prays for forgiveness—"Where I am. I am not. I am far away from those who are around me. I live and move upon a worldwide chasm of separation, unstable as the dew-drop upon the lotus leaf" (185)—there are not quite powerful enough to deconstruct the overdetermination of Bimala as a wife and mother who has destroyed her husband and adopted son. Because Amulya, unlike Sandip, never renounces the ideology of swadeshi and nationalism, and because Sandip departs to worship "your [Bimala's] larger image in a larger temple. . . . Here I had only your favor, there I shall be vouchsafed your boon" (179), one must conclude that the harshest indictment is leveled against Bimala's illegitimate entry into the domain of national politics as a disruptive movement that had turned the world inside out. Woman could enter the modern nation-state only when fully cognizant of her marked difference not only from Western woman but from the new patriarch as well. For according to the formulations of nationalist ideology, successful emancipation depended on woman being able to recognize and endorse the one fixed meaning of "woman"—a cultural signifier of an essential indigenous femininity—as the nation formed itself against the discourses of colonialism.

I turn now to a very different text in terms of both genre and style that offers a repudiation of the interpellation of a certain class of women as the new female subject necessary for the survival of a patriarchal modern nation-state. Rokeya Sakhawat Hossain's *Sultana's Dream* presents a radical transformation of the temporal space carefully shored up in the exclusionary and hegemonic discourse of nation formation. In Hossain's feminist utopia the nation is envisioned as Ladyland, a technologically advanced world where men are placed inside the zenana and women guaranteed complete freedom. *Sultana's Dream* is very short, only twelve pages long, but its date of publication, 1905, and its very self-conscious feminism make it an interesting text to explore in relation to Tagore's *The Home and the World*.

Earlier in this chapter I quoted Liddle and Joshi's explanation as to why the term "women's movement" was favored by Indian nationalists. In *Sultana's Dream*, the issue of colonialism is depicted not as an occupation of a foreign power but as a gendered oppression that has successfully been overturned, with the new nation being run by female inhabitants who underline their feminist ideology to the visitor from colonial Bengal. I suggest that we view Ladyland as East Bengal created by Curzon's partition of the Bengal Presidency in 1905, but one significantly transformed by its female inhabitants. Hossain belonged to an upper-class Muslim family and dedicated her life, as Roushan Jahan points out, "to motivate Bengali Muslim women toward self-realization."[35] Hossain's literary activities revolved around certain fundamental problems regarding the situation of women in India, primarily Bengali Muslim women.[36] If *Sultana's Dream* satirizes life behind purdah by reversing the gender of those imprisoned in sequestered quarters, Hossain's *The Secluded Ones*, a collection of forty-seven anecdotes documenting Hindu and Muslim purdah customs all over North India highlights the "absurdity of the extreme seclusion imposed on the women of North India, especially Bengali Muslim women."[37] Hossain's relentless criticism of the lives of Bengali Muslim women behind purdah and the year of publication of *Sultana's Dream* allow me to read the feminist utopia as an illustration of an imaginary Bengal existing outside the boundaries of British India.[38]

If our entry into Ladyland is necessarily circumscribed by our sociohistorical and ideological temporality,[39] so is Sultana's. Like *The Home and the World*, the text opens in the space of the zenana, but unlike the tragic undertones of the opening lines of Tagore's novel, here we see Sultana thinking of the "condition of Indian womanhood" (7). We leap from this enclosed space of her bedroom to the bustling world outside—a transition never made by Bimala—and realize that Sultana has never before fully confronted a busy street "in broad daylight" (7). The narrator believes at this point that her escort is her friend Sara come to accompany her for a walk in a garden similar to those in Darjeeling.[40] References to such places as Darjeeling and Calcutta allow us to situate this text in its own sociopolitical context, as do the repeated references to purdah. Sultana initially feels awkward because "being a purdanashin woman [she was] not accustomed to walking about unveiled" (8). Both her name and this particular reference to being veiled reinforces my reading of Ladyland as a radically transformed Muslim society. While the general term "purdah" covers a wide range of practices related to female seclusion, including the veiling of upper-class Hindu women, I read the use of the words "veiled" and "unveiled" in this text as a reference to the use of *burqas* by Muslim women. In Ladyland itself, religion is replaced by a code of ethics based on Love and Truth. Lest this sound rather romantic, a strain often found in early utopias, Peter Fitting points out that "utopia and dystopia by their very nature remind us of their connections with the real . . . and [their] deliberate engagement . . . with contemporary issues" (143). If we bear in mind the political and ideological motivation for the partition of Bengal mandated by Lord Curzon, as well as the swadeshi movement, then the eradication of formalized religion in Ladyland could be read as a response to the communal friction of the times. *Sultana's Dream* can then be understood not only as a feminist utopia but also as a manifesto for a truly secular nation.

First and foremost, *Sultana's Dream* is concerned with revealing the twisted logic behind the cultural practice mandating the seclusion of women. Repeatedly in *The Secluded Ones*, Hossain makes us witness the mental and physical degradation of women as a result of purdah. Women run from other women who look different, women become hysterical and fall sick, women allow themselves to be burned to death rather than be seen by strangers, and on and on. But in *Sultana's Dream*, we see the absurdity of the logic when Sara explains to Sultana why men need to be locked up. The zenana is now the *mardana*, where men do all kinds of domestic work including looking after babies.[41] If women need to be sheltered because they are weak and cannot be educated in science and math because their brains are smaller, men are here compared to wild animals and the "insane" who need to be locked up to keep the streets safe (9). Men "are fit for nothing," "they talk too much about their work and do little," and bigger brains do not equate to greater intelligence (9, 10, 12).

This is then borne out by the technological advances that the women had made and the various devices that their queen and female engineers had devised to ease the burden of cooking, facilitate transportation, and master agricultural production.

It is through the satirical representation of the rationale for the mardana that the novella offers a critique of the values of its patriarchal society. The juxtaposition of the two very different spaces in the same historical moment allows Sara to reprimand Sultana for neglecting "the duty you owe to yourselves, and [losing] your natural rights by shutting your eyes to your own interests" (9). Sultana cannot wait to get back and describe women's lives in Ladyland, and Sara encourages her to "tell them all that you see here" (15) in order to estrange women from their familiar surroundings and awaken in them their potential for transforming their present condition. The strategy of defamiliarization,[42] so characteristic of utopias, shocks Sultana into a realization of the strangeness and mutability of all that she had taken for granted. In an essay on American feminist utopias, Dianne Griffin Crowder suggests that the appearance of an unprecedented number of feminist utopias between 1965 and 1985 (with a particular concentration in the years between 1975 and 1979) had to do with nature of the genre—they are "the literature of hope"—and the renewed "possibility of a better world" fueled by the liberation movements of the late 1960s (237). The publication of this singular feminist utopia in English by an upper-class Bengali Muslim woman can be said to be similarly stimulated by the energy of the nationalist movement and Hossain's apprehension of the possibility of a transformed world where the "ideologies of women as carriers of tradition" would no longer "mitigate, compensate, [and] contest . . . women's entry into the public sphere, the labor market and their self-constitution" (Sangari and Vaid 17–18).

In his essay on *The Home and the World*, Ashis Nandy rightly concludes that the violence of a full-fledged Hindu-Muslim riot with which the novel concludes is the "inevitable corollary of Sandip's nationalism." He further elaborates that the "violence is a natural by-product of the strategy of mobilization employed by Sandip and his enthusiastic followers. Such a mobilization requires, Tagore implies, symbols embedded in an exclusivist cultural-religious idiom" (14). The efficacy of such primordial identifications for the construction of a secular nation is what Nandy highlights in his sympathetic evaluation of *The Home and the World*.

What Nandy leaves out is the construction of the female subject and her necessarily fractured relation to the gendered signifier of a religiously inflected cultural and political nationalism.

A similar hollowing out of the character of Bimala occurred recently in the pages of the *Boston Review* wherein Tagore's novel was characterized as quintessentially cosmopolitan. In response to Sheldon Hackney's 1993 call for a "national conversation" about American identity (Cohen 3) and Richard Rorty's critique of the intellectual Left's disdain for the value of patriotism in an Op-Ed piece in the *New York Times* (February 13, 1994), Martha Nussbaum advocates the high moral ground of a cosmopolitan internationalism as the basis for "political emotion and concern" that she sees as the foundation of *The Home and the World*.[43]

She begins her piece titled "Patriotism and Cosmopolitanism" with an indictment of the heroine Bimala, who, according to Nussbaum, is too easily swayed by the passionate rhetoric of nationalism espoused by the charismatic Sandip. In Nussbaum's reading of the novel the tragedy lies in Bimala's belated realization that Nikhilesh's cosmopolitan "morality was vastly superior to Sandip's empty symbol-mongering, [and] that what looked like passion in Sandip was egocentric self-exaltation, and that what looked like lack of passion in Nikhil contained a truly loving perception of her as a person" (6). Whatever the merit of Nussbaum's conviction that "the life of a cosmopolitan, who puts right over country, and universal reason before the symbols of national belonging, need not be boring, flat, or lacking in love" (6), to understand Tagore's novel as primarily a "story of education for world citizenship" (6) is to ignore absolutely the historical and specific character of Tagore's negation of a particular manifestation of nationalist discourse. Tagore's repudiation of the extremist form of Indian nationalism does not necessarily imply that he denied all forms of nationalism; neither does it take into account Tagore's belief in an essential difference between East and West repeatedly emphasized in the essays discussed above. Furthermore, in reducing Bimala to a passive recipient of the competing discourses of the nationalist versus the cosmopolitan, Nussbaum frames Bimala within a paradigm of colonial discourse that objectifies the "other" and represents her without the characteristic features of the "subject."

What happens to woman when she simultaneously embodies the truth of tradition, the shakti of the nation, and the untruth of an authentic indigenous femininity is what my analysis of Tagore's delineation of Bimala seeks to provide. My conclusion of this chapter with a reading of *Sulta-*

na's Dream functions as an intervention and a reminder that the construction of a female subject in a given sociohistorical moment can also operate as a mise en abyme of the larger political problematic. The narrativization of this political scenario demands a normative locus if it is to succeed. Woman becomes the site of this obsession with the norm.

In my final chapter I explore the manner in which a number of contemporary theorists of postcolonial literature and nationalism continue to evade or elide the myriad namings of "woman" in narratives of nation formation. I closely examine two South Asian postcolonial novels written in English to suggest a feminist literary practice different from that which I developed in my analysis of the representations of the Indian woman by two male nationalist and three imperialist writers. As I shift terrain to compensate for what I see as a lack in certain metropolitan theories engaging with nationalism and/in the "third world," I take to heart Spivak's cautionary words: "Varieties of feminist theory and practice must reckon with the possibility that, like any other discursive practice, they are marked and constituted by, even as they constitute, the field of their production" ("Imperialism" 319).

CHAPTER FOUR

New Women, New Nations:
Writing the Partition in Desai's *Clear Light of Day*
and Sidhwa's *Cracking India*

The reading of all third world literature as national allegories proposed by Jameson in his (in)famous essay "Third World Literature in the Era of Multi-National Capitalism" fueled a highly contested debate not only about the primary terms used in the essay—"third world literature," "national allegory"—but also about the geopolitical consequences generated by a socioliterary critical paradigm that strives to be all-inclusive. In this chapter I seek to intervene in the ongoing discussion by focusing on nationalism as a gendered discourse. Nationality and gender, as I have shown in the preceding chapters, are in themselves unstable categories that assume stability through their representation and consolidation in discursive acts. Jameson's essay, some of the responses to it, as well as certain other articles dealing with nationalism and its allegorical representation in third world literature[1] gloss over the problematic relationship resulting from the invidious symbiosis of gender and nationality.[2] My reading of Anita Desai's *Clear Light of Day* and Bapsi Sidhwa's *Cracking India* addresses the sociopolitical predicaments confronted by women whose position as independent, equal citizens in the nation is thwarted by the appropriation of "woman" (and its related gendered significations) as a metonymy for "nation." I chose these two novels for their very different representations of the above relationship as well as their distinct negotiation of the realities of the partition of India. In postcolonial analysis of the Indian nationalist movement, one does not find significant theoretical investigations of the discourse of partition even though scholars continue to refer to the partition as the apocalyptic event for the subcontinent. By examining these two novels, I hope to address the impact of both nationalism and the partition on women.

Discussions of nationalism and gender in third world literature are further compounded when one shifts the location of certain writers loosely grouped under this category to other sites. The two writers I have chosen here could also be classified as writers of the South Asian diaspora and even as South Asian American writers. During the last ten years, Anita Desai has spent a large part of her time teaching at U.S. universities, and her latest novel is set in Iowa. Interestingly, Desai began to gain recognition in the United States only after the publication of *Baumgartner's Bombay* in 1988, although she has been writing since the 1960s.[3] *Baumgartner's Bombay*, according to Desai, was successful in the United States "not because of its Indian material but because of its Jewish material. It's aroused a great deal of curiosity and interest among Jewish readers . . . and people are interested in the element of the war, the Nazis and then the Holocaust" (Jussawalla and Dasenbrock 168–69). Bapsi Sidhwa, a Parsi from Pakistan, moved to the United States in 1983 and has lived in Charleston, Atlanta, Houston, Cambridge, and New York. She had published two novels, *The Bride* and *The Crow Eaters*, before she came to the States, but it was her novel *Cracking India* that introduced her to a North American audience. The novel had originally been published in Britain with the title *Ice-Candy Man*.

It is important to highlight a writer's multiple locations not just to complicate any easy categorization but also to allow for a more nuanced exploration of the praxis of cultural contact, "otherness," marginality, domination, and change. Postcolonial studies in the U.S. academy has often been accused of being preoccupied with things South Asian/Indian. While there may be some truth in that, it is also the case that South Asians have only very recently been included in discussions about "Asians" in North America. As we read and teach postcolonial writers in the United States, we must pay increasing attention to ways in which we classify them to better unpackage categories such as third world, postcolonial, and Asian American and reveal the discursive, contingent nature of such descriptive labels. For example, if *Cracking India* is a particularly inflected postcolonial fictional account of the partition, *An American Brat* by the same novelist is a coming-of-age novel that depicts the trials and tribulations of a young Parsi immigrant woman in the United States. It shares a number of themes and tropes with other, more familiar Asian American novels.

A writer such as Sidhwa may herself state that "I don't know the

Americans very well enough to write of *purely* American characters. I will use people from my part of the world in America—the expatriate, the immigrant experience if you like, how they interact here with the American" (Jussawalla and Dasenbrock 219; emphasis added). Alternatively, she may produce contradictory explanatory frameworks for an evaluation of her writings, as does Desai. In an interview Desai reveals that her recent work is more cross-cultural because after living in the United States, "a screen has come between me and India. I can't simply ignore this experience abroad—it's too overwhelming, it demands to be dealt with, somehow grappled with" (177). At the same time she implicitly refutes this characterization of her work when she asserts that she feels "extremely isolated . . . removed to a society with which I have no *natural* link whatsoever" (179; emphasis added).

It therefore becomes all the more crucial for the postcolonial teacher in a U.S. institution, often herself emblematic of some originary "otherness," to critique the very shoring up of a unique ahistorical American or Indian identity by those very writers who in their fiction set out to delineate the ways in which identities in general are subject to ongoing negotiation and reconstruction. It is incumbent on us consistently to foreground discursive positionings of both reader and writer, to initiate reading strategies that emphasize the ways in which terms such as "postcolonial," "Asian American," "South Asian," or "Indian" are part and parcel of differentially situated micro- and macronarratives that create the need for identitarian and territorializing nomenclatures even as we question those very needs and impulses. With respect to the gradually evolving connections between postcolonial and South Asian/Indian American identity formations in the United States, we need to be vigilant against the creation of facile and seamless links. Even as we demand inclusion of certain South Asian postcolonial texts in discussions of Asian American literature, we must scrutinize the complex and often contradictory socioeconomic and historical realities that constitute the various groups that make up Asian America in terms of patterns of immigration and issues of class, caste, religion, gender, and sexuality.

Although both novels I discuss can be grouped with texts that concern the themes of migration, travel, exile, and repudiation of one's originary community, they must be read in terms of their particular location within the formations of new nation-states in the wake of a specific history of colonization. Furthermore, both novels represent a vision of gendered agency that is intimately tied to a certain class and education which must be taken into account when one generalizes about the condition of the colonial and postcolonial South Asian woman. The depiction of a specific colonial and postcolonial society, upper class and Hindu in one novel and upper class and Parsi in another, might also help us understand the construction of a particular genealogy of South Asian immigration to the United States, a genealogy that privileges the second wave of professional, post-1965 immigrants. My readings of the two novels are situated within the debates about the status and nature of third world literature provided at length in the introduction, and I hope that the brief discussion of the multiply mediated locations of these two writers will extend my own analysis of their representations of gender, partition, and postindependent India.

In my analysis of the novels, I want to emphasize the manner in which a particular construction of the Indian woman haunts the symbolic and material registers of the postcolonial nation-state. My discussion of the two novels allows me to complicate the terms third world and postcolonial, thus forcing recognition of how these terms homogenize multiply constituted histories and disparate territories. Rather than accept these categories as accurate representations, we need to underline how every term has to be specialized, especially in the context of third world nationalisms. Such terms as "motherlands," "mother cultures," and "mother tongues" continue to flourish in this era that is witness to a resurgence of violent nationalist discourses globally. As Susheila Nasta writes, in "the iconographies of nationalism, images of mothers have conventionally invited symbols suggestive of primal origins—birth, hearth, home, roots, the umbilical cord of being—as encapsulated by terms such as 'mothertongue,' 'mothercountry'" (xxi). We need to explore the complexities inherent in a preponderantly masculinist ideology that propagates itself through a heavy reliance on feminine ideals. The essays in the collection *Nationalisms and Sexualities* seek to do this by focusing on the complex and often ambiguous relationships between the idea of nation as imagined community, the emphasis on the "proper" nature of the homosocial bonding that characterizes public discourses of dominant official nationalisms, and the trope of nation-as-woman.[4]

In the discussions of third world literatures as national allegories, however, one finds not only a curious absence of gender as a category of analysis but also an ignorance of the ways in which an analysis of the narratives of third world women and women writers may prove useful in the disruption of a self-deluding complacency that often accompanies readings of overt or covert nationalist (read "primarily heterosexual male") narratives—interpretations that tend to establish an allegorical correspondence between the psychic crisis of the male protagonist and the sociopolitical crisis of the modern nation-state. Perhaps if they turn to other texts—by women, gay men, and lesbians—they might understand how the crisis of individual identity could, as Rhonda Cobham suggests, be read as "a crisis of gender and sexual identities that parallel and intersect with the socio-political manifestations of disorder" (43). The examinations of the numerous ways in which the discourses of imperialism, colonialism, and nationalism have relied on the trope of the feminization of the other has led to innovative studies in the fields of ethnography, history, and literary/cultural studies. As Sara Suleri has cautioned, however, the conflation of gender with "woman" and her stereotypical characteristics can, unless one is very scrupulous in one's critical delineation, produce a curious replication of the desire to shroud the other in an impenetrable "female" mystery, thereby perpetuating the binary grid set up in imperialist, colonialist, and nationalist discourses. Even though I am not entirely convinced by Suleri's general claim that the "geography of rape as a dominant trope for the act of imperialism" is no longer "critically liberating" (17), I do believe that attention to surface configurations of the idiom of gender in many imperialist discourses can erase the sexual ambivalence that often marks them. The trope of rape, along with feminization, is often complicated by the homoeroticism that underlines the confrontations between colonizer and colonized. Suleri focuses on imperialist discourses surrounding empire building in India and on Anglo-Indian as well as Indo-English narratives; in the introduction to her book she argues for a continuous attention to the production of our own post-colonial, feminist critical discourses that should not serve "as the landscape upon which the intimacy of homoerotic invitation and rejection can be enacted" (17).[5] Readings of encounters between men and between men and women of different races could "provide a highly productive field of study for the epistemological limitations—and their concomitant terror—imposed by an imperial contemplation of the multifariousness of culture. Such [studies] could furthermore provide cultural criticism with a terrain upon which to complicate and to question more literal inscriptions of gender-bound metaphors" (16).[6] Perhaps then we can begin to decode the myths surrounding gender, sexuality, and nationalism that so many critics of third world texts continue to endorse through their disrecognition.

By redirecting Radhakrishnan's encompassing observation "that the field of historiography in general needs to acknowledge the reality of the feminist intervention as both micropolitical and macropolitical" (80) toward the discourse under examination here—that is, nationalism—I wish to open up a space that would allow us to question the homogenizing tendency inherent in the discursive realm of nationalist politics that sets itself up as representing a nongendered ethnic majority. Thus I now turn to the novels by Bapsi Sidhwa and Anita Desai, first analyzing Sidhwa's *Cracking India*, a novel set in the city of Lahore during the turbulent religious riots marking Indian independence and the traumatic birth of the new nation of Pakistan.[7]

In a 1994 essay, Susie Tharu suggests:

> In India the partition is rarely conceived (as it seems to be in Pakistan) as a political resolution to the Hindu-Muslim tensions that developed in the late nineteenth and early twentieth centuries—a perspective that would image the violence as regrettable but perhaps unavoidable. . . . Indian accounts are nearly always shot through with a sense of the grotesque and uncivilized violence of human nature that has been desecrated. . . . The 1950s and 1960s position on the partition would certainly include a sense of the culpability of colonial rule. . . . But the extent to which the hold of this interpretation has weakened in the late 1980s and 90s is remarkable. The antagonists now are Muslims, with their "sub/pre-national" religiosity, who take on the role of enemy within and symbolize the evils of a "soft" (Nehruvian/socialist) state. (74–75)

The novel *Cracking India* undermines this simple religious binary set up by the Hindu communal Right and often justified in the new narratives of Indian national reimaginings invariably inflected by the ideological underpinnings of a primarily Hindu, bourgeois, hegemonic order.[8]

Cracking India, as the title suggests, takes as its subject the historical partition of British India into Pakistan and India. The term "partition" implies a neat cartographic creation of a new geographic entity that elides the personal and political vicissitudes accompanying such remappings.

Yet Sidhwa's use of the gerund "cracking" evokes the tortuous birthing of new nation-states through hacking, splintering, and breaking. The present continuous tense and the assumption of some agent deliberately cracking away at the subcontinent makes it clear that such geneses have profound political motives and are inevitably accompanied by ever deepening scars and widening fissures which continue to fracture new nations long after their inception.

The most striking aspect of the novel is its point of view—the partition and its effects on the residents of the city of Lahore and its neighboring villages is related by a most precocious child, Lenny, who turns eight as India moves toward its simultaneous independence and holocaustic partition. The eight-year-old's intellectual distance from the political events allows for some very poignant perceptions of the emotional turbulence of the times. The novel, on the whole, takes a sidelong, yet penetrating look at the events leading up to the partition by choosing to focus on a Parsi rather than the usual Hindu or Muslim family. On the one hand, the essential conflict between Hindu and Muslim is complicated by the involvement of the Parsi community in the diurnal lives of their neighbors, and their desire to stay neutral as the British carve up India.[9] On the other hand, the religious conflicts between the largest groups—Hindus, Sikhs, and Muslims—become the central focus as the novel traces the lives of a multireligious cast of working-class characters. If in the early pages of the novel we might be led to believe that the fraught maturation of an eight-year-old Parsi girl afflicted with polio functions as a mise en abyme for an increasingly divided and sick nation,[10] this belief is deftly circumvented by the novel's increasing focus on the character of a no-name woman who, throughout the novel, is addressed by/as her occupation, Ayah. As the Parsi family survives the horrors of the religious riots, the small group of men who gather around Ayah as she traverses Lahore with her charge are either killed, maimed, or expelled from their home(land). As the city burns and religious tension mounts, friends turn against each other; Hindus convert to save their lives; and Ayah, who had always been able to curb dissension among her male cohorts by threatening to remove her much desired presence if the friendly gatherings became acrimonious, is betrayed and raped by her closest friends.

Unlike the other novels that I have discussed in this book, *Cracking India* does not invoke the mythologization of the upper-class Hindu woman as nation. Rather, the impossibility of a uniform symbol of national identity is what causes the greatest contention among Ayah and her friends who are Sikhs, Muslims, Pathans, and Hindus. Repeatedly, the conversations between Ayah, the Ice-candy-man, Imam Din, Sher Singh, the butcher, and the masseur revolve not around the question of a coherent Indian identity but on the abilities of the Indian politicians and the British successfully to manipulate religious and ethnic identities. According to Benedict Anderson, the modern nation is always "conceived as a deep, horizontal comradeship" (16); in this novel the imagined "fraternal," secular community is a theoretical "modular" enterprise of the privileged colonized intelligentsia—Gandhi, Jinnah, Nehru, Iqbal, and Tara Singh. Lenny, on the other hand, becomes "aware of religious differences. It is sudden. One day everybody is themselves—and the next day they are Hindu, Muslim, Sikh, Christian. People shrink, dwindle into symbols" (Sidhwa 101).

The poignant horror of this contraction of humans into religio-ethnic signifiers is evidenced in gruesome depictions of a frenzied Sikh mob rushing through the streets of Lahore holding aloft a "naked child, twitching on a spear struck between her shoulders, [waving it] like a flag" (101); a group of Muslim "goondas" disrobing a Hindu Banya and running him over with a jeep (101); the arrival of a train carrying "butchered" Muslims from Gurdaspur and "two gunny bags full of women's breasts" (159); the discovery of masseur's mutilated body rolling out of a sack left by the roadside (185–86); the devastation of the Muslims by the Akalis at Imam Din's village, Pir Pindoo (206–20); and Ayah's betrayal by her friends, especially Ice-candy-man (189–95).

The novel relentlessly catalogs the brutality of men as they resort to violent ethnic and communal "cleansing" in the name of a pure nation.[11] And despite the generic killings orchestrated by various religious dominations, the novel emphasizes the particular plight of women as they become the increasing focus of a definitive ethnicity.[12] Men are killed and their bodies mutilated as a result of "the identification of politics with the *self* of a community" (Ranciere 59), but the novel also documents the possibility for the male body to signify one's identification with an-other community and thereby escape death. For example, Hari the gardener's conversion to Islam is easily verified by his newly circumcised penis (along with his ability to recite the *kalma* albeit with the "cadence and intonation of Hindu chants" [192]) and frustrates the vengeful desire of the Muslim mob. Ayah, however, has no recourse to such fundamental anatomic transformations and is dragged away by "harsh hands, supporting her with careless intimacy" (195).

In this book I have repeatedly explored Elleke Boehmer's position that "where male nationalists have claimed, won and ruled the 'motherland,' this same motherland may not signify 'home' and 'source' to women" (5). The generation of new motherlands in already named spaces creates unrepresentable horrors in the lives of people who have to shuttle across newly constructed borders in the name of religious, ethnic, and regional affiliations. *Cracking India* brilliantly represents the manner in which the referent home is unmoored from a localized space and translated into a metaphor—the motherland—in masculine, nationalist vocabularies. Thus, those who measure the inscape of their identity in terms of a narrowly demarcated terrestrial landscape, such as the Muslims of Pir Pindoo, pay a terrible price for their refusal to participate in the creation of an iterative national mythology. Lenny's naïve and comic questioning about the logic of partitions—"India is going to be broken. Can one break a country? And what happens if they break it where our house is? Or crack it further up on Warris Road? How will I ever get to Godmother's then?" (101)—takes on grim overtones when suddenly, by a sleight of the cartographer's hand, Pir Pindoo becomes a part of India. The decision by the Muslims of Pir Pindoo not to abandon the place of their forefathers for an uncertain future in a new nation becomes a plaintive cry as a "two-toothed old grandmother, her frail voice quavering bitterly, shrieks: 'we should have gone to Pakistan!'" (209). A celebration of nationalism as love for one's country is juxtaposed to the brutal annihilation of peoples who are not seen as belonging to the nation. The novel illustrates Ghia Nodia's succinct evaluation of nationalism "as a coin with two sides: one political, the other ethnic. . . . The idea of nationhood is political, and there is no nationalism without a political element. But its substance is irreducibly ethnic. The relationship may be expressed as one of a political soul animating an ethnic body" (14–15). Even though the "flesh of ethnicity . . . can be sublimated into patriotic esteem for the institutions and achievements created by a democratic (not just ethnic) 'we,'" the birth of the Indian nation-state reveals the "failure to tame the ethnic flesh of nationalism" (15); nowhere is the latter more graphically captured than in this description provided by Ranna, a young boy and the sole survivor of the massacre of the Muslims in Pir Pindoo. As Ranna enters Amritsar, an Indian city just thirty miles from Lahore (in Pakistan), he is but a semi-naked specter as he looked in doors with his knowing, wide set peasant eyes as men copulated with wailing children—old and young women. He saw a naked woman, her light Kashmiri skin bruised with purple splotches and cuts, hanging head down from a ceiling fan. And looked on with a child's boundless acceptance and curiosity as jeering men set her long hair on fire. He saw babies, snatched from their mothers, smashed against walls and their howling mothers brutally raped and killed. (218–19)

And once again, with this description, we are subjected to the manner in which women, made to appear in a metaphoric or symbolic role in the nationalist scenario, function as the absolute element of alterity which needs to be violently erased for a given national identity to occlude its position as a "relational term . . . in a system of differences" (Parker et al. 5). The writers of the introduction to the collection *Nationalisms and Sexualities* assert that since the very fact of national identity depends "constitutively on difference [it] means that nations are forever haunted by their very definitional others. Hence . . . the nation's insatiable need to administer difference through violent acts of segregation, censorship, economic coercion, physical torture, police brutality" (5). The novel shows, as I stated earlier, the manner in which, suddenly, friends become marked by their ethnic and religious difference; yet as Anne McClintock, summarizing the points made by Nira Yuval-Davis and Floya Anthias, has shown, women have been variously implicated in nationalisms. Even though they are often active participants in national struggles, the gendered and sexed female body is made to bear the burden of excessive symbolization—"as the biological reproducers of the members of national collectivities, as reproducers of the boundaries of national groups, as active transmitters and producers of national culture [and] as *symbolic signifiers of national difference*" (355; emphasis added). Perhaps the negation of such positive difference is what drives men to commit outrageous violence on women in the name of a putative national unity.

The raped female body encompasses the sexual economy of desire that is denied in the mythologization of the purity of one's own ethnic, religious, and national gendered subject. The inevitability of rape leaves woman with the "choice" of committing suicide so that she can be accommodated within the narrative of the nation as a legitimate and pure—albeit dead—citizen. Those who survive rape are refused entry into the domestic space of the new nation. This denial of legitimate gendered subject positions in the new nation is deemed necessary, for as McClintock has so astutely shown, "nations are symbolically figured as domestic genealogies" (357). The purity of the family mirrors the purity of the nation, and the raped woman cannot be the vehicle of the familial metaphor that enables the narration of the nation. Since "woman's political relation to the nation [is] submerged as a social relation to a man through marriage . . . [for women] citizenship in the nation [is] mediated by the marriage relation within the family" (358). In *Cracking India* these rejected women occupy the house next door to Lenny's, recently abandoned by the Hindu doctor and his wife. The Shankar's house has been converted to a "camp for fallen women" (226), though to Lenny it resembles a jail that confines anonymous women, who "keep to themselves, unobtrusively conducting their lives, lurking like night animals in the twilight interiors of their lairs, still afraid of being evicted from property they have somehow managed to occupy" (202). The novel too seems to strain against the accommodation of these women who remain in our imagination as "dark shapes . . . in shalwar-kamizes moving lethargically between their cots" (202). The unnarratable lives of these women undermine the efficacy of the pedagogical narratives of both nations and reveals the founding ambivalence at the core of every progressive national narrative.

Despite the popular attraction to national sentiment that appears to cut across class barriers, *Cracking India* elucidates the elitist as well as bourgeois underpinnings of the Indian nationalist project. Two fallen woman who are "saved" are Ayah and Hamida, and they can leave the camp because of the intervention of Lenny's extended family. Lenny's mother and aunt get involved in the migration forced on millions by "smuggling rationed petrol to help [their] Hindu and Sikh friends to run away. . . . And also for the convoys to send kidnapped women, like [Lenny's Ayah] to their families across the border" (254). More immediately, they, with the help of Godmother and her connections with the police, enable Ayah to leave prostitution and Ice-candy-man's quarters to return to her family in Amritsar. They also employ a woman from the camp, Hamida, to replace Ayah. Hamida, who had been a housewife, is placed in charge of Lenny and warned never to let her out of her sight. Hamida's platitudinous promise to "guard Lenny like the pupils in [her] eyes" is, as the narrator cynically observes, "grotesque in the obviously strained and abnormal circumstances of her life" (203). Hamida cannot go back; Ayah chooses to return to Amritsar fully cognizant that her family might refuse to accept her and still pursued by Ice-candy-man, who "too disappears across the Wagah border into India" (288–89). The novel ends on this very tentative note. We can only imagine the lives of Ayah, Hamida, and Ice-candy-man in India and Pakistan. The text, however, gives us the "toddler nation greenly fluttering its flag—with a white strip to represent its minorities—and a crescent and star" (286), thereby allowing us a glimpse of the future of our bourgeois Parsi narrator. This future is one that contains marriage and Lenny's induction as a female, minority citizen in the nation of Pakistan. But it is also a future forever marked not only by a realization of the "full scope and dimension of the massacres" (96) but also by the memory of her unwitting yet crucial participation in the destruction of Ayah's life.[13] Her self-flagellation then, punishing her tongue "with rigorous scourings from [her] prickling toothbrush until it is sore and bleeding" (196), now perhaps takes the form of narrating the independence and birth of nations with all its illegitimate undertones and bourgeois betrayals.

Anita Desai's novel revolves around the domestic upheavals of a Hindu bourgeois family in Old Delhi, a family forever transformed by the ideology of a religiously inscribed nationalist movement. Desai depicts two "daughters of independence" (to borrow the title of Liddle and Joshi's book) whose lives seem singularly unchanged despite the rhetoric of independence that gave rise to two nation-states. My reading of *Clear Light of Day* is not offered as a symptomatic analysis of the body of Desai's works, nor do I suggest that all bourgeois women's writings from India *must* be read as *primarily* engendered by the discourse of colonialism and nationalism. But because Desai's text does strategically use the rise of nationalist fervor, the discord between Hindus and Muslims, and the partition and the death of Gandhi in the construction of its narrative, the postcolonial critic can provide a nuanced reading of the complex function of gender in the tropology of this particular postcolonial novel. Hopefully, this analysis will suggest to feminist postcolonial critics the importance of dialogic readings of other bourgeois Indo-English texts which can wrest nation "from the context of easy allegorization" (Suleri 14) and provide more comprehensive examinations of the structural function of gender in the political discourse and performance of colonialism and postcolonialism.

Most critics of *Clear Light of Day* address the links between individual life and history that weave through the book, reading the often violent domestic upheavals in the Das family against the historic background of an Indian nation born in the wake of a bloody partition.[14] Instead of plotting the manner in which certain important domestic episodes are inextricably connected to crucial historical events, thereby suggesting the reflection of the macropolitical in the micropolitical, I investigate how the hegemonic discourse of Indian nationalism presents itself as an equalizing, progressive force wresting authority from colonial government by obfuscating its own complicity in the replication of the paternal signifier in the name of national survival.[15] The occasion for the narrative is the present or, more specifically, a summer in the 1970s, when Tara, the younger sister, returns to the Old Delhi house on one of her regular visits from Washington, where her husband, Bakul, is a functionary in the Indian diplomatic corps. Though Bimala, the older sister, is a teacher of history at a local women's college, her life seems arrested, still circumscribed by the old boundaries that include the Das house and garden and the home of their next-door neighbors, the Misras. Her companion, other than the members of the Misra family, is the silent, psychologically scarred younger brother, Baba, whose only source of solace and entertainment is the reverberating sounds of 1940s Western songs played on a scratchy gramophone.

If during the independence movement issues concerning the rights of women could be strategically included within the immediate nationalist platform, after independence the difference between the genders was effectively deployed to shore up patriarchal power and to establish the firmness of national purpose. The initial demands of freedom for women did generate certain changes in the status of women at the personal and political front,[16] but the alliance between the discourse of nationalism and that of the "woman question" was fraught with contradictions and ambiguities. Even as Indian women were being granted the right to vote (suffrage helped the nationalist cause) and struggling much harder (the fight was long and bitter) for the passage of a Hindu Code that would reform the areas of personal law such as marriage, divorce, and inheritance, woman as repository of an untainted, unchanging "Indian-ness" became the sign of the imaginary feminized nation whose chastity had to be safeguarded by virile nationalists against Western penetration. This difference between woman as sign and women as equal personal and political participants in a nation-state produces an unnegotiable conundrum for women who are constantly struggling to be one and act the other.

This paradox is highlighted by Desai in the character of Bimala, who is the head of a household without being either wife or mother and who has an occupation. She is not suppliant and can participate as an equal in conversations with men; she claims that she loves her pet animals more than any mother could love her children; and she smokes, a vice that further distances her from conventional women. In some ways she resembles an Indian version of the eccentric English bluestocking, attracting men by being handsome, not beautiful. Tara, on the other hand, had married young, and as she acknowledges, her husband "had trained her and made her into an active, organized woman who looked up her engagement book every morning, made plans and programmes for the day ahead and then walked her way through them to retire to her room at night with the triumphant tiredness of the virtuous and the dutiful" (21). Tara does not desire to change her life for Bimala's, but there is an element of self-loathing that refuses to be held at bay when she watches Bimala holding court:

> Tara was pricked with the realisation that although it was she who was the pretty sister . . . it was Bim who was attractive. Bim who . . . had arrived at an age when she could be called handsome. All the men seemed to acknowledge this and to respond. . . . Tara did not smoke and no one offered her a light. Or was it just that Tara, having married, had rescinded the right to flirt, while Bim, who had not married, had not rescinded? No, it was not, for Bim could not be said to flirt. . . . Bim never bothered. (36–37)

Bim never bothered to be somebody else or to please anyone. At least this is what Tara believes is true. We are privy to Bim's discontent, however, to her sense of feeling trapped in Old Delhi where nothing changes, where history has already happened, living a life that stands still, as exciting narratives take place elsewhere—London, New York, Canada, the Middle East, and, closer to home, New Delhi (5). Despite Tara's assertion that she and her family need to come back periodically to be in touch with "eternal India," which will continue long after "Nehru, his daughter, his grandson . . . pass into oblivion," along with other postindependent government malpractices such as bribery, corruption, poverty, and "red-tapism" (35), she is frustrated and frightened by Bim's refusal to distance herself from the past.[17] "Why did Bim allow nothing to change? Surely Baba ought to grow and develop at last, to unfold and reach out and stretch. But whenever she saw them, at intervals of three years, all was exactly as before" (12). But what Tara perceives as Bim's desire to remain rooted in the past is construed by Bim as the inevitable pitfalls of the role she has been forced to play. In 1947, when the Indian nationalists were struggling to generate the narrative of a united Indian nation, Bimala's life was dramatically overtaken by incidents beyond her control. With the death of the parents, her brother Raja's tuberculosis, and the widowed aunt Mira-masi's gradual retreat into alcoholism, Bim by default had to take over the reins of the Das household. A defiant youthful challenge against the inevitable marriage plot that determined the lives of women— "I won't marry. . . . I shall never leave Baba and Raja and Mira-masi. . . . I shall work—I shall do things . . . and be independent" (140)—takes an ominous turn as Raja leaves to become a surrogate son of a Muslim family and Mira-masi dies the horrific death of a hallucinating alcoholic. The desire to be independent now overtaken by the need to nurture Baba and Mira-masi and placate Raja, she is apotheosized by her only suitor, the Bengali doctor, as a self-sacrificing domestic goddess. Thus, instead of a Joan of Arc or even a Florence Nightingale (two of young Bimala's ideals), Bimala's lack of desire for a suitor is revised as a desire to be the female archetype: "Now I understand why you do not wish to marry. You have dedicated your life to others—to your sick brother and your aged aunt and your little brother who will be dependent on you all his life. You have sacrificed your life for them" (97). Bimala finds this speech "horrendous, . . . so leadenly spoken as if engraved on steel for posterity" (97).

Her repression of the doctor's last visit is intimately connected to her denial of this attributed status. Bimala's primal memory of her final encounter (in reality the penultimate one) with the doctor is associated with the assassination of Gandhi; as she flees the doctor's solicitous advances, she stumbles over a cobbler crouching in the dark, murmuring "Gandhi-ji is dead." In her overwhelming need to break the news to Raja, she abandons any pretense at being an interested, subservient girlfriend and rushes off home. There, once the initial shock and grief over the news has died down, Raja turns to Bimala and asks, "And your tea-party, Bim? How was it? Has Mrs. Biswas approved of you as her daughter-in-law?" (94). Bimala is appalled and angered at Raja's obvious assumption that she wishes to be somebody's daughter-in-law and that she could possibly be interested in as shallow a person as Dr. Biswas. Her initial anger, however, gives way to laughter as she brushes off Raja's words as a brother's natural desire to torment his sister. It is much more difficult for her to erase Dr. Biswas's words given his idealization of her as a female "sati savitri" (a North Indian colloquialism, derived from the mythological character Savitri, the epitome of a self-sacrificing woman). Hence her need to suppress the last encounter: "There was one more time, one that she never admitted and tried never to remember" (94).

The narrative of bourgeois morality and respectability that bolsters the nationalist disourse constantly seeks to protect its boundaries by domesticating and circumscribing the economy of power operable in the nonnormative. Nationalist ideology "absorb[s] and sanction[s] middle-class manners and morals and play[s] a crucial part in spreading respectability to all classes of the population" (Mosse 9). Thus Bimala's sexuality, an aspect that is highlighted in an incident in which Bakul, Bimala's brother-in-law, bends to light her cigarette, is denied because it is abnormal and dangerously free not being directed at any one man: "There was that little sensual quiver in the air as they [the men] laughed at what she said, and a kind of quiet triumph in the way in which she drew in her cheeks to make the cigarette catch fire and then threw herself back into the chair, giving her head a toss and holding the cigarette away so that a curl of smoke circled languidly about her hand" (36). Because Bimala refuses the advances of the doctor, he has no other recourse but to inscribe her disdain for his overtures as a defense against anything that might dissuade her from following her natural call to be the angel of her father's house.

Tara, scared of any emotional confrontation, unwilling to understand or accept the implications of Raja's obsessions with Hyder Ali's family, Baba's uncanny silence, and Mira-masi's gradual deterioration, gravitates toward the Misra household through whom she meets Bakul, who dutifully asks Bimala for her sister's hand in marriage, and leaves for foreign shores. Bakul signifies the typical "modern" (read "liberated") Indian man who believes that the true sign of progress is the right balance of tradition and modernity. He courts Tara at the club but respectfully comes to the house to ask for her hand in marraige. Bimala's response is cutting in its sarcasm: "'I'm head of the family now, am I? You think so, so I must be.' . . . I don't think you need to ask anyone—except Tara. Modern times. Modern India. Independent India" (81). Bakul feels his position as a desirable suitor undermined by this abrupt, dismissive gesture, and one realizes that even though a "modern" man of Bakul's ilk might initially be attracted by the likes of Bimala, having her as his wife would prove hazardous to his authoritative presence:

> [Bakul] wondered, placing one leg over the other reflectively, as he had sometimes wondered when he had first started coming to this house, as

a young man who had just entered foreign service and was in a position to look for a suitable wife, *if Bim were not, for all her plainness and brusqueness, the superior of the two sisters, if she had not those qualities—decision, firmness, resolve*—that he admired and tried to instill in his wife who lacked them so deplorably. If only Bim had not that rather coarse laugh and way of sitting with her legs up . . . now Tara would never . . . and if her nose were not so large unlike Tara's which was small . . . and *Tara was gentler, more tender.* (19; emphases added)

The novel, unlike *Cracking India*, does not engage with the violence of the riots or the sudden inhumanity of neighbors turning on each other in the name of religion and ethnicity. Instead, it chooses to focus on the plight of the Das household as a result of Raja's determination not to participate in the Hindu nationalist excoriation of the Muslims. Raja's interest in Mogul culture and his fascination with Urdu language and literature becomes concentrated on the imposing figure of Hyder Ali, the Muslim landlord. His youthful defense of the Muslims against the rabid fundamentalism of his Hindu friends during the precarious days of the last few months of British rule quickly turns into an obsessive concern for the fate of the Ali family at the expense of his own. Even though the novel commends Raja's and Bimala's nonpartisan politics, it also critiques Raja's naïve idealism:

> When the boys at Hindu College found that Raja was one Hindu who actually accepted the idea of Pakistan as feasible, they changed from charmed friends into dangerous enemies. . . . When he spoke to them of Pakistan as something he quite accepted, they turned on him openly, called him a traitor, drowned out his piping efforts at reasonableness with the powerful arguments of fanatics. They so much wanted him [Raja] to join them. He was so desirable as a member of their cause in his idealistic enthusiasm, his graceful carriage, his incipient heroism. (57)

Raja's heroism remains nascent, and he is forced to spend the worse days of the partition ill with tuberculosis, too weak to do anything other than impotently anticipate the inevitable fighting in the streets and the burning and looting of Muslim property. Raja's bravery is expressed only in his fantasies; when one of his terrorist friends places a guard outside the Das house to monitor Raja's contact with his Muslim neighbor, "for a moment, he thrilled at the idea of his importance, his dangerousness. He saw himself as fighting for the Hyder Alis, brandishing a sword, keeping the mob at bay. The very thought made him break into a sweat" (59).

Cracking India describes in graphic detail the horrors that *Clear Light of Day* suggests in a single sentence: "There was rioting all through the country and slaughter on both sides of the new border" (71). Just as Raja's weak body prevents him from imagining the unimaginable calamities that the partition heralds, the narrative too seems unable to speak the unspeakable endured by millions. Hyder Ali is found to be safely ensconced in the Muslim haven of Hyderabad; Raja recovers from his tuberculosis and in keeping with his romantic predilection marries Hyder Ali's daughter. However, Raja can deny the division of India and Pakistan and set himself up as the exemplary Indian in independent India by moving to Hyderabad and marrying Hyder Ali's daughter—Hindu, Muslim bhai bhai! (Hindu, Muslim are brothers)—only by abdicating his responsibilities as the eldest son. Raja's infatuation with the strong masculine figure and presence of Hyder Ali is greatly distinguished from his relationship with his own father, who is presented as aloof and unapproachable. It is not that Raja's father is feminized, but his prolonged absences from the household and his impenetrable self-absorption prevent the consolidation of the paternal signifier as the Law of the Father. By contrast, Hyder Ali becomes for Raja the apotheosis of masculinity in relation to which his Hindu family (including his father) appears emasculated. This specific yoking of two heterogeneous cultures (Hindu and Muslim) undermines the usual binary gendered opposition of colonizer and colonized (English and Indian) as male and female. The alliance between Raja and Hyder Ali assumes a homoerotic cast that is not negated by Raja's marriage to Ali's daughter.

Of course, Raja's eventual departure for Hyderabad and his marriage to Benazir is equally motivated by Hyder Ali's immense wealth. Raja discards one cocoonlike existence for another, exchanging the dazzle "of the impressive figure of the old gentleman with silvery hair, dressed in white riding clothes seated upon a white horse" (47) for the vision of his son disguised in grand Mogul robes riding a toy white horse. Raja's love of theatricality, buoyed by the grim reality of a burning Delhi and a chaotic country split into two, allows him dramatically to abandon all domestic duties at the death of his father. He refuses to "worry about a few cheques and files in father's office" as "everyone [in partitioned India] becomes a refugee" (66). The Das household has to survive, however, and as Bimala, "dour as her father, as their house," harshly asserts: "No, that's only for me to worry about. . . . That, and the rent to be paid on the house, and five, six, seven people to be fed every day, and Tara to be married off, and Baba to be taken care of the rest of his life, and you to be got well again—and I don't know what else" (67). As Raja and Tara depart Old Delhi for allegedly greener pastures, Bimala is left to pick up where Mira-masi leaves off.

And that, ultimately, is the question with which this text leaves us—what is the real difference between Mira-masi and Bimala? Does Mira-masi's life in colonial India parallel Bimala's life in independent India? True, Mira-masi was a poor relation widowed at fifteen, who had lived with her husband's family serving time as a drudge until she was brought into the Das household to take care of Baba so that his parents could return to their bridge games at the club. But the repression of her sexuality so that she would not fall prey to the appetites of her brothers-in-law and the constant demands placed on her by others to fulfill surrogate roles of woman as maid and as nurturer ultimately force her to erase her memory and her body by slowly and silently drinking herself to death. The children's vision of her as a tree with strong roots and green sheltering branches is eradicated by Mira-masi's own anguished nightmare of being wrapped in "long swaddlings as if she was a baby or mummy—these long strips that went round and round her, slipping over her eyes, crossing over her nose, making her breath stop so that she had to gasp and clutch and tear" (77). Her very identity in the Das household, captured in the appellation Mira-masi (Aunt Mira), finally leads to her breakdown. Mira has never been allowed to be just Mira, and her nephews and nieces who demanded so much of her are transformed by her deluded mind into licking flames that gradually grow taller, towering over her, forcing her to cower as they "pricked her like pins, drawing out beads of blood" (78). She dies denuded, ultimately reduced to a handful of ashes at the bottom of the river.

Bimala, by contrast, is educated, financially independent, and unmarried, but the bourgeois moral underpinnings of an Indian nationalist ideology are so mythologized that Bimala is ultimately uncomfortable with the freedom granted women during and after independence. She asserts her independence yet is paralyzed at times by the roles she must enact on demand by relatives. Though she manages the household and signs financial documents for their insurance company, she daily urges Baba to try to go to work, to assume the role that she believes a man should desire.

Despite Tara's belief that Bimala refuses to change things, Bimala constantly tries to coax Baba out of his passivity, to take charge so that she can retire to the background and live her life as the unmarried, protected sister who teaches history at her leisure.

At various moments in the text we find Bimala acutely burdened by her role as mother, sister, and ersatz father, encompassing the sign of the essential woman and representing the oxymoronic nonphallic, paternal signifier. Oscillating between these two sharply divergent extremities, the one signifying an essential indigenousness and the other a nontenable position in the unambiguous discourse of nation-state-fatherhood, Bimala often cries out in anguish, "There is never anybody except me" (61). Will she, unlike Mira-masi, be able to prevent the regression into a second childhood? Can she deny the world outside by enveloping herself in an unpenetrable cocoon as did Mira-masi? Can she withstand the horror of watching her body degenerate and end up "not soft, or scented, or sensual?" Will she in the end refuse to let those around her choke her, suck her dry of substance, reduce her to a desiccated stick or "an ancient tree to which no one adhered"? (111).

Even as the reader notices differences between the passive Mira-masi and the assertive Bimala, similarities keep emerging. Just as we are reminded by Bakul that Bimala does not have the requisite characteristics necessary for a good wife, we recollect that the children, early on, had felt that Mira-masi did not really have "the qualities required by a mother or wife" (110).

> Looking at her, they could not blame the husband for going away to England and dying. Aunt Mira would not have made a wife. Why, they felt, a wife is someone like their mother who raised her eyes when the father rose from the table and dropped them when he sat down; who spent long hours at a dressing-table before a mirror, amongst jars and bottles that smelt sweet and into which she dipped questioning fingers and drew out the ingredients of a wife—sweet-smelling but soon rancid; who commanded servants and chastised children and was obeyed like a queen. (110–11)

The only time that Mira-masi's body is adorned in anything but a white sari is at her cremation; unlike Mira-masi, though Bimala is not forced by tradition to wear white (widows wear white in India), the aching poignancy of the similar trajectory of their superficially disparate lives is captured in Bimala's words to Tara as they reminisce about their childhood aspirations. Tara can laugh at her childhood dream because it has come true—she wanted to be a mother. But Bimala, who wanted to be a heroine, cannot.

> There was a dark shadow across her face from which her eyes glinted with a kind of anger [that frightened Tara]. . . . Bim raised her chin, looked up at her with . . . a horrible smile. . . . "And how have we ended?" she asked mockingly. "The hero [Raja] and heroine—where are they? Down at the bottom of the well—gone, disappeared" [the well was where the cow had drowned and had eventually become marked as an ominous site]. . . . "I always did feel that—that I shall end up in that well myself one day." (157)

The novel ends on a note of narrative harmony. Bim's reflection, occasioned by a memory of the famous line from T. S. Eliot's *Four Quartets*, "Time the destroyer is time the preserver," suggests that she can ultimately draw strength from her "inner eye . . . [through which] she saw how her own house and its particular history linked and contained her as well as her whole family with all their separate histories and experiences. . . . It was where her deepest self lived and the deepest selves of her sister and brothers and all those who shared that time with her" (187).[18] I would argue, however, that the ending strikes a discordant note even if predicated on a peace derived from looking deep into oneself and on an intangible power drawn from a belief in essential familial identity that can synthesize the various conflicting trajectories occasioned by traumatic historical and personal events.

This desire for resolution of domestic upheavals, articulated as it is by Bimala, who throughout the novel has struggled against easy solutions, suggests the difficulties women encounter in trying to break away from " 'the image of [the] woman [who] is no differently perceived: by the father, the husband, and in a way more troubling still, by the brother and the son.' "[19] Perhaps Desai's reluctance to be labeled a feminist writer suggests her own precarious negotiation of gender issues that continue to permeate various discourses concerning the consolidation of an Indian nation. Thus the ending of the novel brackets the plight of Mira-masi and others;[20] we are never shown how Mira-masi's "dead and airless" life is transformed into life-giving sustenance (187). Progressive accounts of both colonial and nationalist historiography similarly produce narratives that chart the superficial progress made by Indian women under the aegis of the Raj or because of the inclusion of women's issues under the nationalist umbrella. But the similarities between a widow in preindependent India and a single, unmarried woman in independent India affirms the obsession with the replication of the ideal woman in the register of the imaginary, thereby reproducing an ever recognizable symbolic economy. The contradictory and often violent lives of real women, as captured in the fictional lives of Bimala and Mira-masi, ultimately represent a gap, an aporia in a nationalist discourse that in representing itself as fighting against outside enemies needs to repress something within; "'woman' becomes the mute but necessary allegorical ground for the transactions of nationalist history" (Radhakrishnan 84). Hence, whether talking about a theory of third world literature or the reading of third world literature as nationalist allegories, one needs to account for the repressed gendered subject that allows a masculinist nationalist discourse to flourish.

EPILOGUE

In 1997, India celebrated fifty years of independence. As I finished work for this book, the idea of India seemed to be looming large in the imagination of diverse peoples all over the world. From conferences on partition literature in Bologna, Italy, to the dedication by the *New Yorker* of "The Fiction Issue" to India; from airlines advertising special fares to Mumbai and Delhi to celebrations in Chantilly, Virginia: one could not help but trip over the subcontinent in some shape or form. The one big gap in all this hype was India itself. If this sounds absurd so baldly put, let me elaborate: How exactly was India "celebrating" this event? What were Indians in India doing to commemorate this moment in history? "Nothing much" seemed to be the standard response. I had traveled to India and seen very little to indicate that 1997 was somehow special or different. My own perceptions were borne out as much by my conversations with friends and relatives in Calcutta, Delhi, and Bombay as it was by the dearth of any media coverage on actual celebrations in Indian cities, towns, and villages on Cable News Network (CNN), Headline News, or even ITN. My aim in raising this question is to direct attention to the manner in which India continues to be mined for consumption by the West.

The moment I write this sentence, though, I am compelled to qualify it. This is not the age of *King Solomon's Mines* or even the Indiana Jones films; if India continues to exist in some minds in the frozen landscape of some spurious B-grade adventure movie, it is more than compensated by those who are better versed in the language and ideology of the "new" India, those who refer to the city of Bangalore as the "Silicon Valley of India," those who realize that the greatest buying power in the twenty-first century could come from the burgeoning middle class in India, and those who know that *Baywatch* is the most popular show among Indian viewers. Many complex reasons exist for this shift in perception from India as a "country in aspic, a picturesque museum" to Ian Jack's assessment that "much of India has become like the rest of the world."[1] The most obvious reason has to do with the economic changes wrought in India during the last ten years. Another, and the one that concerns me here, is the growing number and visibility of Indians in certain parts of the Western Hemisphere and Australia. Here I focus briefly on the Indian diasporic population in the United States and its relationship to India and the United States by drawing attention to certain events in the Washington, D.C., area and their coverage in the *Washington Post*.

In the greater Washington, D.C., area, there had been a yearlong preparation for August 15, 1997. The *Washington Post* "Style" section advertised an Indian Dance Event sponsored by the dance teachers consortium in the area (I believe there are forty dance educators in this organization and about twenty dance schools) a week before the event on August 9. A later edition had a picture (to which I will return) and a write-up of the celebration in Chantilly, Virginia, in its "Metro" section. The Kennedy Center had a weeklong showcase of such Indian art movies as *Genesis, Nishant*, and *Mahatma*. For most it was a time and place to gather with their families and participate in "Indian culture." A student of mine who has been to India only once said she felt she should go because she wanted to know more about India and herself. Perhaps for the generation born and brought up in the United States, the events created an epistemological space wherein they could act out their identity. It was pure, unadulterated enjoyment of intangible "things" such as "our" culture and tradition, made tangible in an-other place and time.

It was definitely not the time to raise the specter of the Hindu Right. Questions about the political climate in India and the rise and consolidation of Hindu nationalism were taboo. One felt it inappropriate to ask if there were many Indian Muslims partaking in these celebrations. I could not help but remember that some of these very Indians celebrating an Indian nation born fifty years ago had, on August 8, 1993, participated in a huge event at the Hilton Hotel in Washington, D.C., called World Vision 2000. This event, in the guise of commemorating the birth of Swami Vivekananda, was actually a political event to promote and fund the Hindu Right, as the tripartite Bharatiya Janata Party (BJP), the Hindu Visva Parishad, and the Rashtriya Seva Sangh (RSS) are commonly referred to. On that day, only about one hundred Indians of various religious denominations, representing various secular and anticommunalist groups from across the United States, stood outside the hotel protesting the meeting to which Indians had flocked from all over the United States. The money being pumped into India by nonresident Indians (NRIs) does not fuel only the economy; the political clout provided by the NRI money is considerable, and a large percentage of it is mobilized in the name of a militant Hindu nationalism.

The narrativization of the agenda of the Indian nation after 1947 by the Congress leadership, generally known as "Nehruvian secularism," was contradictory in its very beginnings. It can be traced back to the marginalization of Gandhi, who stood firmly against partition. The subsequent collaboration between Jawaharlal Nehru and Sardar Patel, respectively described by G. Balachandran as "the impatient statist and socialist modernizer . . . and the staunch defender of a unitary Hindu order" (105), in the making of the Congress Party, which was to be the significant political party for decades, underlines the nebulous vision and status of secular nationalism in modern India. Thus, on the face of it, "India's political leadership has tried implicitly to deflect the thrust of majoritarian nationalism by replacing religion with territory as the basis of nationalism"; in practice, "territorial nationalism in the Indian context is often indistinguishable from religious nationalism" (116). To simplify a long and convoluted history of the rise and decline of the Congress Party, the rise of a number of regional parties as well as left-wing parties, and the egregious manipulation by Indira Gandhi, especially in the 1980s, of the "ethnic/religious card in the guise of upholding secularism and 'national unity'" (122), let me state that the binary opposition set up between the idealized secularism of the Nehru era and the rise of Hindu fundamentalist forces such as the BJP does not quite hold up under scrutiny. A more comprehensive reading is Sumantra Bose's analysis of the relationship between secularism and communalism in postcolonial India as "dialectic" rather than "adverserial":

> Treating "communalism" thus, as the antithesis of Indian "nationalism," frequently results in the post-colonial "secular" state (and the freedom movement before it) being absolved of most if not all culpability in the rise of "communalism," and specifically of Hindutva. . . . Yet there has been widespread reluctance among scholars of contemporary India, and of the growing problems of communalism, to situate the rise of Hindutva within a broader more substantive critique of the modern Indian state. (106–7)

Bose goes on to use a Gramscian analytic framework to explain the rise of Hindu nationalism, focusing on India's democratic and secular regime and relating this "state oriented approach to critically relevant long-term changes in India's social structure and related political economy" (108).

What Bose has called "the organic crisis" (111) of the Indian postcolonial state is not something that affects Indians in India alone. Because of the intimate ties binding a large percentage of Indian immigrants to their "homeland," the rhetoric of the Hindutva movement in its most persuasive form allows Hindus in India and abroad to seek, understand, and claim "a sense of their cultural identity" and, especially for displaced Hindus, authorizes a "mentalscape" for "the enhancement of [their] sense of self-sameness and continuity in time and space." And this identification cuts across gender lines. If earlier incarnations of the Hindu Right allowed mostly upper-caste males a sense of pride and position in their "Hinduness," the movement today enjoys support from a wider section of society and has very visible women leaders and a paramilitary organization for women only. The Hindu Right's delineation of a nationalist-oriented imagined community (Hindu Rashtra) relies heavily on the popularity of the tale of *Ramayana*, and its leaders have successfully rallied the symbol of the mythical god-king Rama for their masculinist Hindu agenda. As Sucheta Mazumdar has pointed out, however, women are increasingly and visibly engaged in the front ranks. During the crisis precipitated by the destruction of the Babri Masjid, it was not surprising to see "female religious preachers, draped in saffron robes, defy the judiciary and police and hold forth on why the temple to Rama must be built, 'even if the waters of the Saryu (local river) turn red with our blood.' ... A door-to-door strategy of 'spreading the word' is increasingly used by the women's networks of the Hindu Right" (Mazumdar 4).

But the month of August 1997, I quickly realized, was not the time to raise questions about the whys and wherefores of the recasting of India as a "Hindu Nation" or to discuss the manner in which gender ideology was being recast and manipulated to aid the growth of the particular political movement in India and among Hindus abroad, at least not in the suburbs of Washington, D.C. Rather, it was a time to exalt "The Rhythms of India" in an elaborate ritualized dance recital; it was a time to open the *Washington Post* and see yet again a reference to India in the form of a Northwest Airlines advertisement. The half-page airline ad (August 20,

1997) in the "World" news section cunningly deploys the traditional oriental image of India even as it showcases the entry of the revitalized subcontinent into the global economy. The top of the ad reads, "WORLD BUSINESS CLASS," followed by "WHILE INDIA MAY BE EXOTIC, MYSTERIOUS AND UNPREDICTABLE, GETTING THERE ISN'T." Beneath these words, no doubt best capturing the essence of the mysterious Orient, is a black-and-white image of the bust of an exquisite woman with a beguiling smile, her face and neck adorned with jewels against the backdrop of a distant Taj Mahal: the image of a Hindu woman foregrounded against the most famous tomb of a Muslim queen. To the left of the image are printed various cities in North America, at the center of the lower portion of the figure of the woman is Amsterdam and to the right the cities of Delhi and Mumbai. The rest of the ad details how one can win five thousand WorldPerks Bonus miles when one flies World Business Class to India, of course, in addition to the usual parade of exotic women and ancient monuments. Lest the picture of the beautiful woman and the historic shrine lead us astray, the rest of the ad reminds the reader that despite the burgeoning economy of India, a wide gulf separates us from them. Travel to India, we are told, "will take on a soothing regularity as the *global alliance of Northwest Airlines and* KLM (emphasis added) begins daily service to Mumbai (formerly Bombay) and Delhi." Enjoy the "spacious comforts" of World Business Class—the last stop for "predictable . . . and quiet enjoy[ment]" en route to India, the land of——; our imagination can easily fill in the blanks. This ad obviously is designed to attract North American investors seeking investment opportunities in India. But as an Indian or Indian American skims through the pages of the newspaper, she too might be tempted to give up flying coach to travel in comfort halfway around the world.

My analysis of the ad returns us to the issue of gendering the nation not only by nationalists and British colonialists but also by multinational corporations seeking to promote the putative borderless economy of the future. And such en-genderings continue to persist even as in the academy and elsewhere the demise of the category of the nation-state is celebrated, rather prematurely I would argue, in the wake of transnational capital and the global flows of culture and peoples. The location of the critic indulging in such celebration is the crucial issue in any such debate. As Rajeswari Sunder Rajan has argued in the introduction to "Gender in the Making: Indian Contexts," a special issue of the journal *Thamyris*:

The nation, specifically identified as the political state and its operations in law, government, and "politics," as such, as well as in terms of contending ideologies of nationalism, is the problematic within which cultural analysis is performed in the context of decolonized nation-space. . . . The internationalization of post-colonial studies in the U.S. academy (in particular) has tended to obscure the existence of, and indeed the need to retain, the frames of nation, and with it, of class, gender, caste and community in contemporary theoretical work in post-colonialism." (*Rajan*, Introduction 5)

And such en-genderings become further complicated as the site from which they emerge shifts. In this book I have concentrated primarily on one site, while in the last chapter I drew attention to the manner in which two South Asian diaspora writers reimagine the nationalist movement and modern India.

The photograph that accompanied the write-up about the celebrations in Chantilly, Virginia, provides us with an opportunity to mark another site of engagement with issues of gender and construction of national identity and its implications for Indians in the United States. The August 17 "Metro" section of the *Washington Post* carried a large picture of Saikantha Raparia, an Indian woman sitting on the ground of the Capital Expo Center in Chantilly with her three-year-old son, Pranav Raparia. The caption reads, "A CELEBRATION OF INDEPENDENCE" in bold print. In the background one can see mostly the lower half of a number of women's bodies dressed in saris and long skirts; the women are identified as "performers at India fest 97." I have chosen to focus on this picture because it clearly highlights the fractured identities and ambivalent relationship to citizenship shared by many Indians living in the United States.

Rather than depict a performance by those faceless women or choose the much smaller picture on the fourth page accompanying the article, which actually has two Indian men dressed as Nehru and Gandhi waiting backstage to "perform a dramatic interpretation of the history of India," the photograph of mother and child describes something quite other than what a typical picture of Indian performers would. The front-page photograph shows the mother dressed in an Indian sari, with the *bindi* (dot) on her forehead, holding her son draped in an American flag. The caption "A Celebration of Independence" now reads quite differently, because the featured national symbol is that of the U.S. flag. One will never know the story behind the picture—how and why it so happened—but the choice made by the editors of the *Post* to use that picture is open to many interpretations: first, the most obvious one, using Indian women, some fragmented, to depict a national celebration; second, the elliptical nature of the caption—marking a celebration of independence without tying it to a nation. Thus, looking at the photograph, one would see the U.S. flag and, perhaps briefly, be surprised at such a celebration in August. The two lines below the picture rectify the omission in the caption. But the picture itself, I contend, capsulizes the double consciousness of much of the diasporic population. By literally wrapping her three-year-old son in an American flag, the Indian mother demarcates her son as separate from and yet tied to her. While the flag legitimizes the son's U.S. citizenship, the marked ethnic difference of the mother points to the alien nature of such citizenship. In this rendition of citizenship, while difference is not cast as absolute, the forging of an attempted commonality across differences cannot yet bypass the power of woman as symbol and allegory. Such a citizenship thus remains in a state of perennial crisis even as it seeks "validation as a constituency" (Radhakrishnan, "Postcoloniality" 764).

The Janus-faced character of the diasporic citizen is heightened for she who is foreign born or for the recent adult immigrant who considers herself a citizen of India. Unmoored and dislocated, her feelings about the condition of the Indian nation-state in the wake of the rise of the Hindu Right and increasing anti-Muslim sentiment is often quite communalist. A July 1993 interview with Huma Ahmed-Ghosh, a social anthropologist and a Muslim woman now living and teaching in San Diego and married to a Hindu, published in the *Committee on South Asian Women Bulletin*, captures the various levels of identification I have articulated above. She talks about the reactions by both Muslims and Hindus in Delhi after the destruction of the Babri Masjid. What is particularly pertinent are her comments about the reactions of Indian immigrants in California. She describes a meeting of the student group EKTA (Unity) at the University of California at Irvine, where a number of scholars were to talk about communalism. The meeting was soon commandeered by members of the VHP, whose younger members "spoke with particular venom about Muslims—how the nation had been plundered and the temples broken down" (28).

In an outrageous usurpation of an oppressed group's history, these young Hindu right-wingers "drew parallels between the situation of Hindus under Moghul rule to the situation of blacks brought to this country as slaves—citing the novel *Roots*, which has been serialized on T.V." (28). The parallel is baffling, to say the least, but the utilization of American slavery and the oppression of blacks to talk about the condition of Hindus under Muslim rule by Indians in the United States sets up a self-serving ethnic and racial identification by those who otherwise share very different sentiments about blacks. Let us not forget that educated Indians challenged the exclusionary nature of U.S. naturalization policy by advancing their Aryan origins as proof of their Caucasian race in the first decade of the twentieth century.

In these few pages, I have tried to narrativize and highlight the continuities in communalist sensibilities from the nationalist era to the present as well as explain the relevance of issues of national identity and the rise of Hindu nationalism for current discussions of citizenship and Indian immigration to the United States. In the book overall I have argued that the discursive construction of the Indian nation by both nationalists and imperialists was often inseparable from their idealization of a Hindu India epitomized in a particular Hindu female figure. Focusing on fictional representations of such figures, I emphasized the intimate connections between nation building, narration, and the novel. From Bankim's Shanti and Taylor's Seeta to Tagore's and Desai's Bimala, I have provided a literary genealogy of sorts for the unfolding and consolidation of the Indian nation. Such literary genealogies are increasingly relevant to those who teach Indian literature (in English) or, more problematic, South Asian literature in classrooms in U.S. universities. For those of us who practice a critical multiculturalist pedagogy and teach so-called postcolonial literature in the United States, we must pay attention to the historical situation of particular postcolonial literary formations.[2] One cannot study literature of the Indian diaspora, for example, without taking into account the formation of the Indian nation and the complex history of British colonialism in Africa, India, and the Caribbean. The celebration of Indian independence in 1947 and its depiction by Indo-Caribbean female novelist Lakshmi Persaud in *Butterfly in the Wind* must be contextualized very differently from Rushdie's Shandyian depiction of independent India in *Midnight's Children*. Ahmed Ali's *Twilight in Delhi*, which renders in evocative prose the decay of daily existence in Delhi in the last days of Muslim rule, has a relation to the history of Indian writing very different from the work of diaspora writers such as Meena Alexander and Rohinton Mistry, who have produced caustic critiques of the emergency era in India. And here I am talking only about literature being written in English. As we encounter more and more writers from the Indian subcontinent writing and living in the United States, as we encourage their study in English and comparative literature departments, as we insist simultaneously on their representation in ethnic studies programs, we must guard against any facile tendencies to elide or erase the intricate histories that these narratives chronicle. As feminist, postcolonial critics we must pay constant and careful attention to developments in international and transnational feminist thought. We must closely scrutinize the connections between feminist theoretical and pedagogical practices and their transformation in and through language. Transnational diaspora studies in the U.S. academy must continue to scrutinize the formations and unravelings of the nation-state in terms of class, caste, religion, ethnicity, gender, and sexuality at the local level so as to engage more cogently with issues such as development ideology, multinational capitalism, deterritorializations, migrancy, hybridity, and postethnicity at the global level. At the very least, we should receive announcements of the demise of the nation with the same skepticism we did proclamations of the end of history.

NOTES

INTRODUCTION

All citations for the primary texts under consideration will be provided in the individual chapter. I have chosen to spell Indian words without potentially cumbersome diacritical marks or combinations of letters.

1 The invitation was extended to me as an Indian professor teaching in the area, and I understand that the idea of an Indian woman teaching English at an American university was, to the ambassador, both intriguing and appealing.

2 The fetishization of identity through clothing, in the ambassador's assertion of cultural veracity, failed to take into account the "Indian" space wherein these women chose to dress as Indian women. The inability often to wear one's indigenous garb in a Western public space was completely ignored by the ambassador, who had to assume that all the Indian women present always dressed as such. In her essay "White Skin/Black Masks: The Pleasures and Politics of Imperialism," Gail Ching-Liang Low addresses the manner in which "clothes act as signifiers within the locus of desire and pleasure" (89) in the phenomenon of cultural cross-dressing in Anglo-Indian fiction—"the fantasy of the white man disguised as 'native'" (83). In a fashion, even though the ambassador was recoding the issue of cultural cross-dressing for different purposes, he reiterated Low's point that "clothes trap the essence of the east; they objectify it" (89).

3 For an interesting evaluation of corporate-style multiculturalism and its influence on the public sphere, see the essays, introduced by Evan Watkins, in *Social Text* 44 (1995).

4 Arjun Appadurai, in "The Heart of Whiteness," writes: "Even as the legitimacy of nation-states in their own territorial contexts is increasingly under threat, the idea of the nation flourishes transnationally. Safe from the depredations of their home-states, diasporic communities become double loyal to their nations of origin" (804).

5 Gayatri Chakravorty Spivak, "In a Word: Interview," in *Outside in the Teaching Machine* 3–4.

6   For example, in *Imagined Communities*, Benedict Anderson, a household name among scholars of nationalism today, addresses the manner in which issues of ethnicity, race, and class are imbricated in the evolution of nationalist beliefs. But his engagement with the axis of gender is slight, to say the least. As Mary Louise Pratt has pointed out, Anderson's use of the "language of fraternity and comradeship" to capture the idea of the modern nation as an imagined community "displays the androcentrism of modern national imaginings." The absence of gender in Anderson's speculation of the rise and growth of the modern nation cannot simply be explained by arguing that "women 'don't fit' the descriptors of the imagined community. Rather, the nation by definition situates or 'produces' women in permanent instability with respect to the imagined community, including, in very particular ways, the women of the dominant class. Women inhabitants of nations were neither imagined as nor invited to imagine themselves as part of the horizontal brotherhood" (131).

7   This consistent oversight by contemporary critics of nationalism is responsible for much of my ambivalence toward their work, which, as Deborah Gordon notes in the context of feminist decolonizing ethnography, produces a kind of subordination that "is not located in marginalization nor does it indicate a conspiracy to silence feminists. Rather it is a management of feminism produced out of a masculinist feminism with specific troubles for feminist ethnographers (or in this case feminist critics of nationalism)" (8).

8   For example, a collection of essays edited by Deniz Kandiyoti, *Women, Islam, and the State*, seeks to attend to the postindependence trajectories of modern states in their various deployments of Islam to shore up different nationalisms and state ideologies. The essays show how both hegemonic and oppositional groups use these various transformations of Islam to control the problematic space designated by the phrase "the woman question." Emphasized are the "ways in which women are represented in political discourse, the degree of formal emancipation they are able to achieve, the modalities of their participation in economic life and the nature of the social movements through which they are able to articulate their gendered interests are intimately linked to state-building [or nation-building] processes and are responsive to their transformation" (2).

9   Renan 13. If, according to Renan, a "nation's existence is [metaphorically speaking] a daily plebiscite" (19), then it is only men who constitute the population that exercises the right to national self-determination.

10   It is quite another thing altogether to read a 1990 essay such as Timothy Brennan's "The National Longing for Form" and discover no engagement with the way in which gender must have troubled his subject, "myths of the nation." A singular belief that emerges from Brennan's essay is that to understand the male agon of nation building and the explication of its principle "one, yet many" in the chosen genre of the novel, one can confidently ignore the gender dynamics of the subject. One has to read Brennan's essay alongside Doris Sommer's "Irre-

sistible Romance: The Foundational Fictions of Latin America" (in the same anthology, *Nation and Narration*) to realize how the discursive repetition of the structure of the nation in the novel (primarily the romance) is equally a "marriage of gen(d)res" (82). Sommer "locates an erotics of politics ... to show how the variety of social ideals inscribed in the novels are all ostensibly grounded in the 'natural' romance that legitimates the nation-family through love" (76).

11   Such an anthology as *Scattered Hegemonies: Postmodernity and Transnational Feminist Practices*, ed. Grewal and Kaplan, on the other hand, articulates critiques of colonialism, nationalism, modernity, and global economic structures by unpacking their complex relation to gender and sexuality. The subtitle of the first part, "Gender, Nation, and Critiques of Modernity," is not a reflection of singular aspects of the essays that follow. Every author, in seeking to engage with the idea of transnational feminist practice situated in a politics of location, is committed to a deep theoretical investigation of the gendered relationships between ideological structures and epistemological apparatuses.

12   Some of the most innovative and interesting work has been done by Gayatri Spivak, Lata Mani, Jenny Sharpe, Sara Suleri, Inderpal Grewal, Rajeswari Sunder Rajan, Tejaswani Niranjana, Kumkum Sangari, Sudesh Vaid, Susie Tharu, and Tanika Sarkar.

13   One of the many anthologies that have emerged in response to the challenge meted out by the Hindutva movement is *Women and the Hindu Right*, edited by Tanika Sarkar and Urvashi Butalia. In many of the essays in this anthology the writers try to revise and rethink feminism's relationship to right-wing movements.

14   A "sepoy" was an Indian soldier in the British colonial army. The British representation of the 1857 uprising as a "mutiny" is a deliberate hierarchical circumscription of the more encompassing effect of the movement as a significant rebellion that challenged the inherent power dynamics of colonial rule.

15   For an annotated bibiliography of mutiny writings in English, see Ladendorf, *Revolt in India*. For an extensive bibliography on mutiny fiction, see Gupta, *India in English Fiction*, and for a review of mutiny novels, see Shailendra Singh, *Novels on the Indian Mutiny* (Delhi: Arnold-Heinemann, 1980).

16   Sara Suleri reads the colonial narrativization of an "English India" "against the grain of the rhetoric of binarism that informs, either explicitly or implicitly, contemporary critiques of alterity in colonial discourse" (3). She further destabilizes the taxonomic power of imperial cultural knowledge by exploring the reinscription of the idiom of English India in the migrant postcolonial narratives of Naipaul and Rushdie. A genealogy of colonial discourse, of the kind developed by Suleri, constantly compounds the double focus of the analytic dimension inherent in a term such as "postcolonial." In her nuanced analysis of the metaphor of travel, Inderpal Grewal suggests "the particular ways in which

knowledge of a Self, society, and nation" were and continue to be formed in colonial, neocolonial, and postcolonial spaces. She reveals the ways in which
"movement within space came to be ideologically inscribed in the nineteenth
century in British culture, and . . . how such ideologies were [then] deployed by
non-Europeans" (4).

17 Here I rely heavily on Chantal Mouffe's essay "Citizenship and Political Identity" 28–32.

18 Nalini Natarajan, "Woman, Nation, and Narration in *Midnight's Children*,"
in *Scattered Hegemonies*, ed. Grewal and Kaplan, 76–77.

19 Roy documents the "phenomenal rise in the popularity of drama and its emergence in the late nineteenth century as the most prolific form of literary production" in Bengal (50). She also contends that this phenomenon has not been ade-
quately investigated.

20 The imposition of disciplinary norms definitely encountered resistance. But it
is precisely the negotiation of the boundaries of taste and respectability that reveals how "national" culture had to be repeatedly legitimized not just in relation to colonial expectations but also in terms of its relation to the "popular."

21 For a discussion of the development of late-nineteenth-century Hindi literature
and its negotiations with the canons of inherited English literary taste and popular demands, see Chadra, *The Oppressive Present*.

22 A. Ahmad 69. See Schwarz and Prasad for contradictory critiques of Ahmad's
position. Because Ahmad does not concern himself with the feasibility of termi-
nology such as "first world" and "third world" or the problems generated by
such distinctions, I guide the reader toward Ahmad's and Prasad's essays for
discussions on the subject. Let me say briefly that Ahmad's assertion that we
live in one world and that the idea of the "third world" is not empirically
grounded (7–9) is not always convincing, because his analysis relies largely on
his own experiences as an intellectual from Pakistan. Despite his marxist affin-
ities with Jameson, Ahmad distinguishes his subject position from Jameson's in
terms that recrudesce the familiar opposition between Western and non-
Western worlds.

23 See Christine Delphy, *Close to Home: A Materialist Analysis of Women's Oppression*, trans. Diana Leonard (Amherst: University of Massachusetts Press,
1984).

24 Sharpe 18. Sharpe goes on to emphasize the tremendous significance of
Spivak's critique and her undertaking in "Can the Subaltern Speak?": "She
[Spivak] identifies the subaltern woman as one who cannot be simply reduced
to her class or caste position. She interrupts the project of making subaltern
classes the subject of history with a 'text about the (im)possibility of "making"
the subaltern gender the subject of its own story'" (18).

CHAPTER ONE

Gender and Nation: Woman Warriors in Chatterjee's
Devi Chaudhurani and *Anandamath*

1   See Mrinalini Sinha, *Colonial Masculinity: The "Manly Englishman" and the
     "Effeminate Bengali" in the Late Nineteenth Century* (Manchester: University
     of Manchester Press, 1994), for a detailed and critically sophisticated historical
     analysis of the culture of masculinity in colonial India.

2   In "Bengal as the Western Image of India," in *Imagining India* Ainslie T. Em-
     bree writes that in "the late eighteenth and early nineteenth century, when the
     British thought they were seeing India, they were in fact seeing Bengal. A spe-
     cific reminder of this confusion comes when we refer to the chief official created
     by the Act of 1773 as the Governor General of India; he was, of course, the
     Governor General of Fort William in Bengal, but our imagination transforms
     the little fort into a subcontinent. One can assert with a fair degree of certainty
     that between the middle of the eighteenth century and up to the 1850s, the im-
     age of India was largely drawn from Bengal society, as it was perceived by the
     British and, indeed, by Indians who were influenced by the West" (101). In fact
     Embree goes on to assert that an accurate understanding of the pattern of
     nineteenth-century imperial government demands a return to "its beginnings
     in Bengal. Out of the responses to Bengal civilization in the first fifty years or so
     of British rule—that is, roughly from 1760—came the attitudes that character-
     ize the self-confident years of benevolent despotism that stretch from the 1870s
     to the First World War" (101). In his novelizations of the historical past, Ban-
     kimchandra Chatterjee almost exclusively imagines Bengal as India. One can
     list other examinations of Indian history that privilege Bengal (and the Bengal
     Presidency) as the geographic equivalent of India. An account of the Muslim
     period in India has as its title *The History of Bengal: Muslim Period,* ed. Sir
     Jadu-Nath Sarkar (Patna: Academia Asiatica, 1973). Similarly, Ishwari Prasad,
     India in the Eighteenth Century (Allahabad: Chugh Publications, 1973), de-
     votes eight out of twelve chapters to Bengal. Raychaudhuri, *Europe Reconsid-
     ered*, takes as his subtitle *Perceptions of the West in Nineteenth-Century Ben-
     gal*; in the preface he notes that "the Bengali intelligentsia was the first Asian
     social group of any size whose mental world was transformed through its inter-
     actions with the West. In 1817, Bengal's social leaders took the initiative to es-
     tablish the first institution of Western higher education in Asia. By then,
     through trade and colonial government, Bengalis had had more than six de-
     cades of close contact with a European nation" (ix). More recently Ashis
     Nandy, in *The Intimate Enemy: Loss and Recovery of Self under Colonialism*
     (Delhi: Oxford University Press, 1983), defends his use of examples from Ben-
     gal to illustrate his version of the psychology of colonialism, "not merely be-
     cause the Bengali culture best illustrated—and dramatized—the colonial pre-

dicament in India's political, cultural and creative life, but also because it was in Bengal that the Western intrusion was the deepest and the colonial presence the longest" (18).

3　I have relied on two translations of *Anandamath*. The first is translated by Sree Aurobindo and Sree Barindra Kumar Ghosh (Calutta: Basumati Sahitya Mandi [1909 ?]). The second is a reprint and adaptation by Basanta Kumar Roy (New Delhi: Vision, 1992). All page references are to the 1992 edition. The latter leaves out the last chapter, a significant omission in terms of the book's appeal to militant nationalists. For *Devi Chaudhurani*, I have relied exclusively on the translation by Subodh Chunder Mitter (Calcutta: Chuckervorty, Chatterjee, 1946).

4　In the eighteenth and much of the nineteenth centuries, the British governed the Indian economy, which was primarily agrarian, by the same methods as those being used in Western capitalistic societies. Benita Parry, in *Delusions and Discoveries: Studies on India in the British Imagination, 1880–1930* (London: Allen Lane, 1972), summarizes the outcome of such gross mismanagement thus: "The most devastating impact of this approach was on land tenure and the village communities. The aim during the nineteenth century had been to introduce a free enterprise, competitive agrarian system by granting proprietary titles to individuals where previously the land had been communally held. Revenues were fixed in money and, if, the assessments were not paid, the sale of land was forced. The purpose of this was to dismember the petrified corporate structure so that it could be rebuilt on western lines. The outcome was the weakening of the village community, traditionally the heart of the Indian social system, peasant indebtedness and massive land alienation from the cultivators into the hands of absentee landlords and moneylenders" (14).

5　The desolation of the land captured in the opening pages of the novel, with its emphasis on starvation—people eating grass, weeds, and even mice and cats— and the inevitable spread of contagious diseases, echoes the sentiments of a poem written by John Shore (Lord Teignmouth), who arrived in Calcutta as a young civilian and who ultimately rose very high in the ranks of British administration in the East:

> Still fresh in memory's eye the scene I view,
> The shrivelled limbs, sunk eyes, and lifeless hue;
> Still hear the mother's shrieks and infant's moans,
> Cries of despair and agonizing moans.
> In wild confusion dead and dying lie;—
> Hark to jackal's and vulture's cry,
> The dog's fell howl, as midst the glare of day
> They riot unmolested on their prey!
> Dire scenes of horror, which no pen can trace,
> Nor rolling years from memory's page efface. (quoted in Hunter 28)

6   Bengal, like the other Indian provinces, was divided into districts, the basic unit of the administrative system devised by the British to rule India. At the head of each district, which would contain a hundred villages and a population of about half a million, was a collector or deputy commissioner. In the early stages of British imperialism, the commissioner collected his revenues through an Indian intermediary who was often corrupt and cared little about the economic situation of the villagers. Even the rich landowners, who refused to compromise their epicurean lifestyle, suffered losses because of the exorbitant tax placed on land by the British. In *Devi Chaudhurani* we see the heroine's father-in-law reduced to bankruptcy as a result of the mismanagement of his funds and his debt to Govindlal, a usurer working as the local revenue collector for his district.

7   In *A Statistical Account of Bengal*, the seventh volume of *The Annals of Rural Bengal*, William Hunter gives us a brief description of the British district of Rangpur, which was constructed as such when it passed under the rule of the East India Company in 1765. Due to excessive mismanagement by the *diwan* (finance minister) of Dinajpur, Raja Debi Singh, the revenues imposed on the cultivators increased tremendously. In January 1783, the Rangpur cultivators rose in rebellion and drove out the revenue officers. Dissatisfied by the concessions made by the collector, they forced the cultivators of Kuch Behar and Dinajpur to join them in their protest. "The insurgents committed several murders, and issued a proclamation that they would pay no more revenue. One of the leaders assumed the title of Nawab; and a tax called *dingkarcha*, or sedition tax, was levied for the expenses of the insurrection" (157–58). Despite the initial defeat of the self-styled Nawab and his groups of rebels by Lieutenant MacDonald in 1783, "banditti, who ravaged the country in armed bands numbering several hundreds," continued to infest the districts (158). In 1784 military force was again used to quell the dacoits who inhabited the "tract of country lying south of the stations of Dinajpur and Rangpur, and west of the present district of Bogra, towards the Ganges," because it was "far removed from any central authority" (158). In 1787 the *Annals* recount a confrontation between Lieutenant Brenan and a notorious leader of the dacoits, Bhawani Pathak, which is depicted in the novel. In his report the lieutenant mentions "a female dakat, by name Debi Chaudhurani, also in league with Pathak. She lived in boats, had a large force of barkandazs [bandits] in her pay, and committed dakaiytis [robberies and murders] in her own account, besides receiving a share of the booty obtained by Pathak" (159).

8   Kaviraj 107. Kaviraj pays very little attention to the mapping of gender in Bankim's writings, and his finessing of the "Muslim question" is disingenuous to say the least.

9   The revolutionary force of Bankim's claims is unmistakable and illustrates Albert Memi's claim that "the colonized's liberation must be carried out through a recovery of self and of autonomous dignity" (128). Bankim's assertion of ba-

hubol as an integral aspect of Hindu character could be said to partake in this general affirmation of subjectivity on the part of the colonized in a colonial situation. Furthermore, Bankim's insistence on the need to rewrite certain historical events to highlight the efficacy of bahubol against a foreign invader articulates the essential need for the colonized to grasp language and make it speak for an oppressed people. But in his emphasis on bahubol as the only determinate factor for the production of an operating Hindu subject, Bankim's interventionist historiography is a "positivistic project—a project which assumes that . . . it will lead to firm ground, to some *thing* that can be disclosed" (Spivak, *In Other Worlds* 202). And this "thing" that can be disclosed and subsequently emulated for a nationalist initiative is a homogeneous Indian subject that elides the heterogeneity of what Spivak calls "demographic difference—which opens the door to deconstructive gestures" (204).

10 Kaviraj shows how "Bankim's language carries the mark of . . . indecision" and how this indecision undercuts his desire to articulate an Indian national identity. For example, Bankim uses the term "jat" or "jati" for diverse identities ranging from castes to Bengalis, to the Hindus, and to Indians. Kaviraj goes on to suggest that this "ambiguity of meaning of jati in Bankim's essays therefore is an index of a historical difficulty of discourse" and is revealed in the manner in which Bankim, failing to invest the word with a particular meaning, has to, in an external footnote, say that for the "purposes of this essay, the term jati means 'nationality,' or 'nation'" (128–29).

11 Quoted in Haldar 104–5. Haldar also translates Bankim Chatterjee's essay "Samya" and in his lengthy introduction provides an evaluation of Bankim's evolving ideas about Hindu society and religion.

12 In his 1994 essay "Tremors of Intent," Dilip Simeon attempts to critically assess communal conflict, "the one element in our 'national' life that seems to carry the burden of perpetual crisis" (225). According to Simeon, the question of national subjecthood was intricately connected to the "construction of a hegemonic culture as a means to countering the claims to legitimacy of the colonial rulers. The ideological well-spring of the national movement was the differentiated but discernible effort on the part of the intelligentsia to evolve that homogenized subjectivity which they considered the ground of a modern nation state" (225–26). And this homogenized subjectivity was repeatedly cast as Hindu by some of the most outstanding litterateurs of the time, such as Harishchandra, Chiplinkar, Pratapnarayan Misra, and Swami Shraddhananda (228).

13 Ranajit Guha has pointed out how the first and last essays of the *kalamka* series were written within sixty and twenty-eight years, respectively, of the Sepoy Mutiny (63). The word "kalamka" or "kalanka" loosely translates as "stain" or "taint," and Bankim, in the series of readings on Indian history, saw the lack of any nationalistic desire in earlier Hindu populations, as well as the absence of any manifestation of bahubol in contemporary Hindus, as a negative trait.

A key essay that addresses these related issues is Bankim's "Bangalir Bahubol, Bharat Kalanka, Bharatbarsher Swadhinata Ebong Paradhinata" (1879).

14   Guha believes that armed resistance is the only way by which to obtain nationhood from a colonial force. Partha Chatterjee explains this aporia in Bankim's nationalist discourse as characteristic of nationalist thought "at the moment of departure. It is born out of the encounter of a patriotic consciousness within the framework of knowledge imposed upon it by colonialism. It leads inevitably to an elitism of the intelligentsia, rooted in the vision of a radical regeneration of national culture. In Bankim's time, the heyday of colonial rule, this vision could not find any viable political means to actualize itself. Instead, it became a dream: a utopian political community in which the nation was the Mother, once resplendent in wealth and beauty, now in tatters" (*Nationalist Thought* 179).

15   From *The Theory of Religion*; quoted in P. Chatterjee, *Nationalist Thought* 66.

16   From *Krishnacharitra*, quoted. in P. Chatterjee, *Nationalist Thought* 70.

17   Partha Chatterjee defines Bankim's notion of dharma as different from asceticism and puritanism. "It does not advocate the renunciation of sensual pleasure. It is a worldly philosophy which makes it a duty to achieve control over the senses. . . . Puritanism is opposed to sensual pleasure: the dharma of the *Gita* advocates neither desire nor abhorrence . . . 'no room for hypocrisy here' " (*Nationalist Thought* 72).

18   According to Partha Chatterjee one cannot accuse Bankim of a nostalgic investment in an ancient, glorious Indian past. In *Nationalist Thought*, Partha Chatterjee argues against reading Bankim's incorporation of Indian practices and the religious overtones in his later novels—particularly *Anandamath* and *Devi Chaudhurani*—as an overindulgence in a "backward looking emotionalism" (80). Any interpretation of the prescriptions of "Hindu orthodoxy" in his later novels as his ultimate surrender to the ties of the heart(h) would be to miss Hindu orthodoxy's "very source of ideological strength, namely, its proclamation of a rational and modern religion suitable for the nation" (80). Partha Chatterjee concludes that since neither the progressives nor conservatives were able to resolve the tensions between the "modern" and the "national" "in any historically specific way," Bankim Chatterjee offers a theoretical program (not really a practical solution) whereby "the modern and the national could be synthesised only in the ideal of the complete man, the true intellectual. But it was hardly possible to devise programmatic steps to achieve that ideal in the realm of politics" (80).

19   On the role of women and femininity in Bankim Chandra, see Ratte 42–59.

20   Spivak, "The Politics of Interpretation," in *In Other Worlds*, 129.

21   Ibid., 130. I have taken the liberty of rearranging Spivak's words. In her essay "The Politics of Interpretation," Spivak is concerned with critically unraveling the political consequences of disciplinary privilegings in various literary, his-

torical, and psychoanalytic essays that rewrite a theory of ideology as individual consciousness and will. In doing so they end up reconstituting a subject of ideology unmarked by race, gender, and class. Such a masculinist, first world, ideological structural apparatus at work is made visble in "conserving the sovereign subject; excluding a monolithic Marx(ism); and excluding or appropriating a homogeneous woman" (118). Spivak's essay seeks to produce a politicized feminist hermeneutic that is capable of critically addressing the structural problem of the exclusion and unproblematic appropriation of sexual difference in various disciplinary discourses that fail to engage with and accommodate the critical subject of ideology.

22   More important, Mahendra's initiation allows for the unveiling of the plight of the Motherland in a series of four representative images of the godhead. The first is the four-armed god Vishnu, who is surrounded by other gods and goddesses and cradles in his lap "an image of enchanting beauty . . . splendid with opulence and lordship" (B. Chatterjee, *Anandamath*, 38). We are told that this image is of the "Mother"(land) in all her innocence, whom Mahendra fails to recognize because she is beyond his imaginative horizon. Next, Mahendra is ushered into the presence of Jagadhatri, protector of the world, who represents the Mother(land) as she was, "in hue like the young sun, splendid with all opulence and empire" (39). The third image is that of Kali, "enveloped in darkness, full of blackness and gloom. She is stripped of all, therefore naked" (39). She symbolizes the Mother(land) today, "a burial ground . . . garlanded with skulls" (39). She is also armed with a club suggesting the importance of armed resistance in the face of the enemy. And finally Mahendra is overcome with the resplendent image of the ten-armed goddess Durga, who embodies "the Mother[land] as she shall be. Her ten arms are extended towards the ten regions and they bear many a force imaged in her manifold weapons; her enemies are trampled under her feet and the lion on which her foot rests is busy destroying the foe" (40).

23   The sage plays an important role in the novel because he suggests that there would be a time in the future when the Santans' (The Children of God's) struggle for liberation would be resumed. This is most probably a reference to 1857. In the serialized version of the novel, Satyananda calls for an attack on both the English and the Muslims. Reference to the English was removed in the first edition. The second edition of the novel also excluded Captain Thomas's interest in Santal (tribal) women. It is interesting that a later translation of the novel into English, published during the height of the nationalist movement, does not include the last chapter. This final chapter contains the admonition by the sage not to fight the British because they were to lead Bengal out of anarchy, hence its omission speaks to the status of the novel as the touchstone for Bengal's armed revolutionaries.

24   A substantial portion of the novel is spent in describing the life led by Prafulla in the heart of the jungle as she follows the strictures imposed by her mentor.

We are exposed to her gradual attainment of knowledge as she learns to read, write, and interpret religious texts. She sees nobody except two women who act as guards and companions; at the end of the fifth year Bhawani returns and submits her to rigorous examination to see if she has learned the "truth" about existence and self-sacrifice. It is only when he is absolutely reassured that he reveals the reason for the five years of hardship.

25 A magnificent scene describes Devi Chaudhurani sailing down the River Trisrota, probably a tributary of the Holy Ganges, in her barge on a moonlit night (this scene evokes strong recollections of Cleopatra sailing down the Nile in Shakespeare's *Antony and Cleopatra*): "The barge was painted in variegated colours with a numberless [sic] paintings of human figures on it. The brass knobs, handles, rods, etc. were all silver plated. a shark's head was engraved at the prow and that was also silvered. . . . On the roof of the barge sat a person of superb beauty and elegance" (117). Devi Chaudhurani is described as being dressed in a superfine piece of Dacca muslin with rich embroideries of gold. "Her bodice [was] set with diamonds and pearls; and the rest of her body was fully covered with gold and valuable jewellery [sic] of precious diamonds, emeralds and pearls. . . . Her raven locks, as they fell circling round her face and other parts of her body, seemed like the broad dark shadows that skirted the white and shining stream" (118). She looked like "a veritable goddess Saraswati playing on her vina or lyre" (118–19).

26 This is the only time that we see her devising a strategy to overpower the lieutenant, commanding the rebels who are always near at hand to her service and actually using her intelligence and resources to instigate an attack on the British.

27 Brajeswar had been told that his wife had died, and to see her alive again releases pent-up emotions. Prafulla too can finally express her tears and display emotions that had been bottled up while under the guise of the Devi. "He could not utter a further word. . . . Almost instantly, Prafulla felt a gush of tears on her eyes passing like a torrent and dismantling her ten years' [sic] old barrier of restraint." Brajeswar, who had discovered that his wife and the infamous outlaw were one and the same, had come firmly resolved not to shed any tears on her account, but "quite unwelcome they came and filled Braja's eyes" (198).

After the emotional storm has passed, Brajeswar brings up her participation in the raids and questions her motives. At that instant Prafulla is reminded of her father-in-law's callous dismissal of her situation as he literally kicked her out of his house. When Prafulla had asked him how she would live if they threw her out, her father-in-law had said, "Go and earn your living by theft or pillage, just as you like" (200). It's on the tip of her tongue to lash out at Brajeswar and say, "Yes, I am a robber no doubt, but why lecture me now? Was it not you people who once advised me to live by plunder and pillage? What I am doing now is simply obeying the mandates of my superiors and nothing more" (200). Being the dutiful wife and daughter-in-law, however, she tries to subdue her anger and pain.

28 Meenakshi Mukherjee writes that the accusations made by modern critics about Bankim's Hindu chauvinism is something that Bankim himself seemed to have anticipated. She argues that it was because of this that he "added a rather gratuitous and defensive postscript to his novel *Rajsingha* (a novel that denounced quite viciously the Muslim ruler Aurangzeb), stating that in this book he had by no means tried to indicate the superiority of Hindus over Muslims" (53). Mukherjee underlines Bankim's ambivalence toward the Muslims by citing his essay "Bangadesher Krishak" (The peasants of Bengal), in which he lashes out against the exploitation of both Hindu and Muslim peasants. She suggests that "one explanation of this inconsistency . . . could be that he regarded the Muslim peasants as Bengalis, whereas the Muslim rulers of Bengal were to him alien people" (53).

29 See Partha Chatterjee's *Nationalist Thought and the Colonial World* and Tapan Raychaudhuri's *Europe Reconsidered*, two books to which I am greatly indebted for their thorough and quite dissimilar evaluation of Bankim's writings on religion and nationalism. For other engagements with Bankimchandra Chatterjee in English, see Nandy, *Intimate Enemy*; Guha, *Historiography*; and Tanika Sarkar, "Bankimchandra."

30 In the hymn, India is identified as the mother goddess who is worshipped as Shakti (strength), and the weapons in her ten arms represent the power that her armed children can use.

31 For a critical evaluation of working-class and peasant women involvement in the Congress-led nationalist movement in the late 1920s and early 1930s and the Civil Disobedience movement, see Tanika Sarkar's essay "Politics and Women in Bengal" 231–40. For a more straightforward and at times uncritical historical assessment of the role of women in various stages of the nationalist struggle, see Kaur.

32 The role of the benevolent queen, idealized/idolized as mother and goddess by the poor and oppressed and considered a fearful adversary by the British, affords her no pleasure. When she meets Brajeswar after ten years, she at once wants to cast off her identity as the Devi. She seeks out Bhawani Thakur and expresses her desire to be freed from any further association with the rebels. She does not enjoy her infamous reputation among the landowners and the British, and as she puts it to the gang leader, "the infamy is sure to continue even after my death" (170). To Bhawani Thakur's assertion that she had not considered her course of action in such a negative light ten years earlier, Prafulla replies, "Quite, my opinion is changed now. These long years you seemed to have cast a spell on me—no more shall I be bound by that spell" (168). The truth, as it emerges in the text, is that Prafulla is never really under a spell. She does what she has to and in a sense atones for her luxurious public display by living fru-

gally in private—she sleeps on hard floors, eats a meal of rice and vegetables only once a day, and dresses in simple clothes. Like Kalyani in *Anandamath*, Prafulla is rewarded for her private penance not just by being reunited with her husband but also by being elevated and valorized by all concerned as a paragon of domesticity.

33 Prafulla's father-in-law, unaware of the identity of Devi Chaudhurani and deeply in debt, acts as a spy for the British to help them capture her. In the end, when her identity has been revealed and the British lieutenant has been defeated, Nishi wants to make the old man suffer for all the terrible things he had done to Prafulla. She wants the father-in-law to accept a marriage beteen his son and the Devi, but she reveals this only after she has humiliated and tortured him with fabrications of the cruel treatment that he could expect at the hands of the Devi and her men for his role as a spy (242–46).

34 Nishi has no memory of familial life and had been sold to a prince before she was rescued by Bhawani Thakur.

35 Perhaps the only reminder of Prafulla's other existence is the denial of the role of mother once she reenters the domestic space. She is a surrogate mother, much as she was the symbol for the motherland. The absence of children conceivably enables the paean to Prafulla as the Devi to function as the open-ended conclusion to the novel.

36 Kalyani is willing to abnegate herself because of her given and to a certain extent desired subaltern position in the hierarchy of discourses that is circulated by the Children (Kalyani demonstrates how enmeshed women are in the fictions about women's place). "I have done well," Kalyani says as she takes the poison. "I was afraid that for my sake you might refuse to follow the path of your own duty" (73). Kalyani sings the song "Bande Mataram" as she dies, and as Mahendra joins in he feels transformed. The gradual ebb of life from Kalyani's body is no longer the focal point of Mahendra's attention. Woman is displaced onto and by the song of a far more important female figure, the Motherland. Kalyani feels virtuous because she is conditioned to believe that it is a wife's duty to aid her husband at the expense of her own life. Her greatest comfort is that she can die in his presence and that he can now follow the chaste path to his and, by extension, the country's salvation: "And it is your duty to fulfill the conditions of your vow with the utmost fidelity. Faithfully with all your body, mind and soul, you must now serve Mother India. Fight for India's freedom with all the forces in your command. This is your path of duty—your dharma. Solely through this path salvation awaits you" (74). Thus, one is led to believe that it is Kalyani's very desire to die and that this kind of willing abnegation of self on a woman's part will be ultimately rewarded. As we see, Kalyani is revived by Bhavan, who possesses infinite knowledge of medicinal herbs, and is then conveniently relocated until she can be united with her husband and daughter. Also, because Mahendra is denied the knowledge of his

wife's and daughter's existence, he can fight courageously without any fear holding him back. Of Prafulla, Kalyani, and Shanti, only Kalyani reflects the feminine cultural norm as such.

37 The latter would be considered very radical because it is a privilege exclusively granted to male Brahmins and functions as a signifier of their holy caste.

38 Bankim critiques Sankhya philosophy with its emphasis on *vairagya*, or "otherwordliness." According to him this philosophy lies at the root of many religions in India, including Buddhism, and fuels otherworldliness and fatalism. Bankim believes that such a belief system is ultimately responsible for the subject condition of the Hindus for the last seven centuries, first under the Muslims and, now, the English ("Sankhyadarshan").

39 Bakhtin, *Rabelais and His World* 10. In "Film and Masquerade" 74–87, Mary Anne Doane uses the essay of Joan Riviere on "Womanliness and Masquerade" to explain the asymmetries of transvestism, suggesting that women have always had to masquerade to participate in a man's world. For a woman to dress, act, or position herself in discourse as a man is easily understandable and culturally compelling, but not the other way around. One can suggest that Shanti's disguised involvement with the Santans has a carnivalesque, subersive quality about it. For an analysis of Bakhtin's notion of the carnival and feminist uses of it, see Russo, "Female Grotesques" 213–29. Russo, summarizing Bakhtin's concept of the carnival, asserts that "the masks and voices of carnival resist, exaggerate, and destabilize the distinctions and boundaries that mark and maintain high culture and organized society. . . . The political implications of this heterogeneity are obvious: it sets carnival apart from the merely oppositional and reactive; carnival and carnivalesque suggest a redeployment or counterproduction of culture, knowledge, and pleasure. In its multivalent oppositional play, carnival refuses to surrender the critical and cultural tools of the dominant class, and in this sense, carnival can be seen above all as a site of insurgency, and not merely withdrawal" (218). For a powerful feminist critique of the carnival, see Glazener 109–29, esp. 109–18. See also Bauer, esp. 1–15.

40 She starts on her journey to join the Children. The song she sings as she travels into the jungle expresses her emotions at being previously thwarted from fulfilling her desires because of her gender. She wishes to plunge into battle and will not allow anyone to stand in her way. The cries of "Bande Mataram" will no longer be stilled, and therefore she reasons, "Who cares to be a woman today?" "Our fight is on," she sings, pleading with her beloved not to leave her behind. Can't the men see how "her warhorse neighs and paws / To go to war, yes, to go to war to free India / From England's yoke." The refrain is haunting: "I cannot—I cannot stay at home any longer / Oh, woman! Who cares to be a woman today?" (117).

41 Butler, *Bodies That Matter* 8. In her introduction to the book, Butler is concerned with the manner in which the category of "sex" is made to regulate the

materialization of the body "in the service of the consolidation of the hetero-sexual imperative" (2). To this effect, she seeks to interrogate the ways in which the materiality of sex is demarcated in various discourses about the gendered body. Such an inquiry might allow us "to think about how and to what end bodies are constructed . . . [as well as] to what end bodies are *not* constructed and, further, to ask after how bodies which fail to materialize provide the neces-sary 'outside,' if not the necessary support, for the bodies which, in materializ-ing the norm, qualify as bodies that matter" (16). I have appropriated Butler's discourse about the construction of the heterosexual, normative body, using it to open up a discussion about the normative, Hindu male body materialized in Bankimchandra's novel.

42 Bagchi, "Positivism and Nationalism" 61. Bagchi's article uses Bankim's knowledge of Auguste Comte's positivism as a point of departure for a feminist reading of *Anandamath*.

43 This scene of revealing one's prowess by stringing a bow is reminiscent of ear-lier epic treatments of this motif. Both Arjun in *The Mahabharatha* and Rama in *The Ramayana* win their beloved, Draupadi and Sita, respectively, by string-ing a bow when others could not. The role reversal here is quite interesting, for it places Shanti in relation to two of India's greatest epic heroes.

44 Because Shanti was young and alone (without a husband), Satyananda's specu-lation about her status as a child widow is not inappropriate. Widows in India had to follow stringent rules and had very strict dietary injunctions.

45 Elam 45. In her wonderfully lucid book, Elam engages the two theoretical dis-courses—feminism and deconstruction—not as a conversing pair to see how they "go together" but to discern "how they are beside each other" (1). In the section from which I have quoted, Elam questions what kind of "category 'women' [have been made] to constitute" in various feminist treatises. Trying to move beyond the fundamental opposition between gender and sex, nature and culture, Elam uses Kant's philosophical distinction between three kinds of judgments to "examine the stakes in the gender/sex distinction [that may lead to an understanding of] woman as a category without recourse to a notion of identity as such" (44).

46 Tanika Sarkar writes that in "Samya," "Bankim came closest to an agenda and voice that had promised to be the most far reaching, the most radically humani-tarian that had emerged so far among the Bengali intelligentsia. Such an agenda was produced, moreover, without any reference to Hindu philosophical re-sources ("Bankimchandra" 194).

47 *Bankim rachanaballi*, quoted in Tanika Sarkar, "Bankimchandra" 197.

48 Tanika Sarkar, who also pays close attention to this passage, reads it in terms of the "eroticization of the spectacle of violent death" ("Bankimchandra" 197). I found Sarkar's essay as I was revising the chapter and decided to use her trans-lation for its greater accuracy.

CHAPTER TWO

Woman as "Suttee": The Construction of India in
Three Victorian Narratives

1   Since I discuss three British imperialist narratives, it seems fitting to use their
    terminology when referring to the Sepoy Rebellion.

2   Sharpe's study, which is scrupulous in its particular delineation of the trope of
    rape "not as an essential condition of the colonial psyche but [as always being]
    contingent upon its discursive production" (3), suggests that Sara Suleri's dis-
    missal of the critically liberating potential of the "geography of rape as a domi-
    nant trope for the act of imperialism" (17) is a bit hasty.

3   Gayatri Chakravorty Spivak, "The Politics of Interpretations," in *In Other
    Worlds* 129.

4   Cixous 252. For a brilliant analysis of the politics and ethics of sexual differ-
    ence that might open up a space wherein the postcolonial feminist may engage
    with certain metropolitan feminists, see Gayatri Chakravorty Spivak, "French
    Feminism Revisited," in *Outside in the Teaching Machine* 141–72.

5   Patrick Brantlinger also argues against the epistemic rupture of the colonial
    project between the early and later periods of the nineteenth century.

6   In the brief section on sati is a curious reference to the issue of what counted as
    felony under British colonial law forbidding the practice of widow burning.
    The new law "treated as felony all participation in the sacrifice of human life
    by the burning or burying alive of women" (286). This sentence is not merely
    prescriptive. Its disciplinary intent is expanded via its descriptive suggestion
    that widow burning was only one of the many kinds of human sacrifices prac-
    ticed by the Hindus.

7   The subtitle of this particular tract is very revealing: "Showing from *Essays
    Published in India and Official Documents* That the Custom of *Burning Hin-
    doo Widows* Is Not an Integral Part of Hinduism and May Be Abolished with
    Ease and Safety." Pegg was a missionary in Cuttack, Orissa. The author at-
    taches a poem at the end of the tract presumably written by an Anglo-Indian
    woman named Ellen. I will quote one verse to reveal what a hold sati had on
    the British imagination: "See how she writhes! hark to her screams, / As now
    the lurid flames enfold her! / But all is vain, no pity gleams / In the stern face of
    one beholder! / Her kindred stand with hearts of stone, / Cased by the demon
    Superstition; / Hear her last agonizing groan, / Nor heave a sigh at her condi-
    tion!" (97).

8   "Governement Circular on Sati Addressed to Military Officers," November
    10, 1828, in Bentinck 91.

9   Mani, "Production" 32. See also Mani, "Construction" 119–56; Mani, "Cul-
    tural Theory" 392–404; Rajan, "Subject of Sati" 1–27; Sabin 1–24; and Yang
    8–33.

10 For an exhaustive list of "fictional" accounts of the mutiny, I refer the reader to the list of published and unpublished sources included in the appendix to Sharpe's *Allegories of Empire*.

11 The Hindu calendar is not only different from the Western calendar but can also differ from region to region. Thus the new year is different for Bengalis than, say, people from Uttar Pradesh in the north.

12 The Sudras would belong to the third tier in the caste system, preceded by the Kshatriyas and the Brahmins. Taylor's choice of a lower-caste woman to represent Hindu India offers an interesting contrast to the figure of the Brahmin woman in both Chatterjee and Tagore.

13 For an intelligent discussion of the ways in which the depiction of women in the epic texts *Ramayana* and *Mahabharata* differ in various renditions, see the interview of Romila Thapar, "Traditions versus Misconceptions" 3–14. Thus in the Buddhist *Jataka* version of the *Ramayana*, Rama and Sita are brother and sister, and after their exile Sita becomes Rama's queen and consort (3). In a southeast version of the story Sita is the daughter of Ravana. And according to Thapar, in the Jaina version *Paumacharyam*, "Sita is a much more assertive person . . . and ravana is not a demon" (4).

14 The reference to Italy is significant here, because Italy functioned in the English imagination as a place where sensuality dominated.

15 Above all, we are told he is not a racist; he does not belong to that class of Englishmen who declare India to be an " 'infernal hole'; who speak and think contemptuously of its people, who deny them their sympathy and help, who hold them as 'niggers' and 'black fellows,' as if they were negro savages, who override them haughtily, who despise and refuse their society, and never even attempt their friendship, and consider themselves demeaned by any concession to their manners or long-existing customs" (70). Brandon definitely thinks the Indians are a cut above the "negro savages" and that India, with its ancient history, is not "the dark continent" (one wonders how Brandon would have behaved in Africa).

16 Thus although the union between Seeta and Brandon could produce a dynamic third space that in its indeterminacy might be capable of fracturing otherwise determinate subject positions in colonial India, it fails to do so precisely by avoiding the issue of an interracial child.

17 For a reading of *Seeta* that foregrounds British "Mrs. Grundyism," see Brantlinger 212–16. Opposition also comes from the Hindu community, and as Brandon is ostracized by the British, so Seeta is scorned by the Indian community. Between British racism and Hindu fanaticism about purity of caste and belief, Taylor suggests, there is little to choose. The easy way out would be for Brandon to take Seeta to be his mistress—that is less scandalous than taking a wife. But Taylor was one of the few Englishman who did not approve of treating Indian women as only mistresses or prostitutes.

18 Brantlinger does evoke the presence of Seeta's English rival.

19 The Rani of Jhansi did play an extraordinary role in the rebellion of 1857, though the details provide much scope for dispute among historians. For a wonderful analysis of the Rani's role in the mutiny and her celebration in India as a legendary figure of epic proportions, see Lebra-Chapman. In British representations of the uprising, the Rani is frequently depicted as an avaricious, violent queen whose only interest lay in protecting her kingdom so that she could exploit her subjects. In Indian accounts she is a great queen who refused to surrender to the British. She has been resurrected in India as an early nationalist and even a pioneer Indian feminist.

20 Lebra-Chapman summarizes the questions raised regarding the Rani's involvement in the rebellion: "Was the massacre of the sixty-six English men, women, and children at Jhansi in 1857 done at her order? Was she in fact aware of the plans of the Sepoys before they were carried out? Could she have done anything to prevent the massacre had she known of it in advance? Whatever the answers to these and other questions about her role in the Jhansi uprising, there can be no doubt about her exploits from late March through June of 1858, when she was engaged in battle at the forts of Jhansim Kalpi, and finally Gwalior, where she died in action" (3).

21 Here we see how the color of Zora's skin distances her from the typical brown woman.

22 This denial of "humanness" to colonized peoples, the reduction of the subjugated race to "things" rather than people, has been described at length by Fanon. In *The Wretched of the Earth* Fanon writes, "At times this Manichean world goes to its logical conclusion and dehumanizes the native, or to speak plainly, it turns him into an animal" (42). In Steel's novel, any desire on the part of the reader to see Jim's affair with Zora as even partially approaching an acceptable sexual relationship between two lovers is denied by Jim's use of the "colonial vocabulary" to describe Zora.

23 Alice ritually visits the grave of her long-dead baby. Furthermore, when she discovers that she is pregnant by Erlton (Kate's husband), she knows that she must divorce her husband and marry the father of her child, because motherhood is woman's first priority. Alice, who repudiates other forms of womanliness, dies saving a white baby. Zora's lack of any real sorrow at the death of her child signifies the colonized woman's "unnaturalness" and unmistakable "barbarism."

24 In this role, he anticpates Kipling's spy-hero Kim.

25 Nancy Paxton examines Steel's contradictory position as white feminist very much interpellated by racist, elitist, and imperialist ideologies. She describes Steel as gynephobic and suggests that she was afraid of female sexuality. According to Paxton, "Steel indicates her fear of uncontrolled female sexuality not only in her assessment of Indian society but describes it as a destructive force in Anglo-Indian society as well" ("Complicity and Resistance" 164).

26　In this she reminds me of Chatterjee's heroine Shanti.

27　In Bushby's tract on widow burning, the shedding of ornaments is emphasized as a crucial ritual for the woman ascending the funeral pyre of her husband.

CHAPTER THREE

Woman as Nation and a Nation of Women: Tagore's
The Home and the World and Hossain's *Sultana's Dream*

1　The novel was initially published in serial form in 1915 and in book form in India in 1916.

2　I will refer to Nikhilesh by the abbreviated form of his name, Nikhil.

3　In *The Rhetoric of English India*, Suleri posits that one needs to acknowledge the "striking symbolic homoeroticism of Anglo-Indian narrative" (17). She calls for a feminist reading of those narratives which construct the histories of the colonization of India that would complicate the "conventional interpretation of the confrontation between a dominating and a subordinated culture" (17) by resorting to the hegemonic trope of rape. She demands that a more complex "gendering of colonial cultural criticism" would need to take into consideration homoerotic sexual symbolism in all its racialized significations (17–19).

4　Partha Chatterjee, "Women and the Nation," in *Nation* 147.

5　Jahan 2.

6　Quoted in S. Sarkar, *Modern India* 107.

7　There are many critical historical accounts of the Swadeshi movement and its aftermath, too many to list here. A few that I have found most helpful include Leonard Gordon, *Bengal;* Sankar Ghose, *The Renaissance to Militant Nationalism in India* (Calcutta: Allied Publishers, 1969); Hasan; David Laushey, *Bengal Terrorism and the Marxist Left: Aspects of Regional Nationalism in India, 1905–1942* (Calcutta: Firma K. L. Mukhopadyay, 1975); S. Sarkar, *Swadeshi Movement;* S. Sarkar, *Modern India;* and J. N. Vajpeyi, *The Extremist Movement in India* (Allahabad: Chugh Publications, 1974).

8　Tagore's revivalist ideas were deeply embedded in the discourse of an Indian tradition in which the Hindu past is glorified in poetic language, reformed, and reconstituted to free it from the taint of barbarism and irrationality. See Tagore's "Samaj-bhed" and "Birodhmulak adrasa" (1901) in *Rabindra rachanabali*, vol. 10.

9　The literal translation of "atmasakti" would be "soul strength" or "inner strength."

10　Raja Rammohan Roy had challenged the orthodox Hindu mores by reforming Hinduism and forging a new identity through the introduction of a new religion, Brahmoism.

11　*Nationalism*, Tagore's collection of three essays, contains two other essays, "Nationalism in the West" and "Nationalism in Japan," and a long poem translated as "The Sunset of the Century." In "Nationalism in the West" Tagore discusses the manner in which India's confrontation with the British was different from its encounter with the Moguls. According to Tagore, "we (Indians) had known them (Moghuls) as human races . . . we had never known them as a nation" (4); with the British "we had to deal, not with kings, not with human races, but with a nation—we, who are no nation ourselves" (5). He then discusses at length the functionalist aspect of the British nation in India that works to undermine the "spirit of western civilization," concluding with a strong condemnation of the ideology of nationalism. In the essay on Japan, Tagore congratulates Japan for "never los[ing] her faith in her own soul, in the mere pride of her foreign acquisition" (33). He cautions against an easy imitation of the West even as he warns against a wholesale condemnation of the West. As he puts it, for Japan and by extension the East, "what is dangerous is not the imitation of the outer features of the west, but the acceptance of the motive force of the Western nationalim as her own" (47). Tagore again derides "nations who sedulously cultivate moral blindness as the cult of patriotism," thereby causing their demise in a "sudden and violent death" (47).

12   Nandy 19. For a critique of Gandhi's appropriation of the symbols and myths of female sexuality to structure his movement of passive resistance and his ambiguous mobilization of women for national liberation, see Ketu Katrak's nuanced essay "Indian Nationalism, Gandhian 'Satyagraha,' and Representations of Female Sexuality," in *Nationalisms and Sexualities*, ed. Andrew Parker et al. (New York: Routledge, 1992), 395–406.

13   Lazarus 199. Lazarus examines anti- (and post-) colonial nationalism and suggests the indispensability of national consciousness to the decolonizing projects (198).

14   Leonard Gordon, writing about Bankimchandra Chatterjee's novel *Anandamath*, points out that Bankim "fuses religious and patriotic symbolism as he mingles the two significant religious traditions of Bengal, Vaishnavism and Shaktism." Gordon provides a succinct summary of Shaktism that I quote at length: "The basic doctrine of Shaktism is that there is a power called 'shakti' underlying and energizing all reality. A female diety, who is usually a consort of Shiva—Durga, Kali, Chandi, or Shakti—may be understood to embody and express this power and may thus be worshipped as the single and highest diety. . . . The concept of shakti underlies a concept of physical strength that emerges as well in the writings of Vivekananda, Aurobindo Ghose, and Rabindranath Tagore" (80). We can see how many aspects of shaktism are manifested in Sandip's emblematization of Bimala as "Shakti" in Tagore's *The Home and the World*.

15   Tagore, "The Way to Get it Done," in *Greater India* 47–48, quoted in L. Gordon 86–87.

16   Tagore's choice of a high-caste Hindu woman is in keeping with his belief in the functionalist virtues of the caste system (see "Brahman," in *Rabindra rachana-*

bali, as well as his fundamental conviction that social change could be best effected from the top down.

17   Frantz Fanon in *The Wretched of the Earth* identifies the contradictory nature of the native intellectual who even when arguing for freedom from the colonizers ends up reconstructing the "superstructure." According to him the native bourgeoisie believes that "the essential qualities remain eternal in spite of all the blunders men may make: the essential qualities of the West, of course. The native intellectual accept[s] the cogency of these ideas, and deep down in his brain you [can] always find a vigilant sentinel ready to defend the Greco-Latin pedestal" (46). It is only when the intellectual regains contact with his people that this "sentinel is turned into dust" (46–47). Bimala has contact with only Nikhil and Sandip, both of whom embody Western notions of idealism, rationalism, and individuality. It is when Bimala meets Amulya and hears from him the truth about Sandip's so-called revolutionary tactics that she begins to formulate her own version of a call to arms in order to save the nation. To quote Fanon, Bimala becomes the type of native intellectual who "takes part in a sort of auto-da-fé, in the destruction of all his [*sic*] idols: egoism, recrimination that springs from pride, and the childish stupidity of those who always want to have the last word" (47).

18   Pateman has assessed one of the fundamental tenets of feminism to be "the dichotomy between the private and the public." She sees this as central "to almost two centuries of feminist struggle; it is, ultimately, what the feminist movement is about" (118).

19   On gender and the "women's question" in the nineteenth century, see Borthwick; P. Chatterjee, *Nation*; Chattopadhyay; Fruzzetti; Karlekar; Shudha Mazumdar, *A Pattern of Life: Memoirs of an Indian Woman*, trans. Geraldine Forbes (New Delhi: Manohar, 1977); Ghulam Murshid, *Reluctant Debutante: Responses of Bengali Women to Modernization, 1849–1905* (Rajshahi: Rajshahi University Press, 1983); Manisha Roy, *Bengali Women* (Chicago: Chicago University Press, 1992); S. Sarkar, *Critique*.

20   Liddle and Joshi provide a very readable history of the dynamic and complex progress of the Indian feminist movement. Besides identifying the contradictions that have beset the movement since its onset, they also provide interesting interviews with a number of representative women across the various classes and castes. The authors identify the "first wave" of the feminist movement as beginning in the first decade of the twentieth century, as opposed to Geraldine Forbes, who believes that the women's movement in India started in the 1880s. I would like to suggest that the women's question appeared as an issue as early as the 1850s and continued to surface sporadically.

21   Karlekar 9. Karlekar concentrates on autobiographical writings, which she calls personal narratives, "an important body of writings which can only be classified as exhortatory literature" (2). She argues that these women authors accepted the need to document the manner in which women's behavior was

subject to transformation as a result of social reforms that affected their lives. Karlekar asserts that a close reading of the texts that she has chosen to translate "helps in a reconstruction of femininity as seen from the point of view of the object, who now becomes a mediating subject" (5).

22 *Bhadramahila* is derived from *Bhadralok*, which has been variously translated as "middle class," "petty bourgeoisie," and "respectable folk."

23 P. Chatterjee, *Nation* 139. Chatterjee distinguishes between *atmacarit* and *smritikatha*. The first autobiographies that came to be written in the second half of the nineteenth century by men were called "atmacarit," a literal translation of the word "autobiography." But, as Chatterjee discusses, "it also carried, more significantly, an allusion to the entire body of carita literature of the classical and medieval eras in which the lives of kings and saints were recorded" (138). "Smritikatha," on the other hand, translates as "memoir"; as a distinctive literary genre, it combined the narrative of personal domestic history with the evolving social history of the time.

24 The anthology consists of six lectures delivered in America between 1920 and 1921. The essays—"What Is Art?" "The World of Personality," "The Second Birth," "My School," "Meditation," and "Woman"—address such varied issues as the nature of art, scientific facts and the creative personality, the supranatural world surrounding us, the philosophy behind Tagore's model school in Shantiniketan, Tagore's belief in the efficacy of meditation, and, finally, his categorization of the essential attributes of women. In all the essays, Tagore reifies the binary opposition between India (East) and the West by affirming an essential Indian core that has shaped his thoughts and attitudes on the above topics.

25 Tagore is insistent on the "depth of passiveness in woman's nature" in which the "potentiality of life is stored." He therefore criticizes what he terms the "restlessness" of women in the Western world as something that is not "the normal aspect of her nature." He feels that both men and women in the West are in constant search for new excitements and "condemn things that are commonplace." By "straining their powers to produce a spurious originality," they end up merely being surprised rather then satisfied. This is, according to him, particularly harmful for women because they have "the vital power more than men," and if they continuously "want something special and violent in their surroundings to keep their interests active [it] only prove[s] that they have lost touch with their own true world" (208–9).

26 There is a homosocial bond between the two that exists before Bimala enters the picture and survives throughout the tangled triadic relationship. In fact Bimala comes out of purdah for the first time to meet Sandip. The implications of the forging of bonds "between men" over women, so astutely analyzed by Eve Sedgwick in the context of Victorian literature, is quite obvious in this text.

27 Henry Schwarz reads the novel in terms of the "difficulty of adapting realism to the colonial context [because of] its unproblematic relationship to the real.

The reality produced by classic western realism is the western reality of a globally-dominant middle class patriarchy, not that of a subjugated and semi-feudal populace with its own specific structure of class and gender relations" ("Sexing the Pundits" 252). Thus Nikhil's equanimity, "which has often been identified with the author's, registers the empirical world with a confident neutrality and faith in the essential stability of the real, and asserts that the reformist tendencies of the semi-modern colonial domesticity emerging in upper class and upper caste Hindu homes can become the model for stucturing society in the outside world" (252).

28 Western adornment is, for example, seen as an artificial trapping that seduces men and sways women from their righteous marital path. When Bimala repents, she dresses simply in the natural fashion of an Indian woman as opposed to her previous vain indulgence in the latest fashions. The description of the countryside is full of expansive green fields and thatched cottages, and Panchu, a peasant, is depicted as a good-hearted, natural fellow. This description is opposed to the manipulations of Sandip and his followers, who constantly resort to artifice to obtain their goals. Finally, Sandip becomes the epitome of all that is artificial and false as we see him pore over the gold coins that Bimala has stolen from her husband to help the nationalist agenda.

29 Despite the conflicts that went on inside the zenana as depicted in the little skirmishes between Bimala and her widowed sister-in-law, there was also a deep respect for the elder women in the household in lieu of an explicit hierarchy.

30 One sees the similarity between the initial stages of a woman's movement in India and the feminist movement in Britain. From such patriarchal fathers as Ruskin to utilitarians like Mill to feminist-utilitarians such as Harriet Martineau, one constantly comes across the argument that women should be educated to make them better wives and mothers.

31 I am greatly indebted to Denise Riley's polemical tract *"Am I That Name?"* where she critiques the ground of both the historical construction of woman and the history of feminism. A number of the questions that I raise regarding the sociopolitical positions and subjectivity of Bimala are influenced as well by Riley's essay "A Short History of Some Preoccupations." In this essay she answers those critics who felt that her critiques of the category of woman, since it erased any possibility of a grounded notion of self-identity, eroded the fundamental value of feminism as politics. To those who raise this problem of identity, Riley poses this crucial question: Wouldn't a feminist politics be more effective "if you knew the different ways in which *you were likely to be heard*, what your assertion of identity was *doing*"? (122).

32 Once again we see an analogy being made between Bimala and Sandip in their aspect as destroyer, a characteristic also of the female goddess in its many incarnations.

33 Bakhtin has pointed out how every character in a novel inhabits a "zone" which is both verbally and semantically autonomous and which is also influ-

enced by the various other zones so that no character's language is ever mono-logic. His theory of dialogic interaction also suggests that a character's voice always encroaches on that of the author as a result of which the author's inten-tion is continuously refracted in and through the zones of the characters she or he creates. What is even more cogent and relevant is that although "hetero-glossia in the novel is by and large always personified and incarnated in indi-vidual human figures" (*Dialogic Imagination* 326), they are simultaneously "submerged in social heteroglossia, . . . [and] reconceptualized through it. Op-positions between individuals are only surface upheavals of the untamed ele-ments in social heteroglossia, surface manifestation of those elements that play on such individual oppositions, make them contradictory, saturate their con-sciousness and discourses with more fundamental speech diversity" (326). Of course, speech is continuously extended in Bakhtin and among Bakhtinians to incorporate various discursive practices.

34 The absence of the red sindoor (vermilion powder) and the white sari was and, in Bengal, continues to be the traditional garb of widows.

35 Jahan 3. For an account of her role as a pioneer Muslim feminist, see Hossain 3–12. According to Hossain, Rokeya started the movement for the emancipa-tion of Bengali Muslim women. Hossain examines Rokeya's first complete work, *Maticur*, which is a collection of essays published between 1903 and 1904 and contains, according to Hossain, "Begum Rokeya's best feminist ide-als and thoughts" (5).

36 For a study of the status and role of Muslim women in India that takes into ac-count the historical context of political, economic, and social changes initiated in the nineteenth century, see Lateef.

37 Roushan Jahan, *"The Secluded Ones"*: Purdah Observed, in Hossain 20.

38 This should not prevent us from imagining Ladyland as a feminist utopia de-picting a generalized futuristic space.

39 Hossain's belief in the positive benefits of technology is not something to which we can now subscribe that easily. Our awareness of the exploitation of women through technology makes us wary of equating women's liberation with a knowledge of science and mathematics. However, during Hossain's time, when women were discouraged from learning mathematics, her insistence on women's mental abilities needs to be read as an affirmation of woman's equal-ity in all spheres.

40 Darjeeling is a hill station in the northern part of what is now West Bengal.

41 *Mard* in both Bengali and certain other North Indian languages translates as "men."

42 In her essay "Beyond Defensivenes," Daphne Patai cites Victor Shklovsky's no-tion of defamiliarization, as elaborated in his essay "Art as Technique," as a key device used in utopian fiction.

43 For a very different ideological analysis of the future of patriotism beyond the hyphenated union of nation and state in an American context, see Appadurai.

CHAPTER FOUR
New Women, New Nations: Writing the Partition in Desai's
Clear Light of Day and Sidhwa's *Cracking India*

1 The term "third world" is still highly contentious and its significations never absolute. The essays I discuss seek to highlight the dubious and unstable nature of the category by putting it within either quotation marks or parenthesis; Jameson often capitalizes the two words, which lends it much more stability and authority than I find desirable. Even as I recognize the provisionality of the semiotic status of the formulation third world, I choose to make the essay less cumbersome by erasing the quotation marks around this much beleaguered category.

2 Besides Ahmad's and Prasad's essays that I briefly discuss here, see Schwarz, "Provocations" 177–201. For an elaborate exchange of often divergent positions regarding the phenomena of nationalism, see Balibar and Wallerstein. Except for one essay by Wallerstein titled "The Ideological Tensions of Capitalism: Universalism versus Racism and Sexism," which suffers from a formulaic marxist reductivism, the remaining essays fail to address the simultaneous polarization and congruence of the categories of gender and nation. In "The Island and the Aeroplane," on the contrary, Gillian Beer brilliantly explores the gendered mapping of political space in the interstices of patriarchy and imperialism. For a provocative though brief essay on the politics of citizenship, see Mouffe, as well as the "discussion" that follows the essay. I have deliberately mentioned only some of the more recent contributions because the list is too cumbersome. Any one of the books or articles mentioned provides extensive references.

3 Anita Desai belongs to the second generation of Indian authors writing in English, and after Rushdie she is probably the most recognized both in India and abroad. Her first novel, *Cry the Peacock*, was published in 1963. The first generation of authors writing in English began to work in the 1930s. They included Raja Rao, R. K. Narayan, Mulk Raj Ananad, and G. V. Desani. Anita Desai is a particularly interesting figure; with a Bengali father and a German mother, she grew up in Delhi, where she has lived for most of her life and which she still calls home.

4 The anthology *Nationalisms and Sexualities* is a groundbreaking collection that explores the intersections of the discourses of gender, sexuality, and nationality in diverse areas. A few of the essays pertinent to the issue of gender and nationalism in third world cultural productions include those by R. Radhakrishnan; Gayatri C. Spivak, "Women in Difference: Mahashweta Devi's 'Douliti the Bountiful'"; Geraldine Heng and Janadas Devan, "State Fatherhood: The Politics of Nationalism, Sexuality, and Race in Singapore"; Ketu Katrak, "Indian Nationalism, Gandhian 'Satyagraha,' and Representations of Female Sexuality"; Mary Layoun, "Telling Spaces: Palestinian Women and the

Engendering of National Narratives"; and Valentine M. Moghadam "Revolution, Islam, and Women: Sexual Politics in Iran and Afghanistan."

5   Fanon, in *Black Skin, White Masks,* presents an elaborate psychoanalytic study of the relations between black men and white women, black women and white men, and black men and white men, uncovering the complex ways in which "discourses of rationality are forced to give figurative articulation to the nightmares that the dreams of colonial rationalism may produce, thus indicating the gender imbrication implicit in the classification of culture as an anxious provenance partitioned between the weakness and strength of men" (Suleri 17). In *The Wretched of the Earth* Fanon also discusses the manifestations of male sexuality in relations between the colonizer and colonized. The chapters titled "Concerning Violence," "On National Culture," and "Colonial War and Mental Disorders" are particularly relevant.

6   Malek Alloula's *The Colonial Harem* is one such excellent study that unravels the various modes and nodes of transformation of the colonial scene by collecting, arranging, and annotating picture postcards of Algerian women produced by the French in Algeria during the first thirty years of the twentieth century. As Barbara Harlow writes in her introduction, *The Colonial Harem* does not merely expose the analogical links that connect "the imperializing project of colonizing other lands and peoples with the phantasm of appropriation of the veiled, exotic female. The similarity between penetrating the secret, tantalizing recesses of the harem and making the masquerading pilgrimmage to Mecca and the holy Kaaba of Islam, which nineteenth-century travellers . . . did, reveals the many guises under which imperialism penetrated the Arab world" (xvi).

7   For a historical account of the birth of Pakistan, see Chaudhri Muhammad Ali, *The Emergence of Pakistan* (New York: Columbia University Press, 1967). For a different analysis of Hindu-Muslim discord in India that goes beyond the usual theories—that the intrinsic hostility between the two religious groups was heightened during the heyday of colonial rule with the prospect of independence bringing this hostility to the forefront, and that the British, faced with a rising anticolonial movement, deliberately heightened minor differences to hold on to their Indian colony—see Syed Nassar Ahmad, who seeks to explain the growth of Muslim consciousness in India in terms of the rise of the capitalist world economy in the sixteenth century, which was instrumental in its creation of "peoples." His argument is "that the initial cultural differences between the Hindus and Muslims widened and gained social significance as a consequence of the structural impact of India's integration into the world system" (1).

8   For an interesting account of the role of the Parsis in Indian politics and society, see Eckehard Kulke's *The Parsees in India.* In this study Kulke documents the fact that the Parsi community, which had lived relatively unnoticed in India for over a thousand years, showed remarkable changes after the advent of the British. He examines, among other things, the role of the Parsis in Indian politics on the local, national, and imperial levels.

9   The in-between status of the Parsi community is caught in a brilliant serio-comic moment very early in the novel. Colonel Barucha, Lenny's surgeon as well as the local leader of the Parsi community, in an attempt to console Lenny's mother, who blames herself for her daughter's affliction, "roars a shocking postscript: 'If anyone's to blame, blame the British! There was no polio in India till they brought it here!'" (25). Lenny is aghast at this criticism of the British and narrates: "As far as I am concerned this is insurgence—an open declaration of war by the two hundred Parsees of Lahore of the British Empire! I am shocked because Colonel Barucha is the president of our community in Lahore. And, except for a few designated renegades, the Parsees have been careful to adopt a discreet and politically naive profile" (26).

10 Early in the novel, after Lenny's cast has been removed, she recollects a child-hood nightmare in which children are dismembered in a warehouse: "Children lie in a warehouse. Mother and Ayah move about solicitously. The atmosphere is businesslike and relaxed. Godmother sits by my bed smiling indulgently as men in uniforms quietly slice off a child's arm here, a leg there. She strokes my head as they dismember me. I feel no pain. Only an abysmal sense of loss—and a chilling horror that no one is concerned by what's happening" (31).

11 For a succinct definition of ethnic groups and their relationship to the nation, see Kellas, esp. chap. 8. Kellas attempts to do the impossible—assess the complex inter- and intrarelations between ethnicity and nationalism in the world in about two hundred pages. Despite my many problems with Kellas's book, I find his denotation of the term "ethnic group" helpful: "'Ethnic group' and 'ethnocentrism' are comparable with 'nation' and 'nationalism.' The difference between them is that 'ethnic group' is more narrowly defined than 'nation,' and 'ethnocentrism' is more rooted in social psychology than is 'nationalism,' which has explicit ideological and political dimensions. Ethnic groups are generally differentiated from nations on several dimensions: they are usually smaller; they are more clearly based on a common ancestry; and they are more pervasive in human history, while nations are perhaps specific to time and place. Ethnic groups are essentially *exclusive* or *ascriptive*, meaning that membership in such groups is confined to those that share inborn attributes. Nations on the other hand are more *inclusive* and are culturally or politically defined. However, it is often possible to trace the origins of nationalism to ethnic groups or their ethnocentric behavior" (4).

12 Early in the novel the connections between ethnicity (or regionalism), class, and gender are raised in a conversation between Ice-candy-man and Ayah. Ayah, we are told, is a Punjabi, but she chooses not to wear "Punjabi" clothes because that would mark her as a cheaper commodity in the employment market. As she says: "Do you know what salary ayahs who wear Punjabi clothes get? Half the salary of the Goan Ayahs who wear saris!" (38). If the sari increases her worth in the labor market, it also makes her more accessible to men's sexual advances. A conversation about regional identity soon turns into

a comic scene of sexual foreplay when Ice-candy-man's "ingenuous toes dart beneath Ayah's sari" (38). Ayah soon puts a stop to this, and at Ice-candy-man's disingenuous question, "Are you angry?" Ayah retorts brusquely, "You have no sense and no shame!" (38). Later in the novel, this droll exchange becomes ominous when Ice-candy-man betrays Ayah as an impure Hindu woman to the violent mob.

13 Ice-candy-man, whom the young Lenny recognizes as friend, seduces her into betraying the whereabouts of Ayah.

14 See Dieter Reimenschneider, "History and the Individual in Anita Desai's *Clear Light of Day* and Salman Rushdie's *Midnight Children*," *World Literature in English* 23 (1984): 196–207; Graham Huggan, "Philomela's Retold Story: Silence, Music, and the Post-Colonial Text," *Journal of Commonwealth Literature* 25 (1990): 12–23; Alamgir Hashmi, "*Clear Light of Day* between India and Pakistan," in *The New Indian Novel in English: A Study of the 1980s*, ed. Viney Kirpal (New Delhi: Allied Publishers, 1990), 65–72; and Shirley Chew, "Searching Voices: Anita Desai's *Clear Light of Day* and Nayantara Sahgal's *Rich Like Us*," in Nasta 43–63. The last essay is particularly provocative in its use of Spivak's "Rani of Sirmur" essay as a theoretical tool for an illustration of the character of the widowed aunt.

15 Certain other texts could also generate interesting readings: Ama Ata Aidoo's *Our Sister Killjoy* (Ghana); Merle Collins's *Angel* (Grenada); Bessie Head's *A Question of Power* (South Africa, Botswana); and Sara Suleri's *Meatless Days* (Pakistan), to name just four.

16 See Liddle and Joshi for a full-scale discussion of the rise and sporadic development of the feminist movement in India.

17 Tara's desire to return in order to stay in touch with "eternal India" echoes the desire of many Indian immigrants in North America who continue to have close ties with their "homeland." In some ways Bakul's treatment of his wife and his ideas of what an Indian woman should be and reflect parallel those of the Indian ambassador in the anecdote with which I began this book.

18 I thank Samir Dayal for drawing my attention to this passage.

19 Assia Djebar, as quoted by Barbara Harlow in her introduction to Alloula on page xxii.

20 The plight of two Misra sisters is similarly shelved and also undercuts the finality of the too easily achieved harmonious ending of the novel. These two married sisters are forced to return to their father's house because they have failed to produce children. They keep house and eke out a living for their family—the brothers either squander money on ridiculous business ventures or in their endless pursuit of the excellence of Indian classical music—by teaching music and dance to young children. We are never quite sure of their marital status because the text never makes clear if they are actually divorced. Their husbands, one presumes, have married again and are living a comfortable and probably bigamous life.

1   Back cover blurb, *Granta* 57 (spring 1997); Ian Jack, introduction, *Granta* 57 (spring 1997): 10.

2   In this context one could (should?) take seriously Spivak's recommendation that "in the post-colonial context, the teaching of English literature can become critical only if it is intimately yoked to the teaching of the literary and cultural production in the mother tongue(s). In that persistently asymmetrical intimacy, the topos of language learning, in its various forms, can become a particularly productive site" ("Burden of English" 295).

WORKS CITED

Ahmad, Aijaz. "Jameson's Rhetoric of Otherness and the 'National Allegory.'" *Social Text* 17 (1987): 3–25.

Ahmad, Syed Nassar. *Origins of Muslim Consciousness in India: A World System Perspective*. New York: Greenwood, 1991.

Alloula, Malek. *The Colonial Harem*. Trans. Myrna Godzich and Wlad Godzich. Minneapolis: University of Minnesota Press, 1986.

Anderson, Benedict. *Imagined Communities*. Rev. ed. New York: Verso, 1991.

Appadurai, Arjun. "The Heart of Whiteness." *Callaloo* 16 (1993): 796–807.

Bagchi, Jasodhara. "Positivism and Nationalism: Womanhood and Crisis in Nationalist Fiction; Bankimchandra's *Anandamath*." *Economic and Political Weekly* 20 (1985): 60–65.

———. "Secularism as Identity: The Case of Tagore's *Gora*." In *The Nation, The State, and Indian Identity*. Ed. Madhusree Dutta, Flavia Agnes, and Neera Adarkar. Calcutta: Samya, 1996. 47–67.

Bakhtin, Mikhail. *The Dialogic Imagination: Four Essays by M. M. Bakhtin*. Ed. Michael Holquist. Trans. Caryl Emerson and Michael Holquist. Austin: University of Texas Press, 1981.

———. *Rabelais and his World*. Trans. Helene Iswolsky. Cambridge: M.I.T. Press, 1968.

Balachandran, G. "Religion and Nationalism in Modern India." In *Unravelling the Nation: Sectarian Conflict and India's Secular Identity*. Ed. Kaushik Basu and Sanjay Subrahmanyam. New Delhi: Penguin, 1996. 81–128.

Balibar, Etienne, and Immanuel Wallerstein. *Race, Nation, Class: Ambiguous Identities*. Trans. Chris Turner. London: Verso, 1991.

Bauer, Dale. *Feminist Dialogics: A Theory of Failed Community*. Albany: State University of New York Press, 1988.

Beer, Gillian. "The Island and the Aeroplane: The Case of Virginia Woolf." In *Nation and Narration*. Ed. Homi Bhabha. New York: Routledge, 1990. 265–90.

Behdad, Ali. *Belated Travelers: Orientalism in the Age of Colonial Dissolution.* Durham: Duke University Press, 1994.

Bentinck, William Cavendish. *The Correspondence of Lord William Cavendish Bentinck.* Ed. C. H. Philips. Vol. 1. Oxford: Oxford University Press, 1977.

Bloom, Allan. *The Closing of the American Mind.* New York: Simon and Schuster, 1987.

Boehmer, Elleke. "Stories of Women and Mothers: Gender and Nationalism in the Early Fiction of Flora Nwapa." In *Motherlands: Black Women's Writing from Africa, the Caribbean, and South Asia.* Ed. Susheela Nasta. New Brunswick: Rutgers University Press, 1992. 3–23.

Borthwick, Meredith. *The Changing Role of Women in Bengal, 1849–1905.* Princeton: Princeton University Press, 1984.

Bose, Sumantra. "'Indian Nationalism' and The Crisis of the Indian State: A Theoretical Perspective." In *Nationalism, Democracy, and Development.* Ed. Sugata Bose and Ayesha Jalal. Delhi: Oxford University Press, 1977. 106–70.

Brantlinger, Patrick. *Rule of Darkness: British Literature and Imperialism, 1830–1914.* Ithaca: Cornell University Press, 1988.

Brennan, Timothy. "The National Longing for Form." In *Nation and Narration.* Ed. Homi Bhabha. New York: Routledge, 1990. 44–70.

Burton, Antoinette. *Burdens of History: British Feminists, Indian Women, and Imperial Culture, 1865–1915.* Chapel Hill: University of North Carolina Press, 1994.

Bushby, Henry Jeffreys. *Widow-Burning: A Narrative.* London: Longman, Brown, Green and Longmans, 1855.

Butler, Judith. *Bodies That Matter: On the Discursive Limits of "Sex."* New York: Routledge, 1993.

———. "Imitation and Gender Insubordination." In *Inside/Out: Lesbian Theories, Gay Theories.* Ed. Diana Fuss. New York: Routledge, 1991. 13–31.

Certeau, Michel de. *The Writing of History.* Trans. Tom Conley. New York: Columbia University Press. 1988.

Chadra, Sudhir. *The Oppressive Present: Literature and Social Consciousness in Colonial India.* Delhi: Oxford University Press, 1992.

Chakravorty, Dipesh. "Marx after Marxism: Subaltern Histories and the Question of Difference." *Polygraph* 6–7 (1993): 5–15.

Chatterjee, Bankimchandra. *Anandamath.* Trans. Sree Aurobindo and Sree Barindra Kumar Ghosh. Calcutta: Basumati Sahitya Mandi, [1909?].

———. *Anandamath.* Trans. and Adapted by Basanta Koomar Ray. 1909. Reprint, New Delhi: Vision, 1992.

———. *Devi Chaudhurani.* Trans. Sobodh Chunden Mitter. Calcutta: Chuckervorty, Chatterjee, 1946.

———. *Letters on Hinduism and Devi Chaudhurani.* Calcutta: n.p., 1940, 1949 [?].

———. "Samya." Trans. M. K. Haldar. In *Renaissance and Reaction in Nineteenth-Century Bengal.* Calcutta: Minerva, 1977. 187–99.

————. "Sankhyadarshan." In *Bankim rachanaballi*. Ed. Joges Chandra Bagchi. Vol. 2. Calcutta: Sahitya Samsad, 1965. 221–34.

Chatterjee, Partha. *The Nation and Its Fragments: Colonial and Postcolonial Histories*. Princeton: Princeton University Press, 1993.

————. *Nationalist Thought and the Colonial World: A Derivative Discourse*. Minneapolis: University of Minnesota Press, 1993.

Chattopadhyay, Kamaladevi. *Indian Women's Battle for Freedom*. Delhi: Abhinav Publications, 1983.

Chaudhri, Muhammad Ali. *The Emergence of Pakistan*. New York: Columbia University Press, 1967.

Cixous, Hélène. "The Laugh of the Medusa." In *New French Feminisms: An Anthology*. Ed. Elaine Marks and Isabelle de Courtivron. New York: Schocken, 1981. 245–67.

Cobham, Rhonda. "Misgendering the Nation: African Nationalist Fictions and Nuruddin Farah's *Maps*." In *Nationalisms and Sexualities*. Ed. Andrew Parker et al. New York: Routledge, 1992. 42–59.

Cohen, Joshua. "Editor's Note." *Boston Review* 19 (1994): 3.

Court, Dianne Griffin. "Separatism and Feminist Utopian Fiction." In *Sexual Practice, Textual Theory: Lesbian Cultural Criticism*. Ed. Susan J. Wolfe and Julia Penelope Stanley. Oxford: Blackwell, 1993. 235–48.

Courtwright, Paul B. "The Iconographies of Sati." In *Sati the Blessing and the Curse: The Burning of Wives in India*. Ed. John Stratton Hawley. Oxford: Oxford University Press, 1994. 27–48.

David, Deirdre. *Intellectual Women and Victorian Patriarchy: Harriet Martineau, Elizabeth Barrett Browning, George Eliot*. Ithaca: Cornell University Press, 1987.

Derrida, Jacques. *Margins of Philosophy*. Trans. Alan Bass. Chicago: University of Chicago Press, 1982.

Desai, Anita. *Clear Light of Day*. London: Penguin, 1980.

Doane, Mary Anne. "Film and Masquerade: Theorizing the Female Spectator." *Screen* 23 (1982): 74–87.

Elam, Diane. *Feminism and Deconstruction: Ms. en Abyme*. New York: Routledge, 1994.

Embree, Ainslie T. *Imagining India*. Delhi: Oxford University Press, 1989.

Fanon, Frantz. *Black Skin, White Masks*. New York: Grove, 1967.

————. *The Wretched of the Earth*. Trans. Constance Farrington. New York: Grove, 1968.

Fitting, Peter. "The Turn from Utopia in Recent Feminist Fiction." In *Feminism, Utopia, and Narrative*. Ed. Libby Falk Jones and Sarah Webster Goodwin. Knoxville: University of Tennessee Press, 1990. 141–58.

Fludernik, Monika. "Suttee Revisited: From the Iconography of Martyrdom to the Burkean Sublime and the Discourse of the Sentimental Novel in Representations of Widow Immolation." 1996.

Foucault, Michel. "Governmentality." In *The Foucault Effect*. Ed. Graham Burchell et al. London: Harvester Wheatsheaf, 1991. 67–82.

———. *History of Sexuality*. Vol 1. Trans. R. Hurley. London: Allan Lane, 1979.

Fruzzetti, Lina. *The Gift of a Virgin: Women, Marriage, and Ritual in a Bengali Society*. Delhi: Oxford University Press, 1990.

Glazener, Nancy. "Dialogic Subversion: Bakhtin, the Novel, and Gertrude Stein." In *Bakhtin and Cultural Theory*. Ed. Ken Hirschkop and David Shepherd. Manchester: Manchester University Press, 1989. 109–29.

Gordon, Deborah. "Writing Culture, Writing Feminism: The Poetics and Politics of Experimental Ethnography." *Inscriptions* 3–4 (1988): 7–24.

Gordon, Leonard. *Bengal: The Nationalist Movement, 1876–1940*. New York: Columbia University Press, 1974.

Grewal, Inderpal. *Home and Harem: Nation, Gender, Empire, and the Cultures of Travel*. Durham: Duke University Press, 1996.

Grewal, Inderpal, and Caren Kaplan, eds. *Scattered Hegemonies: Postmodernity and Transnational Feminist Practices*. Minneapolis: University of Minnesota Press, 1994.

Guha, Ranajit. *An Indian Historiography of India: A Nineteenth-Century Agenda and Its Implications*. Calcutta: K. P. Bagchi, 1988.

Gupta, Brijen. *India in English Fiction, 1800–1970: An Annotated Bibliography*. Metuchen, N.J.: Scarecrow, 1973.

Haldar, M. K. *Renaissance and Reaction in Nineteenth-Century Bengal*. Calcutta: Minerva Associates, 1977.

Hasan, Mushirul. *Nationalism and Communal Politics in India, 1916–1928*. Delhi: Manohar Publications, 1979.

Hawley, John Stratton. "Introduction." In *Sati, the Blessing and the Curse: The Burning of Wives in India*. Ed. John Stratton Hawley. Oxford: Oxford University Press, 1994. 3–26.

hooks, bell. *Art on My Mind: Visual Politics*. New York: New Press, 1995.

Hossain, Rokeya Sakhawat. *"Sultana's Dream" and Selections from "The Secluded Ones."* Ed. and trans. Roushan Jahan. New York: Feminist Press, 1988.

Huggan, Graham. "Decolonizing the Map: Post-Colonialism, Post Structuralism, and the Cartographic Condition." In *Past the Last Post: Theorizing Post-Colonialism and Post-Modernism*. Ed. Ian Adams and Helen Tiffin. Alberta: University of Calgary Press, 1990. 125–38.

Hunter, William W. *The Annals of Rural Bengal*. Vols. 1, 7. London: Smith, Elder, 1897.

Husain, Shahanara. "Begum Rokeya Sakhawat Hossain: Pioneer Muslim Feminist of Bengal." In *Women, Development, Devotionalism, Nationalism: Bengal Studies, 1985*. Ed. John Thorp. East Lansing: Michigan State University Press. 3–12.

Inden, Ronald. *Imagining India*. Oxford: Blackwell, 1990.

Jahan, Roushan. *"Sultana's Dream": Purdah Reversed*. In *"Sultana's Dream" and Selections from "The Secluded Ones."* Ed. and trans. Roushan Jahan. New York: Feminist Press, 1988.

Jayawardena, Kumari. *Feminism and Nationalism in the Third World*. London: Zed, 1986.

Jussawalla, Feroza, and Reed Way Dasenbrock, eds. *Interviews with Writers of the Post-Colonial World*. Jackson: University Press of Mississippi, 1992.

Kandiyoti, Deniz. Introduction. *Woman, Islam, and the State*. Ed. Deniz Kandiyoti. Philadelphia: Temple University Press, 1992. 1–15.

Karlekar, Malavika. *Voices from Within: Early Personal Narratives of Bengali Women*. Delhi: Oxford University Press, 1991.

Kaur, Manmohan. *Role of Women in the Freedom Movement (1857–1947)*. Delhi: Sterling Publishers, 1968.

Kaviraj, Sudipta. *The Unhappy Consciousness: Bankimchandra Chattopadhyay and the Formation of Nationalist Discourse in India*. Delhi: Oxford Univerity Press, 1995.

Kellas, James G. *The Politics of Nationalism and Ethnicity*. New York: St. Martin's, 1991.

Kulke, Eckehard. *The Parsees in India: A Minority as Agent of Social Change*. Munich: Weltforum Verlag, 1974.

Ladendorf, Janet. *Revolt in India, 1857–58*. Zug, Switzerland: Inter Documentation, 1966.

Lateef, Shahida. *Muslim Women in India: Political and Private Realities*. London: Zed, 1990.

Lazarus, Neil. "National Consciousness and the Specificity of (Post)Colonial Intellectualism." In *Colonial Discourse/Postcolonial Theory*. Ed. Francis Barker, Peter Hume, and Margaret Iverson. Manchester: Manchester University Press, 1994. 197–220.

Lebra-Chapman, Joyce. *The Rani of Jhansi: A Study of Female Heroism in India*. Honolulu: University of Hawai'i Press, 1986.

Leonard, Gordon. *Bengal: The Nationalist Movement, 1876–1940*. New York: Columbia University Press, 1974.

Liddle, Joanna, and Rama Joshi. *Daughters of Independence: Gender, Caste, and Class in India*. London: Zed, 1986.

Low, Gail Ching-Liang. "White Skin/Black Masks: The Pleasures and Politics of Imperialism." *New Formations* 9 (1989): 80–94.

Macaulay, Thomas B. *The Works of Lord Macaulay*. Vol. 1. Ed. Lady Trevelyan. London: Longmans, Green, 1866.

Mani, Lata. "The Construction of Women as Tradition in Early-Nineteenth-Century Bengal." In *Cultural Critique* 7 (1987): 119–56.

———. "Cultural Theory, Colonial Texts: Reading Eyewitness Accounts of Widow Burning." In *Cutural Studies*. Ed. Cary Nelson and Lawrence Grossberg. New York: Routledge, 1992. 392–404.

———. "The Production of an Official Discourse on Sati in Early-Nineteenth-Century Bengal." In *Europe and Its Others*. Vol. 1. Ed. Francis Barker et al. Colchester: University of Essex, 1984. 107–27.

Martin, Biddy. "Feminism, Criticism, and Foucault." In *Feminism and Foucault: Reflections on Resistance*. Ed. Irene Diamond and Lee Quinby. Boston: Northeastern University Press, 1988. 3–20.

Martineau, Harriet. *British Rule in India: A Historical Sketch*. London: Smith, Elder, 1857.

———. *Eastern Life, Present and Past*. 3 vols. London: Edward Moxon, 1848.

———. *Illustrations of Political Economy*. 9 vols. London: Charles Fox, 1832.

———. *Society in America*. 3 vols. London: Saunders and Otley, 1839.

Mazumdar, Sucheta. "For Rama and Hindutva: Women and Right-Wing Mobilization in Contemporary India." *Committee on South Asian Women Bulletin* 8 (1996): 4–5.

McBratney, John. "Images of Indian Women in Rudyard Kipling: A Case of Doubling Discourse." *Inscriptions* 3/4 (1988): 47–57.

McClintock, Anne. *Imperial Leather*. New York: Routledge, 1995.

Memi, Albert. *The Colonizer and the Colonized*. Boston: Beacon, 1967.

Mohanty, S. P. "Us and Them: On The Philosophical Bases of Political Criticism." *Yale Journal of Criticism* 4 (1989): 5.

Montrose, Louis A. "Professing the Renaissance: The Poetics and Politics of Culture." In *The New Historicism*. Ed. H. Abraham Veeser. New York: Routledge, 1989. 15–36.

Mosse, George. *Nationalism and Sexuality: Middle-Class Morality and Sexual Norms in Modern Europe*. Madison: University of Wisconsin Press, 1985.

Mouffe, Chantal. "Citizenship and Political Identity." *October* 16 (1992): 28–32.

Mukherjee, Meenakshi. *Realism and Reality: The Novel and Society in India*. Delhi: Oxford University Press, 1994.

Nandy, Ashis. *The Illegitimacy of Nationalism: Rabindranath Tagore and the Politics of Self*. Delhi: Oxford University Press, 1994.

———. *The Intimate Enemy: Loss and Recovery of Self under Colonialism*. Delhi: Oxford University Press, 1983.

Nasta, Susheila. Introduction. *Motherlands: Black Women's Writing from Africa, the Caribbean and South Asia*. Ed. Susheila Nasta. New Brunswick: Rutgers University Press, 1992. xiii–xxx.

Nodia, Ghia. "Nationalism, Ethnic Conflict, and Democracracy." In *Nations and Ethnic Conflict*. Ed. Charles P. Cozic. San Diego: Greenhaven, 1994.

Nussbaum, Martha. "Patriotism and Cosmopolitanism." *Boston Review* 19 (1994): 6–7.

Padikkal, Shivarama. "Inventing Modernity: The Emergence of the Novel in India." In *Interrogating Modernity: Culture and Colonialism in India*. Ed. Tejaswani Niranjana, P. Sudhir, and Vivek Dhareshwar. Calcutta: Seagull, 1993. 220–72.

Pandey, Gyanendra. *The Construction of Communalism in Colonial North India.* New Delhi: Oxford University Press, 1990.

Parker, Andrew, et al. Introduction. *Nationalisms and Sexualities.* Ed. Andrew Parker, et al. New York: Routledge, 1992. 1–20.

Parry, Benita. *Delusions and Discoveries: Studies on India in the British Imagination, 1880–1930.* London: Allen Lane, 1972.

Patai, Daphne. "Beyond Defensiveness: Feminist Research Strategies." In *Women and Utopia: Critical Interpretations.* Ed. Marleen Barr and Nicholas Smith. New York: University Press of America, 1983. 148–69.

Pateman, Carol. *The Disorder of Women: Democracy, Feminism, and Political Theory.* Cambridge: Polity, 1989.

Paxton, Nancy L. "Complicity and Resistance in the Writings of Flora Annie Steel and Annie Besant." In *Western Women and Imperialism.* Ed. Nupur Chaudhuri and Margaret Strobel. Bloomington: Indiana University Press, 1992. 159–76.

———. "Mobilizing Chivalry: Rape in British Novels about the Indian Uprising of 1857." *Victorian Studies* 36 (1992): 5–30.

Peggs, J. *The Suttee's Cry to Britain.* London: Seely and Son, 1828.

Prasad, Madhava. "On the Question of a Theory of (Third World) Literature." *Social Text* 31–32 (1992): 57–83.

Pratt, Mary Louise. *Imperial Eyes: Travel Writing and Transculturation.* New York: Routledge, 1992.

Radhakrishnan, R. "Nationalism, Gender, and the Narrative of Identity." In *Nationalisims and Sexualities.* Ed. Andrew Parker et al. New York: Routledge, 1992. 77–95.

———. "Postcoloniality and the Boundaries of Identity." *Callaloo* 14 (fall 1993).

Rajan, Rajeswari Sunder. Introduction to "Gender in the Making: Indian Contexts." *Thamyris* 4 (spring 1997).

———. *Real and Imagined Women: Gender, Culture, and Postcolonialism.* New York: Routledge, 1993.

———. "The Subject of Sati: Pain and Death in Contemporary Discourse on Sati." *Yale Journal of Criticism* 3 (1990): 1–27.

Ranciere, Jacques. "Politics, Identity, and Subjectivization." *October* 16 (1992): 58–64.

Ratte, Lou. "A Dangerous Alliance: Anglo-Indian Literary Criticism and Bengali Literary Production." *Genders* 2 (1988): 42–59.

Raychaudhuri, Tapan. *Europe Reconsidered: Perceptions of the West in Nineteenth-Century Bengal.* Delhi: Oxford University Press, 1988.

Renan, Ernest. "What Is a Nation?" In *Nation and Narration.* Ed. Homi Bhabha. New York: Routledge, 1990. 8–22.

Riley, Denise. *"Am I That Name?" Feminism and the Category of "Women" in History.* Minneapolis: University of Minnesota Press, 1988.

————. "A Short History of Some Preoccupations." In *Feminists Theorize the Political*. Ed. Judith Butler and Joan W. Scott. New York: Routledge, 1992. 121–29.

Roy, Tapti. "Disciplining the Printed Text: Colonial and Nationalist Surveillance of Bengali Literature." In *Texts of Power: Emerging Disciplines in Colonial Bengal*. Ed. Partha Chatterjee. Minneapolis: University of Minnesota Press, 1995. 30–62.

Russo, Mary. "Female Grotesques: Carnival and Theory." In *Feminist Studies/Critical Studies*. Ed. Teresa de Lauretis. Madison: University of Wisconsin Press, 1986. 213–29.

Sabin, Margery. "The Suttee Romance." *Raritan* 11.2 (1991): 1–24.

Said, Edward W. *Culture and Imperialism*. New York: Alfred Knopf, 1993.

————. *Orientalism*. New York: Vintage, 1979.

Sangari, Kumkum, and Sudesh Vaid. Introduction. *Recasting Women: Essays in Indian Colonial History*. Ed. Kumkum Sangari and Sudesh Vaid. New Brunswick: Rutgers University Press, 1990. 1–26.

Sarkar, Sumit. *A Critique of Colonial India*. Calcutta: Papyrus, 1985.

————. *Modern India, 1885–1947*. Madras: Macmillan, 1983.

————. *The Swadeshi Movement in Bengal, 1903–1908*. Delhi: People's Publishing House, 1973.

Sarkar, Tanika. "Bankimchandra and the Impossibility of a Political Agenda." *Oxford Literary Review* 16 (1994): 177–204.

————. "The Woman as Communal Subject: Rashtasevika Samiti and Ram Janmabhoomi Movement." *Economic and Political Weekly* (1991): 2057–62.

Saunders, Rebecca. "Gender, Colonialism, and Exile: Flora Annie Steel and Sara Jeanette Duncan in India." In *Women's Writing in Exile*. Ed. Mary Lynn Broe and Angela Ingram. Chapel Hill: University of North Carolina Press, 1989. 303–24.

Schwarz, Henry. "Provocations towards a Theory of Third World Literature." *Mississippi Review* 49–50 (1989): 177–201.

————. "Sexing the Pundits: Gender, Romance, and Realism in the Cultural Politics of Colonial Bengal." In *Reading the Shape of the World: Toward an International Cultural Studies*. Ed. Henry Schwarz and Richard Dienst. Boulder, Colo.: Westview, 1996. 224–60.

Schweinitz, Karl. *The Rise and Fall of the British Empire: Imperialism as Inequality*. New York: Methuen, 1983.

Scott, Joan W. *Gender and the Politics of History*. New York: Columbia University Press, 1988.

Sharpe, Jenny. *Allegories of Empire*. Minneapolis: University of Minnesota Press, 1993.

Sidhwa, Bapsi. *Cracking India*. Minneapolis: Milkweed, 1991.

Simeon, Dilip. "Tremors of Intent: Perceptions of the Nation and Community in Contemporary India." *Oxford Literary Review* 16 (1994): 225–44.

Sinha, Mrinalini. *Colonial Masculinity: The "Manly Englishman" and the "Effeminate Bengali" in the Late Nineteenth Century.* Manchester: Manchester University Press, 1994.

Sommer, Doris. "Irresistable Romance: The Foundational Fiction of Latin America." In *Nation and Nationalism.* Ed. Homi Bhabha. New York: Routledge, 1990. 71–98.

Spivak, Gayatri Chakravorty. "The Burden of English." In *The Lie of the Land: English Literary Studies in India.* Ed. Rajeswari Sunder Rajan. Delhi: Oxford University Press, 1993. 275–99.

———. "Can the Subaltern Speak?" In *Marxism and the Interpretation of Culture.* Ed. Cary Nelson and Lawrence Grossberg. Urbana: University of Illinois Press, 1988. 271–313.

———. "Imperialism and Sexual Difference." In *The Current of Criticism.* Ed. Clayton Koelb and Virgil Lokke. West Lafayette: Purdue University Press, 1987. 310–415.

———. *In Other Worlds.* New York: Routledge, 1988.

———. *Outside in the Teaching Machine.* New York: Routledge, 1993.

———. "The Rani of Sirmur." In *Europe and Its Others.* Ed. Francis Barker et al. Vol. 1. Colchester: University of Essex, 1984. 128–51.

Steel, Flora Annie. *The Garden of Fidelity.* London: Macmillan, 1929.

———. *On the Face of the Waters: A Tale of the Mutiny.* New York: Macmillan, 1911.

Suleri, Sara. *The Rhetoric of English India.* Chicago: University of Chicago Press, 1992.

Tagore, Rabindranath. *The Home and the World.* Trans. Surendranath Tagore. London: Penguin, 1985.

———. *Nationalism.* Reprint, Madras: Macmillan, 1950.

———. *Rabindra rachanabali.* 26 vols. Calcutta: Visra-Bharati, 1958.

———. *Personality.* Madras: Macmillan, 1980.

Taylor, Meadows. *Seeta.* London: Kegan Paul, Trench, Trubner and Company, 1872.

Thapar, Romila. "Traditions versus Misconceptions." Interview with Madhu Kishwar and Ruth Vanita. *Manushi* 42–43 (1987): 3–14.

Tharu, Susie. "Rendering Account of the Nation: Partition Narratives and Other Genres of the Passive Revolution." *Oxford Literary Review* 16 (1994): 69–92.

Thomas, Nicholas. *Colonialism's Culture: Anthropology, Travel, and Government.* Princeton: Princeton University Press, 1994.

INDEX